D0393943

Sleeping in Temples

Sleeping in Temples

Susan Tomes

THE BOYDELL PRESS

© Susan Tomes 2014

All Rights Reserved. Except as permitted under current legislation
no part of this work may be photocopied, stored in a retrieval system,
published, performed in public, adapted, broadcast,
transmitted, recorded or reproduced in any form or by any means,
without the prior permission of the copyright owner

The right of Susan Tomes to be identified as the author of this work has
been asserted in accordance with sections 77 and 78 of the Copyright,
Designs and Patents Act 1988

First published 2014
The Boydell Press, Woodbridge
Reprinted 2015

ISBN 978 1 84383 975 0

The Boydell Press is an imprint of Boydell & Brewer Ltd
PO Box 9, Woodbridge, Suffolk IP12 3DF, UK
and of Boydell & Brewer Inc.
668 Mount Hope Ave, Rochester, NY 14620–2731, USA
website: www.boydellandbrewer.com

A catalogue record for this book is available
from the British Library

The publisher has no responsibility for the continued existence or accuracy
of URLs for external or third-party internet websites referred to in this
book, and does not guarantee that any content on such websites is, or will
remain, accurate or appropriate.

This publication is printed on acid-free paper

Contents

Acknowledgements

I would like to thank my daughter Maya Feile Tomes and my husband Robert Philip for all their wonderful advice, support and encouragement, and Michael Middeke at The Boydell Press for his wise editorial guidance.

Prelude

This is the fourth book I've written about the music I love. With every passing year the task seems to become more important as the world in which we live seems to have less and less time for anything that demands patience, perseverance and long-term thinking.

These are at the heart of what 'classical' music is all about. Ever since I took up the piano as a child, I've found that this kind of music is not only beautiful and entertaining, but is a serious mental resource. It tries to do something which cannot be done by the three-minute song. The best classical music is long-form music, reflecting upon how things are transformed by time. We still need ways to help us think about the experiences that life requires us to undergo. There may be a lot of short-term thinking around at the moment, but life itself hasn't changed. It still presents us with complex extended experiences we seek to understand. Long-form classical music, with its intricate layers and messages, is a wonderful way to symbolise our experience because of the way it unfolds in time, as our experiences do. Understanding when to look back, when to look forward, what part memory plays in it all – this is one of life's greatest tasks. Perhaps music is the best of all the arts at representing this process. It acts as a powerful symbol of how things change, how small beginnings have big results, how moods are altered, how conflict arises, how it can be resolved, and how satisfying it is when things return, seemingly the same, and yet wiser because of what's happened to them as we listened.

Being a classical musician is something that mystifies people, including the musicians themselves. It's a profession and a way of life which delights and challenges in equal measure. I often find it helps me if I attempt to explain it to myself, as I've tried to do here.

Giving people memories

I recently came across the torn and battered copy of Mozart's D minor Piano Concerto from which I learned the piece as a young teenager in Edinburgh. It contains the pencilled remarks of my then piano teacher, Michael Gough Matthews. It's always interesting to be reminded of the advice your teacher gave you years ago, and chastening to discover that sometimes it makes more sense to you now than it did then. Or perhaps it did then too, but you didn't yet know quite how to pick up that particular ball and run with it.

In the middle of the serene slow movement of Mozart's D minor concerto, there's a stormy passage. The mood suddenly changes, and the pianist breaks out into anguished, jagged arpeggios. Evidently my piano teacher had become frustrated with my inability to sense the required atmosphere of this passage. He had written 'dev'essere drammatico!' over it.

Seeing these Italian words many years later, I couldn't help wondering what on earth I would have made of them at the time. There I was, a shy Edinburgh girl who had hardly ever been outside of my home country. I didn't speak Italian, as my teacher no doubt knew because he had to explain to me the various Italian words (allegro, andante cantabile, vivace, etc.) which Mozart was in the habit of using to indicate the speed and character of his music. Was it simply in this spirit that my teacher decided to go with the flow and tell me that 'dev'essere drammatico!'? He could simply have written 'it must be dramatic!' in English, the language we both used, if he wanted to be sure I understood. But he didn't, and seeing his artistic handwriting on the fragile pages many years later, I had the glimmering of an idea why.

But first I want to stay with the memory of the young me, enjoying my Saturday afternoon piano lesson in a sunny top-floor corner room in the Royal Scottish Academy of Music in Glasgow. It has since moved to a new location a few blocks away, but at that time we were in its old building, the Victorian 'Athenaeum' in St George's Square. Like all the UK's principal music colleges, the RSAM ran a junior academy on Saturdays for children and teenagers. Ordinary schools in the UK run until the mid- or late afternoon, and children have a lot of homework as well as after-school clubs, so there is very little weekday opportunity for music lessons. Every Saturday I went through to Glasgow on the train from Edinburgh and had a whole day of music lessons – piano, violin, percussion, harmony and counterpoint, chamber music, orchestra. The heart of the day was my weekly piano lesson. I considered my teacher to be a dashing and handsome figure. His well-cut tweed jacket, his stylish haircut, his aftershave, his elegant soft leather shoes were outside of my sartorial experience at the time. Shoes which were beautiful rather than sensible, for heaven's sake! I was probably wearing my black school shoes, as I did every day of the week.

One of my teacher's jobs was to try and give me some idea of the right performance style for the various piano works I learned with him. When I look back I realise what a tall order this was. We students had little acquaintance with performing styles of any kind, let alone an appreciation of historical traditions. We occasionally heard one another play, but our exposure to professional players, let alone to international performing artists, was minimal. In the days before the internet, it was not at all easy to hear a range of performers from different countries. You couldn't just type a name into a search engine to conjure long lists of their videos and recordings for immediate sampling. At home we had a record player and a small collection of mostly non-classical records. If we had a classical record of something, it would certainly be the only recording I had heard of it, and I would listen to it over and over again. The repetition eroded the notion that there might be other ways of playing that particular piece, and I daresay the way that (for example) Eric Heidsieck played Mozart's D minor Piano Concerto on our LP of it was imprinted forever on my young mind as 'the way to play it', underlying and in a sense annulling any conscious thoughts I later had on the matter.

By that stage I was also attending the Friday night concert series of what was then the Scottish National Orchestra, under their principal conductor Alexander Gibson, in the Usher Hall. This was my first chance to hear artists of stature or performers from outside the UK. For a while I had the habit of collecting autographs after these concerts. Along with a number of other similarly smitten teenagers, I ran backstage after the concert to queue outside the green room, pink autograph book in hand. Slowly we were allowed to file in and get the soloist's or conductor's signature. Some of them were nice, some haughty; some were excitingly dishevelled, some bored and business-like as they scrawled a quick flourish which my school friends would later dismiss lightly with a comment that the signatures 'could have been anyone's really'.

I could tell from these international artists' way of playing that there were ingredients other than the ones I was used to, but I had no idea what to make of it. On the whole we regarded any unusual behaviour as 'antics'. Sometimes performers swayed around tremendously and made all kinds of flamboyant gestures. They leaned back from the piano and gazed at the ceiling. They scrunched forward and bent their head low over the keys as if prostrating themselves in front of a deity. Sometimes they played with far more pedal than I was used to. Sometimes they played dryly and delicately in works of the classical era, and I supposed they were after some particular effect, but I didn't know what or why. I remember occasional visits from female pianists whose platform manner was a cultivated stillness. They made a virtue of plainness, a severity in dress and gesture, a refusal to play to the gallery. This too was surprising and hard to interpret, yet I remember being struck by performers like the Hungarian pianist Annie

Fischer whose quietly intense manner and deliberately unadorned appearance was very much to my taste. In the view of those around me, she hadn't dressed up enough. Why was her hair pulled back in a severe bun? If she was famous, where were her jewels? My fellow piano students and I looked forward to hearing the occasional lumbering Russian 'bears' who would hammer the living daylights out of the piano, glowering from beneath their tousled locks as if they hated us. Why did they do that? We girls had been told to smile prettily and brush our hair when we played in public. Hating the audience was intriguingly dissident. It was an intimation of other values out there, of performers who had grown up with other traditions; I deduced that there must also be foreign audiences whose expectations were different from ours.

Cheap air travel had not yet been invented and nobody in my circle had travelled much abroad. My own family had had one foreign holiday, the stuff of legend in the wider family. We took our own car and drove all the way through France and Switzerland to Italy and back, staying in youth hostels. It was hard going because none of us spoke any foreign languages. Our vocabulary was restricted to, 'Une baguette, s'il vous plaît' and similar beginners' phrases. That holiday gave us an alluring glimpse of European ways of doing things, but we had very little idea of why these customs had arisen, or what they meant; the Michelin Guide wasn't informative on such everyday matters, and there was a limit to how deeply we could communicate with people in mime.

In fact it was not until I went to university that I became better acquainted with the literature on performance traditions – not that the topic was a very hot one amongst us students at the time. We were not yet interested in what recordings could tell us about playing styles of the past, and how those styles might influence us. Everyone around me played as their teacher had trained them to play, and generally speaking our performance manners were modest and predictable. There was a deeply ingrained dislike of 'show-offs'. We didn't yet have much experience of more Mediterranean customs such as dressing in a revealing manner and appearing on the platform with lots of cleavage and shoes so high-heeled that the wearer infringed all the pedagogic rules about balance and the correct use of weight. On the contrary, I remember being scandalised by a female pianist who brought a white lace handkerchief onto the platform and tucked it into a corner of the piano behind the music desk. A white lace hanky! This was the height of exhibitionism. As for tousled locks, these were anathema to our tutors. My Edinburgh piano teacher believed that my hair should be drawn off my forehead and secured neatly in place with a clasp so that the audience could clearly see my face. To hide behind a curtain of hair was considered selfish and ill-mannered, even sinister. What facial expression were you trying to hide?

So it came as a surprise to learn that there were parts of the world where, even in classical music, the performer was traditionally much more of a shaman. Instead of being there merely to entertain or to be ambassadors for beautiful music, performers might rather seem to be lightning rods to carry powerful emotions thrown down by divine composers in thunderbolts from heaven. Performing artists were a bridge between mortals and higher beings, expressing feelings which ordinary members of the public were not able to give voice to. Their platform manner might purposely be designed to titillate, to shock, to intrigue or even annoy. Their hair might be deliberately frothed up into a waterfall hiding their face. They might cultivate a persona of grandeur and isolation, stalking on stage with an air of despising the orchestra and conductor who had invited them to come and play. Evidently there were places where this was not frowned upon.

Although I had always revelled in the relaxed and friendly atmosphere of the RSAM junior academy, where rival pianists would eat bacon sandwiches together, I learned that there were music conservatories elsewhere where the business of preparing for the music profession was horribly competitive. I was reminded of this in later years when I once or twice went with my friend Krysia Osostowicz to play to the Romanian pianist Radu Lupu, whom we both revered. Krysia and I were part of the group Domus at the time. Radu came to a couple of our concerts and commented sadly afterwards that we had seemed to be having fun. When we asked if this was surprising, he explained that in his years of training in Moscow, the opportunity to play in concerts was only given to those who had bested their rivals in internal or inter-college competitions. People schemed and plotted, with their teachers' help, to push their way to the front of the queue. Your fellow pianists would sit in the front row of your performance with copies of the musical scores on their laps. They would 'brief against you' if they got the chance. If you hoped to be a soloist, you knew that you could only hope to play outside of Russia if you fought your way to the top of the pile. The atmosphere was very different and so were the motivations. 'Having fun' was no part of it. Everyone knows what a high standard those conservatories could attain, but at some cost perhaps to the youngsters' innocent love of music.

It seems to me now that it took a long time for news of the outside world to glimmer through to me, even though I was playing the music of many different composers from all over Europe, and sometimes from even further afield. I don't mean simply that the facts took a long time to filter through; I mean a sense of how things were done in other places and why. When my piano teacher wrote 'dev'essere drammatico!' on my Mozart concerto, it was an appeal to my imagination. It was shorthand for '*Think big* and realise that there are excitingly different ways of doing things out there in the world, you little Scottish girl in your home-knitted cardigan!' I believe that subtle provocations do actually work in the student's mind like a little piece of grit inside an oyster shell.

It took a long time for me to understand that beyond the notes themselves, there were appropriate ways of playing the music of different composers, ways that took account of their times and customs and beliefs, as well as factoring in a knowledge of the instruments available to them. These things are now a major part of my thinking when I prepare a piece of music for performance. Surely they must have figured in my piano lessons when I was a child? Yet I don't remember much discussion of different performance options and the reasons one might adopt one or the other. In a way I can understand this, because I and my teachers had quite enough on our hands (as it were) with the basic task of mastering the notes and producing a pleasing sound. Indeed it occupied us for years, as it does most young musicians. It takes such a long time to lay down neural pathways in the brain, to develop coordination and control, to acquire good posture as you play your instrument. It takes time to learn the notes of every new piece accurately, to play with good tone and to follow the composer's instructions regarding fast and slow, loud and soft and all the things in between. And there are lots of pieces to learn and memorise, perhaps especially if you're a pianist. Even before you get on to the fine details of interpretation, there is a tremendous amount of work to be done, and plenty to talk about in lessons.

As you follow the composers' tempo instructions and dynamic markings you are, naturally, making interpretative decisions, but as far as I remember, I didn't consider it like that. Although all my teachers were pleasant, they were also quite authoritarian. They thought there was a right way to do things and directed the student's efforts accordingly. My sheet music was covered in pencilled (or penned, if I was unlucky) admonitions from teachers: 'Too fast!', 'Count!', 'Don't slow down', 'Remember the rests!', 'Left hand accuracy!', 'Ssh!!', and so on. One of my early teachers often wrote, '*My* fingering please!!', an indication that I was continually going off-piste. On a somewhat higher level of nuance there were constant exhortations to 'Phrase!' and to 'play with feeling'. Sometimes teachers would follow the irritating habit of composers to write 'Espressivo!' on the scores, though I gradually came to realise that being told to play expressively is not much help without an indication of *what you are to express*. Composers might as well pepper their scores with reminders to 'play well!'

Quite what I made of all that, I don't remember. I think that when I saw the word 'espressivo' I had a sort of Pavlovian reaction, as many musicians do, switching on a kind of automatic current of benign emotion, perhaps three parts insistence to five parts melancholy and two units of pleading. This seemed plausible in a surprising number of contexts and was demonstrably different from 'neutral'. I probably hadn't wondered whether the right kind of espressivo might be something else entirely: angry, bitter, or funny, for example. Nor had it occurred to me that all music is in essence 'espressivo'. It seems funny to me now to highlight particular passages as 'espressivo', as though the rest of the music isn't. In itself this probably speaks of a performance tradition where a certain manner of playing was taken for granted. Composers cannot have meant that only the passages marked 'espressivo' were to be played with feeling. They must have meant the word as an intensification of some kind.

Behind all my teachers' pencillings lay the assumption that there was a right way to do things. Your teacher *curated* this 'right way', standing at the portal which admitted you to the inner sanctum. You didn't question their approach, but worked hard to follow their instructions; if you did, they were pleased, and that was more or less the end of the process. You could move on to learn another piece. If you went in for competitions, used your teacher's formula and won a prize or were singled out for praise by an adjudicator, your teacher was vindicated. Beautiful tone, accuracy and 'feeling' were sufficient. And quite right too! Those things were hard enough to achieve. You could rest easy if you had managed to achieve them.

Except, of course, that – as I discovered years later when I started to teach – there were many things of which my teachers did not speak because they were difficult to speak of, or terribly hard to put into words. Essentially these concerned the relation between music and one's mental landscape. They were matters of emotional maturity and the ability to enter the composer's inner world, of artistic expression and the movement of the spirit which prompted it. These urgings went well beyond expressing happiness, sadness and beauty. They encompassed a sense of music as architecture, as mathematical system, as psychological map, as language capable of saying things which words could not. It probably felt pointless, or at any rate premature, to speak of such things to youngsters with little experience of the world. At any rate, we didn't speak about them. But it turned out that, as my teachers must have known, music went on doing its work long after we had left each piece behind, and in many cases kept up a leisurely conversation with the musician. All kinds of music lodged deep in the young musician's mind and gradually became part of that interior store of images and shapes that we use when we need to think about the world.

Every musician will know how scraps of music swirl around in their head all the time, whether they consciously summon them up or not. Sometimes there is an obvious explanation: the piano piece you're working on will go through some kind of process of internalisation on an imaginary music-player in your head. Often there isn't an obvious explanation; bits of music float up in response to outward triggers, and sometimes stay with you for days on end. They occur to you in the middle of the night, ravelling and unravelling themselves in your head whether you like it or not. You discover that a work heard long ago, to which you didn't realise you had paid particular attention, has in fact been securely archived in your memory. The beginning of a symphony will suddenly 'play' in your head, and you find to your surprise that you recall the whole of a movement you never consciously memorised. And yet you have memorised it, because it made sense to you. In some mysterious way it was swallowed whole, even when you weren't aware of paying close attention. In my case I find that works I may only have heard in a single performance, for example at the Friday night subscription series of the SNO, went straight into some kind of aural memory bank and stayed there dormant for ages until something evoked a phrase from that piece and I found that, like pulling on the loose end of a ball of wool, I could follow it right to the end.

I also realised that when you teach, you spend a lot of time passing on insights that will probably not make a great deal of impact on the student at the time. Saying the right thing at the wrong time, or at a time when the listener isn't ready to hear it, is a commonplace of teaching. It may well be that my piano teachers said all kinds of wise things which went in one ear and out the other as I sat there vaguely wondering whether my mum had made a fruit cake that would be ready to eat when I got back, or whether I had enough cash left to buy a magazine to read on the train. I probably wasted many opportunities to absorb good advice. In later years, however, when I attended masterclasses, I was often very struck by the master's advice and remembered it without effort, though very likely had the same piece of advice been uttered ten years earlier I might not have 'heard' it.

But when I heard it at the right time, in connection with a piece of music I was familiar with, it suddenly made sense to me in a very organic way. I can only think that that was because the music itself had not been dormant in my brain, but had continued to mature and change along with me, if I could put it like that. Having music in your head is not a static situation, as any musician will tell you. In some mysterious way, the units of musical meaning become accessible to you as units of meaning more generally. And this in turn must be because when composers feel compelled to express their thoughts as musical 'cells', those cells take the outward form they do because they correspond to some kind of thought process in our brains. Lodged in our brains, these musical cells seem to become available to us in some kind of analogous way as tools to think with. I've often thought that music, with its continuous activity of notes at the 'micro' level and its simultaneous organising of those notes into larger and larger phrases which we apprehend without effort at the 'macro' level, has a great deal of affinity with how our thoughts behave.

Music doesn't exist independently of us. It is created by us, produced by us, using processes that exist inside our own heads and our own bodies, even if those processes are obscure or inaccessible to our conscious minds. If someone is motivated to express a thought or a feeling in music, that music is in some way a template of the thought or feeling: not an exact analogy, of course, but its partner at some deep level. I don't mean simply that music can evoke the sound of a sigh, an angry outburst or a declaration of love. Nor do I mean simply that musical melodies go up and down as people's voices do when they speak. I mean rather that music can be the counterpart, in sound, of some internal process of analysis. Analysis of what? Of what happens to us, of what we perceive. I've gradually come to think that as well as working outwards from the feeling to the music, one can also work backwards, from the music to the feeling. Even if the music was produced by someone else, someone from a different time and place, it still seems to be possible to hear it and apprehend the thoughts and feelings inside it as though they were our own. It's more than a matter of appreciating the beauty of the sound. It's recognition of the force which drove the music to be expressed in the first place, a force which we often understand instinctively. This

I think is why really good musicians can often give the audience the feeling that they are *conveying information* as well as simply entertaining us with attractive sounds.

I was intrigued to read recently that psychologists have found it possible to convince people that they 'remember' things which did not, in fact, happen to them. There seem to be many reasons for people to acquire or construct memories not their own. Sometimes it is a matter of unconscious power play with a family member. Brothers and sisters can fight for years over who has the more accurate recall of events in their childhood. The memory of events they shared can be distorted so that one or other person appears in a more positive or a less positive light in retrospect. Siblings, especially twins, are sometimes convinced they remember something which actually happened to the other one. A process of sympathetic identification with someone close to us can make us feel that we remember things that were important to them. A vivid description can conjure up such a compelling picture in the mind's eye that we may store that image as if it were our own memory. Psychologists have found that under experimental conditions they can manipulate people into misremembering things they witnessed.

The subtle memoirist W. G. Sebald recounts in his book *Vertigo* the experience of the French writer Stendhal (real name Henri Beyle) who crossed the Alps as part of Napoleon's army in 1800. On descending from the Alps one afternoon they saw the Italian town of Ivrea in the afternoon sun, a sight which etched itself into Beyle's mind. Other soldiers of Napoleon's army were impressed by the scene as well, and subsequently an engraving of the townscape of Ivrea became popular as something to put on the wall back home. Years later, Beyle revisited the scene and was astonished to find that it was not as he remembered it. In fact, he realised that what he had remembered all these years was the view of Ivrea depicted in the engraving, not the view of Ivrea he actually saw. As he descended from the Alps he would have seen the town from a certain angle, but the engraving showed it from another angle and included things which he could not have seen from his Alpine viewpoint. Yet he 'remembered' seeing those things. The art was more memorable than the real thing. Amusingly, one of the things Beyle concluded from this is that one should not buy engravings of scenes one wants to remember. I've often thought that there's an analogy for music-lovers: that one should not buy recordings of concerts one wants to remember.

Many people's memories of a long-ago family occasion are retrospectively influenced by photographs taken by other people, probably making them 'remember' things they didn't notice at the time, or more poignantly, making it easier to forget things not included in the photographs. People can be influenced to remember as well as to forget, and it is undoubtedly possible to 'give people memories'. I have vivid pictures in my mind of events described to me by friends to whom these events actually happened. As I listened to their tales, I couldn't help visualising the scenes they described, to the point of feeling that I 'remember' them. I don't find it hard to keep in mind that I didn't actually witness those scenes, but to be honest, there isn't much difference between the quality of image conjured up by a friend's vivid recollection and one of my own images. The same is true of friends who recall me telling them about some particular event. They sometimes remember details which I had completely forgotten, and can remind me that somebody said this or that, or behaved in this or that way, or that I reacted at the time in a way which has since faded from my memory. It's a strange feeling that someone else has become the curator of a memory of an incident starring me, an incident they sometimes remember in more detail than I do, even though they weren't there. Who knows, maybe sometimes the recounting of an incident is not so much a way of fixing it in your memory as a way of getting it out of your own head, lessening the weight by sharing it with someone else. You and your listeners become co-curators of certain memories.

I'm working round to saying I believe that music may function like a memory you have been given. Good pieces of music lodge easily in the brain; they have their own organic shape, their own integrity, and a trajectory which makes the listener feel they have been on a journey, witnessed things happening, seen conflicts arising, understood how certain situations have been resolved, and ended up a little changed. Though even short pieces of music can compress such 'journeys' into a small space, long-form music offers far more opportunity to reflect on the workings of time, simply because music is expressed in the medium of time, as our experiences are. When you know such a piece well, you understand that themes and motifs return and are altered; things crash into other things and get blended with them, or have to fight for their own identity. Things get worked up, but they also simmer down and attain resolution. It's not like the memory of something you've seen or actually been involved in, but it's the memory of an experience nonetheless, or the symbol of an experience, if I could put it like that. It sometimes seems as if music enables you to remember someone else's experience – all art does that to some extent, I suppose, but because music is concerned with time, uses time as its medium, it seems to work on the listener's imagination in a particularly potent way. With a really deep piece of music, it often feels as if the composer is making sense of something on your behalf.

Much of the enjoyment of listening to this kind of music depends on memory skills. Music unfolds in time, but when you attend a performance, the time is not under your control. You can't stop the proceedings and turn back to page 12 to remind yourself what happened at that point, or to refresh your memory of the characters involved. You can't turn around and look at the painting again. To get the most out of long-form music and the journey it describes, you need to be able to remember important things you heard earlier. Of course, you can simply let music pour over you like a melodious stream of consciousness, an eternal present. Nothing wrong with that – but it will be a far deeper experience if you are able to remember what you already heard, so that you can appreciate how it interacts with things later, and whether it returns, and if so, whether it has come through unscathed or not. Understanding things in context is a crucial part of the enjoyment and gives depth to the experience, just as with any novel, film or play.

In fact, the skill of listening is quite a tall order for audiences. They probably don't have long acquaintance with the printed music like musicians do. Musicians use their eyes as well as their ears when getting to know a new piece. They can look ahead at the score and see what's coming. They can study it analytically if they wish. By the time they come to perform the piece, they have digested many kinds of information about it, and are ready to act as pilots steering us through its waters. Listeners, however, are not in the same position. They're the ones who have to hear and remember instantly, for they may not have a second chance, and in the days before recording, they often didn't. The ability to recognise patterns in music is fortunately one that nearly all of us seem to possess to a very sophisticated extent, whether we are musically trained or not. Patterns in music are more than superficial; they often behave as little units of thought.

The literary scholar and Proust expert Malcolm Bowie, a great music-lover, wrote movingly in his essay 'Remembering the Future' of 'those complex acts of remembrance that works of art invite us to perform'. For me this is a wonderful way to sum up what I feel is happening when I play or listen to classical music. I'm continually being borne forward, but also reminded to look back, and to appreciate the sense of renewal that comes when familiar things return and give new meaning to the present. 'A novel, a sonnet, a symphony', Malcolm wrote, 'is a mnemonic device inside which, intricately coiled and coded, are an elaborate set of instructions. These tell us, time-bound creatures that we are, how to handle the time dimension in which all artworks unfold; when to look back, when to look ahead in expectation, and how to layer and interconnect different time-levels inside the onrush of artistic experience. Recognising these instructions in one encounter with art, we are soon able to apply them elsewhere.'

We all know how powerful the memory of music can be, almost like the memory of a dream which affects your waking mood and plays on your mind, twining itself around later events. Music can colour events in a similar way. There can be a strange amalgam between recollected music and present events, making those events seem almost like ingredients of the music you're thinking about, or illustrations of it at some unknown level.

For many people, I think music acts in the brain in much the same way as fairy tales do, which is to say as archetypes, providing keys which help you to open mental locks. Fairy tales we've learned in childhood famously come back to us when our own situations seem to mimic elements of theirs. It's not that we actually think our father *is* a king tricked out of an actual kingdom, that our child is truly lost in the woods or that our husband has a blue beard and a corridor full of locked rooms, but those stories act as mnemonics for things we know at an unconscious level.

Pieces of music can work like memories do. You can call them out of your memory store, look at them again, revisit the sensations they gave you, ask them questions and get some answers. Maybe 'answers' is too strong a word, but you can certainly get hints, and intimations that you're not alone, often a very important experience. We don't have all that many opportunities to ask other people for help in making sense of our experiences. Even when those opportunities exist we are shy of taking them, reluctant to show weakness, or simply unable to describe what is bothering us. In that sense, music can be a surrogate counsellor. It offers you a heart-to-heart – or a head-to-head, if that's what you need – with someone else who has pondered their experience deeply. The fact that they pondered it and set it out a century or two centuries ago may be consoling, rather than alienating. It can give you a wonderful sense of perspective. Recalling music can free you from mundane 'clock time' and enable you to experience the healing effect of time not moored in the present, or attached to the past, but floating in the collective imagination, a 'time' which could be Mozart's or Schubert's as much as yours. Such music can be available to you as an experience which, deeply internalised, can help you to forge meaning.

The right tool for the job

My dad was a keen gardener, proud of his flower borders bursting with colour and his pristine, weed-free lawn, which he mowed himself every week in the summer with a heavy old hand-pushed lawnmower without benefit of either petrol or electricity. Dandelions sometimes had the nerve to appear in the lawn, and on his way out to work, Dad would whisk a screwdriver out of his jacket pocket and use it to lever the villain out of the grass. The sight of him bending down to make a surgical strike on a dandelion with his trusty screwdriver stuck in everyone's minds. We all laughed about it and said it was typical of him to be too impatient to go to the garage and get a proper gardening tool. But as time went on and we acquired lawns and weeds of our own, we secretly tried out the screwdriver as a gardening tool when nobody was looking, and one by one we concluded that it was the right tool for the job.

What made my father's use of a screwdriver as a weeding tool especially funny was that the screwdriver was actually the tool of his trade (he had a 'sales and repair' radio and television shop). We were more accustomed to seeing the screwdriver being used to take the back off a Bush or Ekco TV. So it was a bit like seeing a surgeon whip out his scalpel to excise a dandelion – you just didn't expect to see that particular tool being used for that purpose. And what was even better was that the humble screwdriver, such a versatile companion, could be bought for a few shillings and would last you for fifty years.

Sadly the same is not true of the tool of my trade, the grand piano, which at the time of writing can cost over £100,000 to buy new. Even more sadly, pianos depreciate like cars do from the moment they leave the showroom. In the wider context of musical instruments, pianos are nowhere near the most expensive to buy – string instruments have long ago eclipsed them with stratospheric prices running into millions of dollars for a fine old Italian violin or cello by one of the master makers. String instruments have become international collectors' items and art market commodities, with prices being pushed up and kept high by dealers who have no interest in bringing the prices within the reach of mere players. Despite the financial crash of 2008, prices of string instruments continue to rise, and I recently saw an advert in *The Guardian* promoting an art auction with a photo of a fine old French violin, clearly a symbol of something especially covetable. Players who manage to get their hands on such a violin usually can only do so with the backing of a syndicate of investors whose interest in the project is primarily financial, even if they are happy to hear the instrument used on the concert platform. No investors are interested in buying pianos, however, because it is well known that pianos drop in value as well as condition as the years go by, no matter how much you spend on maintaining them. My grand piano, for which I had to take out a mortgage of £11,000 in 1988, is probably worth less than that now, despite the fact that I have spent more than that in maintaining it over the years.

But the piano is the right tool for my job. I learned to play violin and percussion too, and I liked both; they appealed to different sides of my musical personality. But the piano has always seemed to me the instrument on which I could most easily be myself. Some people say the piano is a percussion instrument (because of its hammers) but I've always thought of it more as a string instrument (because of its strings). In fact, it's a brilliant blend of the two, a kind of 'stringcussion' instrument, offering the possibility of precise attack as well as beautiful sonority and resonance. It can go 'Pow!', 'Boom!' and 'Zing!' but it can also purr, chant and roar (not to mention trickle and pour). Even better, it can do those things at the same time. For me, the piano has always seemed a wonderfully *complete* instrument. I'm always offended when I hear pianists described as being 'at the piano', because *at* seems entirely the wrong word. Some years ago, after a concert in Germany, I was delighted when someone said that the piano and I gave the impression of being somehow *one thing*. I had never consciously thought of it like that until someone else articulated it, but since then I've been alert to the way that good pianists seem able to embrace the piano in their mental field, creating a sort of giant amalgam of player and instrument, like a musical equivalent of a centaur.

It's fascinating to see who plays what instrument, and how their alliance began. I've often wondered whether people are drawn towards a certain instrument because it represents an aspect of their character, or whether it's the other way round: that playing a certain instrument gradually moulds your character. It's a little like dogs and their owners, who often seem to resemble one another in some way – shape, gait, energy, friendliness, the look on the face – but one never knows whether people are drawn to choose dogs who resemble them, or whether life together makes them come to share aspects of personality. The same is true of pianists and pianos. I don't mean they grow to look like one another (heaven forbid) but it often seems that there is a 'pianist type', a type distinct from other instrumentalists. I've never known whether that type of person is attracted to the piano, or whether playing piano music makes you into that sort of person. It isn't only a historical thing: I notice it all the time in the younger generation, such as when I follow competitions like the BBC's Young Musician of the Year. When you get attuned to the 'type' you can spot pianists easily. I used to play a game with myself when I met a new chamber group, to see if I could guess which one was the pianist before I saw them in action. I didn't cheat and plump for the only one who wasn't carrying a violin or cello case, by the way – I'm talking about when I met them in a social situation, or saw a photo of them without their instruments, walking on a beach or raising their glasses at a party. There's a 'look' about a pianist, or perhaps it takes one to know one. I'm also, by the way, pretty good at guessing who *isn't* the pianist in the group.

The piano is special. It's one of the few instruments where you can be self-sufficient, playing melody and harmony yourself, with no need of anyone else to complete the musical picture. This makes the piano the perfect instrument for loners, and many composers (probably loners themselves) have chosen the piano for some of their most thorough explorations of interior drama. Not only does the piano have a huge range, from the growly low notes in the deep bass to the tinkling treble notes so high that you almost can't determine their pitch, it also has an enormous range from extremely dry and soft to thunderously loud and resonant. Because there are ten fingers on a pianist's hands, there are countless possibilities for making different hammers strike the strings with different intensities at the same time, so that some notes are made to stand out in relief from others and lead the ear through a forest of resonating notes with narrative clarity. For me the piano offers the greatest possibility of *balance* of any instrument I know: balance between melody and harmony, between rhythm and sustained lines, between treble and bass, between different strands of music in play at the same time, and between the notes of an individual chord.

Most of the instruments in a symphony orchestra have to be held in the air or supported to some degree by the player. Their notes have to be created by shortening a string, by stopping holes in a column of air or changing the length of the column with valves. On the piano, the notes are already there, pre-tuned, or at least pre-tunable. There are eighty-eight notes on a standard piano, each with an ivory-covered key attached to a lever which operates a mechanism that ends with a hammer striking a metal string stretched over a soundboard attached to an iron frame. This mechanism is a very heavy one and supports its own weight. The pianist just has to walk up to it and touch the keys to make notes sound. Pianists are free from the task of holding up and supporting an instrument, and each hand can be independently active. On the piano you can play different notes with different hands; you can play ten different notes at once (more if you use your whole palm or lean on the keys with your arms, as some composers ask you to do).

This makes for a crucial difference between piano music and music for single-line instruments, such as the violin or clarinet, where the player has to produce the notes and control the pitch. (I should of course mention that although string instruments are primarily melodic, there is also the possibility of double- and triple-stopping, playing several strings at once to create chords). Anyone who plays a single-line instrument will tell you that there is no end to the subtlety with which the pitch can be varied according to the harmonic and dramatic context, and in response to the underlying harmony played by other instruments. Then of course there is the infinite question of tone, whether produced by the breath, or by a bow on a string. Mastering tone and pitch is an endless challenge for anyone playing a single-line instrument and can be a life's work as well as a life's obsession. A beautiful melody played on a fine string instrument by a master is one of music's most iconic sounds. The fact remains, however, that music for such instruments is never as *intricate* as music written for the piano. I do have personal experience of this, having played the violin to a fairly high level before I decided to concentrate on the piano. I played violin in the National Youth Orchestra of Great Britain, and when I auditioned for the Royal Scottish Academy of Music at the age of seventeen I was offered scholarships on both violin and piano (I took the piano one). So although I didn't ultimately pursue my violin studies as far as my piano studies, I do feel equipped to compare the two.

Why did I plump for the piano? It was 'the right tool for the job', the one most physically suited to me, an important consideration when choosing your tools. When I played the violin I felt I was twisting my hands into slightly painful positions. My hands used to ache at the end of violin practice. Perhaps I never encountered a teacher who could show me what I was doing wrong or how to alleviate the pain; at any rate, I felt I couldn't face a long future with the violin, whereas the piano seemed to come naturally to me and was physically pleasant to play. (I have admittedly had phases in my professional life where I felt that my fingertips were becoming painfully sensitive to the constant 'hitting' actions of my fingers on the piano keys, but this was linked to the perceived requirement to 'project tone' more forcefully for larger concert halls.) The decision about which instrument to favour was not only about the physical challenge of playing the violin. I played in orchestras all through my teenage and university years, so I knew how it felt to be in 'the violin section', one of many playing the same musical part and depending on other people to supply other parts. Although it was tremendous fun and I wouldn't have missed it, I felt it was on the whole less satisfying than playing an instrument where you could supply all the melody and harmony yourself. Despite the thrill of participating in a great orchestral work, I never quite got used to the sensation of not being able to hear myself when I played in a violin section with a dozen other people all playing the same part.

A pianist can use the percussive nature of the piano to introduce rhythm alongside the melody and harmony, and piano music makes full use of this possibility, providing melody, its harmonies, and complementary rhythmic elements all at once. Thus the piano can produce musical texture of a sophistication far beyond that which is offered by most instruments. We pianists may not be able to make the immediate sensory impact of a glorious violin melody or a pungent saxophone solo, but the enormous range of things a piano can do is ample compensation. We feel that the piano can speak as well as sing.

The Austrian pianist Artur Schnabel once said that the piano was the most expressive of instruments – a surprising thing to say, on the face of it. How could a piano, a mechanical thing of levers and hammers, possibly be more expressive than, say, a cello or a clarinet? I think it's to do with the difference between types of expression. We have song (and singing instruments) to express grand, lyrical emotions. Sustained singing lines are carried by vowel sounds above all. But the piano's way is more akin to speaking, often just as expressive in its own way as singing. The impression of 'speaking' is given by the way each note on the piano is produced – by depressing one end of a lever (the key) to make a felt-covered hammer strike a string. There is great variety in how the end of the lever can be touched: slow, fast, gently, with energy. Each note has its own 'leading edge' (or 'starting transient') created by the weight and speed of attack the player uses on the keys. The percussive element is not necessarily brute force; it can be used with great subtlety to define the beginnings of notes as if they had their own consonants or vowels.

Notes in a piano melody are a little like words in a spoken sentence: distinct, separate, each with its own emphasis and rhythmic character, yet joined together in a chain of units which create meaning. When a good pianist plays, it often feels as if someone is speaking to you, giving you finely detailed information. Listening to a pianist is perhaps more like listening to an actor than a singer, although naturally there are also times when one seems to hear a singer. The piano is not the only instrument which can appear to speak as well as sing, but it's one of the few which can tell you something while also providing the background to the story *and* conjuring up the atmosphere. The enormous repertoire for the piano, larger I imagine than for any other instrument, is proof of how much composers have valued the piano's multi-faceted personality.

It is sometimes said, usually by non-pianists, that the piano cannot 'sing'. The effect of singing may be an illusion produced by the infinitely skilful gradation of tone between notes, and careful handling of 'transient noise' at the start of notes, but the singing is a convincing effect nonetheless and one that many listeners would swear they hear. From time to time, arguments break out in the music press about whether or not the piano can 'sing' and have even made their way into non-musical journals, such as when the pianist and writer Charles Rosen got into a spat with readers in the *New York Review of Books* in 1999. Rosen had mentioned the 'delusions about the production of a beautiful sonority' in piano-playing, and had asserted that 'a single note on the piano cannot be played more or less beautifully, only more or less forte or piano. In spite of the beliefs of generations of piano teachers, there is no way of pushing down a key more gracefully that will make the slightest difference to the resulting sound. … The graceful or dramatic movements of the arms and wrists of the performer are simply a form of choreography.' This was disputed by readers. While it may be the case that one single note played very quietly by Sviatoslav Richter is measurably the same as the note played very quietly by a robot, the information is hardly illuminating since the pianist's art consists in creating relationships *between* the notes, or between notes and silences. Notes in context are what we hear, and experience shows that as soon as one note is followed by another, or is played as part of a chord, beauty and tone quality can be created by subtle gradations. It seems pedantic to narrow the debate to a single note, since nobody ever attends a performance at which only one note is played. I've noticed that sometimes, when a person believes that an instrument 'cannot do' this or that, their playing is an unconscious demonstration of that belief. If someone's piano tone is dry or cold, it's hardly surprising to hear that that person does not believe that the piano can produce a beautiful sonority. You often have to believe that something is possible in order to try for it, and this is something I find myself saying more and more to my students.

Players of single-line instruments would never swap their ability to create tone and pitch for the complexity of piano parts, and this is where individual temperament comes into the picture. What makes a person value one kind of musical role over another? Why does one musician long to be the one playing the beautiful melody, while another is drawn to be a 'supporter', and yet another is motivated by the prospect of being the one with the best overview? I've never seen graphs of the activity in musicians' brains as they play, but I have no doubt that the tasks which preoccupy players of different instruments would make the 'reading' of a pianist's brain somewhat different from a violinist's, a clarinettist's or a drummer's. When a string instrument is played with a bow, for example, each hand has a totally different task – left hand on the fingerboard of the violin, right hand holding the bow. On the violin, viola and cello, the player's hands operate on planes at right angles to one another, which makes physical co-ordination even more complicated. At least with the cello the left hand is in a natural position, because the cello's fingerboard is parallel to the cellist's body. In the case of violin and viola the situation is complicated by the fact that the instrument is held under the chin with the tuning-pegs at the far end, necessitating a twist on the player's left arm to get the fingers into the right position on the fingerboard. Yet the two tasks have to operate with utter coordination to produce one single musical line. When a pianist reads from two musical staves simultaneously, playing different music with each hand and different notes with each finger, it must be a different process for the brain than one in which both hands co-operate to produce a single line. I don't mean to imply that the process of playing the piano is more impressive, just that it must be *different*. Those different processes seem to suit different people, perhaps because of neurological differences. At any rate, it is safe to say that a pianist has to be someone who is happy about dwelling in the realm of intricacy.

I've often wondered whether it's neurologically challenging for pianists that so much piano music calls for octave or unison passages. At a casual glance you might think that such passages are easier because the two hands are doing the same thing, but anyone who has been made to learn two-handed 'scales' on the piano will be aware that when scales are going up, they begin with the little finger of the left hand and the thumb of the right, and when they come down it's the reverse. The use of the hands is not symmetrical in that sense; although the hands are moving in the same direction, up or down, one hand is always on its 'weaker' side while the other is on its stronger. Even advanced pianists have trouble with this when climactic scale passages, rushing up the keyboard as on the final page of Chopin's First Ballade, require them to arrive with a mighty flourish on the weakest finger of the right hand. (I enjoyed reading about the pianistic terror of this final coda as discussed in Alan Rusbridger's *Play It Again*, an account of a year he spent in trying to learn the G minor Ballade while steering the *Guardian* newspaper through turbulent developments in international news.)

Because piano music is the way it is, pianists have to get used to being music's overseers. Many composers use the piano when they compose, treating it as a handy substitute for an orchestra. For a long time, it was standard practice for a new symphony or major chamber work to appear as a piano duet or arrangement for solo piano shortly after the orchestral version was published, for the benefit of the many people who didn't have access to concerts or orchestras. Piano duet versions were the way they got to know large-scale music. Cultured households routinely had pianos in them, and taking piano lessons was part of a good education. It was taken for granted that the piano was the bedrock of any musical training, even for those who wished to take up other instruments eventually. The piano was so useful for learning about harmony, and acted as a portal to a vast amount of repertoire either written for it or arranged for it. Norbert Brainin, first violin of the Amadeus Quartet, told a marvellous story to the magazine *Ibykus* about an occasion when the violinist-composer Georges Enescu played all the Beethoven string quartets to them on the piano:

> Enescu said, 'Have you got plans for the afternoon?' We'd planned to rehearse, but of course I said, 'No, nothing, nor have my colleagues.' Thereupon, Enescu replied that 'I'd very much like to show you how to play Beethoven's quartets, but unfortunately, it will have to be on the piano.' After lunch, the five of us appeared in the recital hall, and Enescu sat at the grand piano with his back to the 'audience,' and began to play. He played by heart; each tone was absolutely precise, and his expressiveness was a sheer phenomenon. He began with Opus 18, No. 1, and then he played straight through all the quartets, including the late quartets. ... He ended by playing the C-Sharp Minor Quartet, Op. 131. The thing took the entire afternoon, straight through to evening. Meanwhile, word had got about in the Conservatory that 'Enescu is playing the Beethoven quartets on the piano for the Amadeus Quartet, one after the other.' The students tiptoed into the hall, sat down quietly, and listened, without Enescu ever noting their presence. As he concluded the C-Sharp Minor Quartet and turned round 'to us,' he saw everyone sitting there, and the entire room broke out into wild applause. It was incredible. Enescu knew the four voices of each quartet, and played and articulated them very precisely. As a pianist, he was so unbelievably good, I do believe he was a finer pianist than a violinist!

Perhaps because many composers were pianists and/or composed at the piano, it's the custom in chamber music for the piano part to contain everyone else's part as well, printed in smaller type above the piano staves. The other players in the group have only their own single lines, thus making their parts much shorter – a few pages as opposed to the dozens in the pianist's score. In orchestral music, similarly, each person plays from a part containing only their own notes (which is one of the reasons why they need a conductor). I've always found it odd that each musician should have only a part with their own notes in it – almost like the Elizabethan theatre, when Shakespeare's actors worked from individual parts containing only their own lines and cues. That custom was superseded by actors working from the complete text, but the same has never happened in orchestras. Of course it would be impractical for each person to play from a big score, but as far as I can see from my occasional involvement in orchestra rehearsals, great inertia results from the fact that nobody sees (or knows) any part other than their own. In these days of technological sophistication, there would surely be a way round it.

In rehearsals of chamber music the pianist usually ends up as the *de facto* conductor, though without the status. A pianist can see at a glance what everyone else is supposed to be playing, and is the only person in that position. I have often thought this single fact accounts for much of why a pianist develops differently from players of single-line instruments. There's something about the experience of working from the whole score, in a context where nobody else does, and where they rely on you to know, which has a profound influence on you. At least I find it so.

I've discussed the situation with people who always play from single parts, and I've found that they actually *prefer* to learn by ear what everyone else is playing, as they find it a more practical and 'lively' kind of knowledge. However, this kind of 'learning on the job' can only be done once the group is assembled. By contrast, long before the first rehearsal, pianists have had to become familiar with the whole score. Because the piano part, always the most complex and containing hundreds of times as many notes, cannot generally be sight-read at the first rehearsal, pianists have to embark on the learning process well ahead of time. It's possible to sight-read piano parts, and some people do it brilliantly, but it's a rare pianist who can put their fingers on all the notes when sight-reading at speed, and most prefer to have prior warning. When playing for the string classes at music courses, I had to sight-read many a piano part in front of an audience. Luckily I'm a good sight-reader, but I quickly had to develop the supplementary art of knowing what to leave out, so that the underlying chord changes kept pace with the other player in real time, even if some of the faster passage-work was missing.

As pianists practise the piano part of a chamber work they usually have all the other parts in front of them as well, and have the opportunity to develop firm ideas about how the piece should 'go'. This often leads to a certain tension at the first rehearsals. It is not fun to have to wait while everyone else discovers what the piece contains, no matter how good they may be at assimilating that knowledge. I don't mean to claim that only prior study of the piece gives you the right to have opinions, for that wouldn't be true; there's a valuable contribution to be made by people reacting in real time to what they hear, 'catching the joy as it flies'. In good rehearsals, both types of understanding work together, fuelling an interpretation with both mature and spontaneous insights. But of course there are many boring rehearsals where the pianist just has to wait while other players figure out what's going on.

You might ask, why don't musicians cut through all that nonsense by printing string/wind parts which also contain the other parts? Then everyone would know what the pianist knows, and groups could start their rehearsals on a level playing-field, as it were. I've occasionally seen string quartets playing from full scores, especially in tricky modern music. But in piano-based groups, it often feels as if single-line players have grown to depend on the pianist to put them right if need be. They are quite content to play from single-line parts, even when an alternative is available. Some years ago there was an initiative from a Swiss music publisher to produce chamber parts where every part contained the whole score. Each person's own part was printed in larger type, with the other lines in smaller type, just as in a traditional piano score. At last, everyone could be playing from the score

– hooray! I acquired a few of these new editions and took them along to rehearsals, only to be told to take them away again. 'Too confusing to read', 'Too many pages to turn', 'I can't keep looking up and down across the lines like that – I lose my place', 'I prefer to get to know it by ear, not by eye', etc. All of which is understandable, except that it still leaves the pianist in the unsought position of being the one in possession of most information.

Despite what others might imagine, this is rarely an amusing position to be in. Even when everyone has got to know the music by ear, if something goes awry in performance, and someone loses their place, or jumps a line, only the pianist can instantly see what has happened, take an overview of the situation and decide whether to jump forward, back, fill in a missing part by playing it on the piano, or whatever. I've got used to this situation, but I still think it has re-grettable human consequences. Pianists are often resented for being 'a bit of a know-all', which they can hardly help but be. Personally, I would prefer everyone to have the whole score in front of them, or for rehearsals to begin when everyone knows the score. In fact, I am not sure I have ever experienced this. It's much more common, at least in my experience, that the pianist has been practising the piano part for months before rehearsals begin, whereas single-line players often leave it until close to the first rehearsal, or even to the first rehearsal itself, to look at their part. This is particularly so with wind players, who don't have to consider the alternative fingerings available to string players, and who can often get away with sight-reading at the first rehearsal.

A while ago I was playing a fiendishly difficult piano part in a chamber work by Spohr. I had been learning my part at home for months in order to have it 'up to speed' (literally so in this case) and more or less by memory. I say 'by memory' because if your nose is glued to the score, you can't look around the group as you play, and I like to be able to do that. As I was getting my music out at the first rehearsal, I heard one of the wind players say to another, 'Have you got a part for me? I've not played this', and the other player answering, 'Don't let Sue hear you say that!' Such experiences can make a pianist feel isolated. Non-pianists dislike pianists knowing more, and pianists wish that everyone else would know as much they do. In chamber music there's an assumption that everyone is equal, but as Menahem Pressler (the pianist of the Beaux Arts Trio) recently said to me, the pianist is inevitably 'primus inter pares', first among equals.

I sometimes feel that life as a *woman* pianist has brought its own special challenges. If one accepts that the pianist is often a kind of authority figure, then from what I've observed I suspect it is easier to occupy that position if you're a man. Chamber groups do replicate some aspects of family dynamics, and I've sometimes felt as if my dual role of pianist and older woman/mother has made me twice as annoying, or to put it more coolly, has introduced a 'beat' of complication. At the time of writing this book, there was a lively debate going on in the press about whether, even now, women have established the right to be acknowledged as authorities or whether, when they have reached such positions, they can assert their authority without being judged 'strident', 'nagging' or 'whining'. Women working in the music profession are of course not exempt from that difficulty.

In one important respect the music profession *is* different, though, because piano parts themselves are gender-blind. In other performing arts – theatre, dance, movies – roles are usually designed for specific genders, and are not interchangeable. Recent productions in the UK such as Matthew Bourne's all-male *Swan Lake* ballet, or Phyllida Lloyd's all-female *Julius Caesar*, have played intriguingly with the idea of men playing women's roles and vice versa but have not displaced the originals, and indeed some of the frisson comes from onlookers being jarred by the 'dissonance'. In music, by contrast, instrumental parts are abstract, not specifically designed either for women or for men, and not at all dependent on the way you look. Even if a composer writes a new work for a specific chamber group, the individual parts are not tailored towards this or that player being a woman (at least I've never come across such an approach). If a composer discovers that a man is to be playing the piano part of his composition on such-and-such an occasion, he does not add manly jumps and displays of muscular strength to the part, nor does he alter it to include beautiful arabesques and pirouettes for a woman.

In classical music, the music remains basically the same no matter who is playing it. Although at first glance this may appear to be restricting, I find it tremendously liberating – that as a musician you simply have to step forward and inhabit the role no matter who you are, man or woman, introvert or extrovert. In the pianist's position you have no choice about *what* to say – because it is set down by the composer, who usually casts the piano in a leading role. There can be no argument about whether it's appropriate for *you* to say those things, or whether you should say them in different words because of who you are. Mozart and Beethoven don't change the script if they know a female person is to be playing the role. As far as I'm concerned, that is a great blessing.

My life as a pianist has been dominated by the fact of playing such a *large* instrument. The phrase 'you can't take it with you' (usually referring to money) has always had a special resonance for me, because it reminds me of always having to leave my piano at home when I go to play a concert. A piano is a big piece of furniture in any home, and indeed is sometimes bought *as* a piece of furniture, simply because it looks elegant and hints at artistic leanings. I remember the arrival of my first 'boudoir grand' piano (not a full-size grand) in my child-hood home – it seemed to take up half of our living-room, and I'm not sure if my parents were excited or wanted to weep with vexation at the encroachment on the children's playing space. In fact, in every house I have lived in, my grand piano has eaten up an uncomfortable amount of space. Its imposing size also means that it's very difficult to transport, and most pianos stay put.

There are one or two pianists in the world who have been in a position to take their own pianos on tour, but they are very rare. Most pianists have to accept that they will need to get used to a new instrument at every concert, and this is a constant challenge. When it comes to sheer tone quality, then of course you're at the mercy of the instrument. But luckily for pianists, the art of 'speaking' the music can be achieved on almost any kind of piano. That's because some vital ingredients of music-making – the art of timing, for example, or a mastery of rhythm – are independent of tone quality. In other words, you can still convey an awful lot without the luxury of gorgeous inbuilt tone. Music, thank heavens, isn't choked off by a mediocre piano. Sviatoslav Richter used to enjoy the challenge of playing very basic pianos – sometimes upright pianos – when he was touring in the Russian provinces. Every good pianist knows that it's possible to find your own voice to some extent on any piano, because rhythm, articulation and timing are such crucial elements in how music affects us. When you're trying to find 'your own sound' on an unfamiliar piano, mind over matter is a very useful tool. You can learn to rise above a disappointing sound, and you can use your imagination to coax things from the piano which it didn't know it could do. It's very important not to let the musical effect sink to the level of a substandard instrument.

In my life as a chamber pianist I usually go to the concert hall ahead of everyone else to get to know the piano, and this often eats into the time which others are able to use to rest after a journey, a rehearsal or whatever. There has to be an element of improvisation about pianists' relationships with the instruments we play, as we have only a short time to figure out what a new piano can do and what it can't, and what may have to change accordingly. For example, a pianist may respond to an old piano with a thin tone by deciding to play a certain piece faster than usual. A new piano with a heavy action will require a bit of negotiation as to where in the programme one can spare some energy by playing more gently. On pianos with uneven tone, you have to know which registers are softer or louder, or which individual notes may 'stick out'. Sometimes an unknown piano can be a delightful surprise, suggesting tonal possibilities which hadn't occurred to you on your piano at home. A piano with an unusually rich tone or especially good voicing may suggest different ways of playing things, but those new ways will need to be worked out on the spur of the moment, and may never be repeated. My way of bonding with an unknown piano is to enter into negotiation with it, though I'm starting to feel that the younger generation of pianists prefer to rely on a technique robust enough to subdue any piano, and powerful enough to project to the back of any hall. (A colleague of mine commented recently that none of his students seemed to want to learn how to play with a true *pianissimo*.) The change is perhaps similar to the development of technique always being commented on in, say, tennis playing, where everyone – men and women – hits the ball harder than they used to, and relies on sheer power more than they did in the serve-and-volley era.

We pianists are an unusual group of musicians for whom the tools of our trade can never become 'extensions of ourselves', moulded by constant contact with our very own hands. In his novel *The Third Policeman*, the Irish author Flann O'Brien puts forward the whimsical theory that when you walk long distances, 'the continual cracking of your feet on the road makes a certain quantity of road come up into you'. I think many string players feel that way about walking a thousand musical miles with their very own instruments: that they gradually absorb bits of one another. Not for us pianists, however, the sensuous bond which develops between (for example) a violinist and their violin. Pianists and pianos advance and retreat from one another like partners in a minuet. We have to know how to let go, to say 'Hail and farewell' to the instruments we play. Learning to be that little bit detached, in order to remain flexible about the parade of unknown instruments passing in front of us, probably has quite a profound effect on pianists' psychology, making us the appraising, quizzical people we often seem to be.

Play the contents, not the container

This enigmatic piece of advice was given by the Hungarian professor György Sebök, whose masterclasses I attended in Switzerland, Canada and Holland in the 1980s. Like many of his aphorisms it was casually delivered with a wry smile, a curl of cigarette smoke and a look that said, 'If you think about this for as long as I have, it may make sense to you.'

I used it as the title of a talk I gave not long ago at King's College, London, where my academic audience was vexed by Sebök's words. For them, the division into 'container' and 'contents' cut across the fashionable theory of semiotics, the study of sign and communication. Music is an example of a 'sign'. The 'sign' can be divided into the 'signifier' (in the case of music, the sound) and the 'signified' (the sense). Some think that music, the least representational of the arts, has no 'sense' of its own, and that it is only we who feel an irresistible need to give it meaning. Certain composers have appeared to lend weight to this argument by refusing to say what the meaning of their music is, or even by claiming that there is none. Stravinsky, for example, said, 'I consider that music is, by its very nature, essentially powerless to express anything at all, whether a feeling, an attitude of mind, or psychological mood, a phenomenon of nature, etc. ... Expression has never been an inherent property of music.' But most music-lovers would beg to differ, and Stravinsky probably didn't mean that music was meaningless. It is possible to enjoy music simply as organisation of sounds with no reference to anything beyond itself – indeed, some music is designed to be like that, and can be intellectually satisfying – but that's not what music usually feels like. The emotions one experiences when playing or listening to music certainly *feel* as if they come from the music. Even if they are not specific emotions, they still feel like the stirrings of emotion at a deeper layer. If I find tears coming into my eyes at the opening bars of a Beethoven string quartet, is that because I have hurried to 'give it meaning' which doesn't belong to it? If I catch my breath at the perfectly timed ending of a Mozart piano concerto movement, is the perfection bestowed on it by me alone? It doesn't feel so, and I don't see the benefit in maintaining that it is so.

'Play the contents, not the container' has worked in my mind over the years like a depth charge. It seems a very simple observation, but its simple language is deceptive. What can it mean for musicians? Sebök said it to a piano student whose playing seemed to be stuck at the level of playing the notes – a very common thing, which can easily be a default setting for musicians of every kind, no matter how expert. It takes effort of the imagination to enter into music, and sometimes it's easier not to, especially when there's more than enough to think about with 'just' the task of playing the notes. But if music is to convey more than just a superficially pleasing pattern of notes, the player has to go beyond its external form and try to feel what underlies it. As Sebök said, 'music is understanding in action'. That too was a philosophy summed up in a few words.

That 'music is understanding in action' is true in an ideal world, but although playing and listening to music are different sorts of experience when there is understanding, music does also exist without that understanding. Sometimes the beauty of music is quite perceptible just through its outward form, and with certain kinds of music, where the performer's involvement and emotion are less crucial, music can even benefit from a neutral approach. J.S. Bach is said to have told a pupil to 'practise diligently and you will do very well'– and he went on to say that, 'there's nothing remarkable about playing the organ ... all you have to do is hit the right notes at the right time'. That was practically Sebökian in its sly wisdom, for how do you know what 'the right time' is without a great deal of experience?

There's a less-is-more element to some kinds of performance, but probably not one that the performer can manipulate very successfully into being so. In my experience as a listener, anyone who actually sets out to deliver a 'hands off' performance will probably produce an example of 'less is less'. I still remember a performance of a Bach cello suite by a cellist who had decided not to interfere, not to have a plan or a personal interpretation, 'just to play the notes'. The motivation was admirable – to let the music speak for itself, untainted by the performer's ego. The goal was a sort of Zen-like purity, but it wasn't successful – everyone just felt bored or disappointed, despite the right notes being played. There are true enigmas in the strange business of performing music.

I came to think of Sebök's remark in this way: the 'container' was the external form of the music, but it encompassed also the concert situation and its ingredients – everything, in other words, apart from 'the contents' of the music. The relationship between container and contents can have all sorts of meanings and nuances, and doesn't apply only to music. Let's take the analogous example of houses, which can be very significant *containers* for people's dreams and fantasies. Houses are primarily physical containers, but they are spiritual containers too. If you've ever gone through the process of house-hunting you'll know how sensitive you get to how each possible house makes you feel, and it's often a very strong sensation. People project their dreams and wishes onto specific houses, and sometimes convince themselves that everything in their life will be put right if only they could live in a certain house. Who knows what causes people to form this instant fantasy bond with a house, sometimes on the basis of just a brief visit. Many house-hunters recount the experience of setting eyes on a certain house and instantly deciding that 'this is it', 'this is where I could be me', sometimes before they've even set foot inside it, and often in defiance of things which they can plainly see are wrong with it. Sometimes they can't even put into words what it is about the house that strikes them as so ideal. At some deep level it seems that a house can represent a kind of psychic landscape. The house is not just a desirable container. It has content too – not only its architectural features, but its own way of interacting with time and space, regardless of anything that a temporary owner might impose on it for a short while. House-hunters sense this and want to be part of it.

I had a little epiphany about houses when I was in an Italian village one summer, sharing a house with a group of musicians in return for giving some free concerts. Many of the village properties were rented out to foreign visitors in summer, often to families who kept returning year after year to the same houses. The houses varied in how the space was divided up internally. Some had a formal living room at the front and a kitchen at the back. Some had the kitchen in the main room. Some had a small room at the front and a larger family living room at the back, giving onto the garden. As we got to know some of the families it occurred to me that their personalities, and perhaps also their nationalities, were linked in some mysterious way with the houses they had chosen. Some people liked to look out into the garden from inside the house, while others preferred to be outside looking in. Some people felt happy cooking in the room nearest the street, with the front door propped open and people popping in and out. Others felt happier to retreat to the back of the house to cook in private. Some families liked to sit on the front step, watching the village life go by in the lane. Others had chosen houses where they could gather in a courtyard at the back, unobserved by the village. I began to feel that in a surprising number of cases the disposition of the physical space matched the disposition of the inhabitants. They were gravitating, I felt, towards a house whose outward form was some kind of template of an inner reality.

In later years, visiting other historical properties, I enlarged my understanding of these 'inner templates' when I realised that I myself was often drawn to parts of the building which were not the grandest, the most flamboyant or the most public. For example, I always feel mysteriously at home in the cloisters of mediaeval churches and monasteries, their sheltered walkways enclosing a little garden or courtyard above which you can see the sky. I know that in olden days the cloisters were used by monks for reading, writing, copying and illuminating manuscripts. There's something about these peaceful organised spaces, at the heart of the building yet invisible from the exterior and set aside from the main hub of activity, a quiet interface between the inside and the outside, which I feel I recognise, as though the architecture is mapping out and giving material form to a situation I 'know' at a deep level.

It may not be too far-fetched to draw a comparison between a house and a piece of music. Most musicians who engage with a great work of music over a period of time would probably agree it feels as if they 'live there'. A good piece of music is also an architectural structure, designed to function in a certain way and to contain certain processes. Just like a real house, a piece of music can become a very significant container for the player. It allows the player to project onto it their own dreams, such as the dream of communicating with the audience, the dream of being in the spotlight, or the dream of being immersed in a meaningful human experience with other people. These wishes can be projected onto a piece of music quite independently of what the piece of music itself is all about.

Unlike a house, though, a piece of music is dynamic, and although some people are lucky enough to be able to read a musical score and hear the music in their heads, most people would agree that a piece of music doesn't really exist until someone brings it to life by playing it. When they do play it, they often succeed in making 'the content' into something of their own, as well as something of the composer's. When you think back to the best performances you've heard, they often seem to be a blend of wonderful music with a wonderful performer who has willingly taken up the composer's blueprint and 'inhabited' it. They've learned to live in the music. That's a process that can't be rushed, but I am quite sure that audiences can sense when a musician is *inhabiting* the music, rather than walking around the outside of it, pointing things out as they go. As a player I can also affirm that it feels quite different to perform a piece that you feel you 'live inside'.

Another analogy might be with actors and their scripts. The script of a play is, you might say, the container, just as a page of musical notes is. We've all seen, or heard on the radio, 'wooden' performances of plays where the words are spoken accurately, but seem to remain on the surface. If you're watching a wooden performance, it's impossible to *get past the words*. We all know the sensation, when reading a book for example, that our eyes are taking in the words and we know what they mean, but the narrative doesn't 'flow'. We remain on the surface, irritatingly aware of individual words, and can't sink down into the meaning. Sometimes I've made myself persist with a book that's been recommended to me, even though I find it hard going. I have the sensation of paying attention to the words on the page, and this activity is in the forefront of my consciousness. But then there may come a point where, without quite knowing how, I cease to be aware of individual words and seem to sink down to a less effortful technique of reading and a deeper layer of meaning. The meaning is accessed through the words, and of course wouldn't be accessible without them, but the words somehow suddenly become linked together and at the same time transparent, so that I can see through them to the thought which underlies them. Instead of being little separate units, the words join together in longer units which make sense and cause me to forget the individual words. Exactly the same thing applies to music, with notes instead of words.

Many people enjoy being involved in music for reasons not much to do with its content. As a one-time amateur violinist and percussionist, a member of school groups and youth orchestras, I've experienced first-hand the enjoyment of collective music-making where it hardly seemed to matter to most people what piece we were playing. The main thing was the *process* of making music, the social interaction and the shared enterprise, for which music provided a melodious background hum. The effort of playing an instrument while counting the beats and 'keeping together' with everyone else often seemed sufficient to provide a kind of music therapy. But it's possible for those efforts to make the participants slightly deaf to the music itself, as I've discovered when asking amateur musicians what pieces they are currently playing, and realising that they can't name them. Does it matter, if they're enjoying themselves? I'm still not sure, but I can't help feeling that amateurs often stop short of what I would call the real work, the exploration of what the music is trying to say and how it could best be said. I attend amateur chamber music concerts quite regularly, and though I completely understand that it is just a hobby for the participants, many of whom are high-flying professionals in other fields, I'm nevertheless surprised at how blank the performances often are, almost as though they feel they are not yet advanced enough to start putting in the music, or as if there is some strong force-field which prevents them from breaking ranks and trying to express what they feel. The expression 'tall poppy syndrome' often comes to mind. In my mind's ear I can hear the voice of Mr Sebök saying, 'Too many people wait far too long to start asking themselves what the music means. You have to look for the meaning *right away!*'

For more advanced performers, musical performance can be a container in other ways. It offers the chance to show off instrumental skills, to experience the spotlight, to have the opportunity to fight with nerves and memory, to bond with the audience, to explore the limits of personal communication skills. It can be a chance to explore and push against the limits of one's control. All these matters could fill many books, and indeed often do. These days I sometimes have the sense that performers are being more and more encouraged to be aware of these 'personal communication' skills instead of focusing on the message of the music. We are constantly told that classical music will fade away unless it wakes up to the fact that we live in a highly visual, connected world. It's a world obsessed with celebrities, media-savvy and skilled with publicity. Performers of very limited talent appear on 'talent shows' and manage to become rich and famous on the basis of carefully managed publicity alone. Poor old classical music, with its long years of dedication and training. How can it survive unless classical musicians wake up to the fact that we live in a world of image, of promotion machines and Svengalis with the power to elevate an ordinary individual into a star? Sometimes it even seems that their very lack of talent is what endears talent show competitors to their adoring audiences.

It sometimes feels as if today's audiences are more focused on appearance, entertainment and escapism than they are on the music itself. Perhaps these things have always been important to concert-goers of every kind, but today they seem more central than ever. Many performers, even classical performers, feel they have to play up to these expectations and put more and more effort into the outward signs that they're having a good time. We players are often complimented on the fact that we look as if we're really enjoying ourselves. I don't mind being told this, but I do feel strange if it's the *only* thing that people say after a performance. It's nice that people notice when I seem to be enjoying myself, but I don't want them to *count on me* to sell them that impression. It's distracting to have to think about that as I play. For me there's no link between a musician 'looking as if they're enjoying themselves' and being a convincing, satisfying performer. Indeed, it sometimes seems as if there's an inverse link between musical intensity and showy enjoyment.

When I was a young musician, practically no thought was given by me or my teachers or my parents to 'the image' side of the business. Performing music was, for the most part, all about what the composer had asked us to do. When I was old enough to go to masterclasses, I heard nothing but discussion of the content of the music and how to bring it alive. Some of the people doing the talking would certainly not have passed muster for their clothes sense, body shape or haircuts. They gave no thought to that side of the business, and we young musicians accepted them the way they were. They weren't style icons and they didn't advise us on fashion choices and public relations either. Now young musicians have to attend courses on 'selling themselves'. They learn the use of social media, how to craft 'a brand' through their choice of clothes, portfolios of photos and attracting sponsorship. We've all seen those YouTube promotional videos where the performer's body language has clearly been practised in front of a mirror or requested by an art director. The pendulum has definitely swung away from the content to the container.

Even without the pressures of our celebrity-obsessed age, it has always been hard to move beyond the 'container' stage of playing music. We're all good musicians in our heads, in the bath and in our dreams, but in reality we have to master instruments before we can play them. There's an enormous terrain of instrumental skill which has to be mapped and traversed before the player can get to 'the grail', the music itself. How to control an instrument is of overwhelming focus and interest, the subject of countless hours of practice at all stages of a career. Indeed the task is so absorbing that it often seems to become the main point of a performance. As you listen you may sense that a performance is primarily a forum for showing off bow control, super-fast vibrato, the ability to move about a keyboard at great speed, etc. As concert halls have grown larger, the ability to project a big, glossy sound has become highly prized and is often admiringly mentioned in reviews. But make no mistake: gorgeous sound can become 'the container', and this is often evident in the way that reviewers, especially in certain countries, speak of it as if it is the be-all and end-all of a performer's prestige.

I know a cellist who hero-worshipped the Russian cellist Mstis-lav Rostropovich and had perfected a very accurate imitation of his sound, including his vibrato. I think it was intended more as a homage than an imitation: Rostropovich's sound had become the lens through which his admiring acolyte viewed every piece of cello music. To the listener, however, everything sounded the same. I'm not suggesting that *Rostropovich* always sounds the same, but his big-hearted, gravelly sound and his unique bow contact with the string – 'gripping' in more senses than one – had become a goal in itself; his awestruck imitator was so obsessed with it that he hardly seemed to register what the music was 'about'. Occasionally I would ask, 'Why are you doing it like that?' and got the answer, 'Because Rostro plays it like that!'

At the opposite end of the spectrum is the player who understands the content very well, but doesn't have the instrumental skill to do justice to it. If their control of their instrument is shaky, if their tone is scratchy, if their phrasing is lumpy or fragmented, if they can't breathe well enough to keep the tone flowing, can we still perceive the content of the music properly? Very occasionally one hears a player whose identification with the music allows them to put it across despite physi-cal problems. Yehudi Menuhin in his later years, when he suffered from a trembling bow arm, was an example of this. I heard him once in

Switzerland and was astonished by how much I got out of the music, despite his obvious nervousness. My experience in the concert hall seems to show that both types of player, the one obsessed with a particular kind of tone and the one who doesn't have control over tone, can cause the content of the music to be veiled as far as the listener is concerned. The relationship between the player and the instrument (good or bad) becomes 'the container' in this kind of performance, and is the thing the audience is most conscious of.

Even without the rather extreme example of a player who aspires to sound like his hero in every musical situation, there are many good instrumentalists for whom performance seems to be 'about' the struggle to feel physically comfortable and at ease with their instrument. Music becomes the arena in which they strive not to feel aches and pains, or in which they conquer their fear of wrong notes and memory slips. These are in the front of their mind when they play, and if these things go well then their main performance goal has been realised.

In some arduous performance situations, such as making a record, even very good players can become focused on the surface of the music when they realise that the microphone is mercilessly picking up and remembering every little inaccuracy. Not wishing these flaws to be immortalised on disc, they become super-conscious at the level of finger on key, sometimes at the same time trying to keep in mind that they must not stamp on the pedal, make a noise when they turn a page, or squeak their chair as they shift their weight about. I've experienced these situations many times, and I admit that when the going gets tough, and you are worrying about every little thing, it can be hard to stay focused on the emotion inside the music. No matter how well you know it, and how deeply you are immersed in it, you may feel yourself being dragged up again to a conscious level, to the level where music can deconstruct from phrases into individual notes. You might imagine that, having reached the stage of understanding the deeper and longer units of the piece, you would not be capable of going backwards and reverting to an unhelpful awareness of each note, but it turns out that both sorts of awareness can be present at the same time.

There are many ways of focusing on the periphery instead of

the contents. I recently gave a coaching session on a Mozart trio to a very good young professional group with members from different countries. As they unpacked their instruments we had a chat, and I was happy to see that they were all in a good mood. Then, to my astonishment, when they launched into the music, I saw the Japanese pianist assume a tortured look. Her body bent forwards into a gesture of abasement in front of the piano, and her face took on an agonised expression. Her whole body was a mask of tension as she played. After a while I stopped her and asked her what it was about the music which inspired this look of agony. She laughed with embarrassment and didn't know what to say. But I think I had an idea of the answer: her foremost thought was that she was in a masterclass, being judged for her seriousness. Mozart is high art, which is serious and painful, and one's body language should reflect this. This for her was 'the container'. The fact that she was playing a merry, high-spirited piece, written for eighteenth-century friends to have fun with, was less meaningful to her than the opportunity to express deep devotion to her art – regardless of whether or not this put a nonsensical gloss on the music. When I told her that her task for today was not to express any anguish except for anguish she found *in the music*, she sat up straight and stopped looking tortured. Soon we were able to talk about the music's content.

In collaborative music-making between two people, such as classical duos of a string player and a pianist, I have often grieved to see the players becoming focused on an external form which has nothing to do with the content of the music. This is when two people try to inhabit the roles of 'soloist' and 'accompanist' because of (I believe) erroneous messages fed to them during their years of music education. The 'container' in this case is a hierarchical situation which duo partners strive to assert without really understanding why. For reasons they could not articulate, they feel they must fall into the roles of a Don Quixote (the 'soloist', or hero, played by the string player) and a Sancho Panza (the servant, played by the pianist).

Often duo pianists subordinate the musical content of the piano part to the desire uppermost in their mind, the desire to be a good and self-effacing supporter. They actually strive to remain less in focus than 'the soloist', and that can be evident in everything from body language and platform demeanour to what tennis players would call 'shot selection', their choice of tone and touch on the keyboard. When I was teaching a very good cello and piano duo at the Guildhall School of Music and Drama recently, I asked the pianist how he saw his role in the Brahms F major Sonata for Piano and Cello, which has a huge piano part. Nodding towards his cello-playing partner, the pianist said, 'To set him going and then to step back and be a good supporter.' The cellist beamed in agreement. I asked the pianist why he thought so. 'Because it is a cello sonata,' he answered. 'Why do you call it a *cello* sonata?' I asked. 'Because the cellist has the main role,' he answered. 'Does he?' I asked. 'What makes you think that?' The pianist smiled and shrugged. So I suggested we look at the score to see who presented the main themes. We looked at the density of notes in the piano part and the amount of musical information lodged there. We found that sometimes the cello stated the theme and sometimes the piano did. Sometimes the piano was the first to state a theme and the cello echoed it. We looked at how the instruments weave in and out, how sometimes one is the leader, sometimes the other. We noticed that for longish passages, for example in the development section of the first movement, it's the pianist who outlines the main argument, while the cellist provides only a kind of harmonic shading. From the evidence, it certainly didn't look as if the piano part was *meant to be in the background*.

I asked the pianist whether it was *from the music* that he took his understanding of his role. He admitted that it wasn't. In fact, when we talked in more detail, it turned out that his understanding of his role was a product of that long-standing conservatory tradition where a string teacher uses a 'class pianist' to play for all their students. It's a convenient way of enabling students to encounter lots of repertoire, but it also sends a very unfortunate message about what this music really is: a partnership between equals. Many of the great duo sonatas were written by composer-pianists who would have been aghast to discover that the piano part had come to be viewed as 'in the background'. But unfortunately after years in educational settings, many young instrumentalists come to see the pianist as being a dogs-body, always there like the chair that Queen Victoria knew would be behind her when she wanted to sit down. There may be good practical reasons for how the 'class pianist' situation has evolved, but I believe it's had a very regrettable impact. String and wind players go out into the profession regarding their duo partners as 'repetiteurs' and themselves as the heroes. And they often maintain this outlook for the rest of their professional lives, passing on to their students the same unhealthy attitude.

Early in my career, the group Domus experimented a lot with 'the container'. We had our own portable concert hall, a geodesic dome-shaped tent that could seat 200. Within it, we arranged the seating as we liked, on the ground, on cushions, around the players, and so on. In our concerts, we tried all kinds of formats from playing without saying anything to introducing pieces at length and telling people about ourselves. We played standing amid the audience, on a stage, on a high platform under the roof, or arranged in a ring round the edge of the tent behind the listeners. In rehearsal we pretended to be other people (such as favourite famous musicians) to jolt ourselves out of being always the same. We tried different seating positions, such as sitting with our backs to one another, or playing with our eyes shut, to see if we could sense one another's movements and intentions. We tried different outfits from formal wear to white hippy smocks to baggy jumpers. The motive was to get rid of stuffy old conventions and make ourselves and our listeners feel free.

As time went on, though, some of us started to feel that all this experiment wasn't actually helping us to get to the core of the music we loved. It was definitely building bridges with certain kinds of listener. It was also raising our profile as individuals, for we were more personally known, recognised and even cherished by our audiences who had heard us speak about all sorts of music-related and non-music-related things. They loved the fact that they had met the person behind the normally un-meetable artist. They loved coming into the dome to find us serving beer or making sushi for them. All this did no end of good to our feeling of usefulness and being part of the community. However, it didn't have much to do with making our interpretations better or our grasp of Mozart and Beethoven deeper. In fact, most of the peripheral stuff was distracting, as our former professors occasionally hinted when they came to hear our concerts.

It turned out that to go deeper into the music, we had to cut down on our surface concentration on what the audience was looking at and thinking. We had to spend more time developing our instrumental skills. Sadly, there seemed to be a kind of inverse relationship between conscious bridge-building to the audience and the depth of the musical experience. Sometimes we had guest players who had not been involved with all the work of building the dome, spending the day in a field in the rain, interacting all day long with visitors, and so on. They had 'only' been practising in a quiet room somewhere else. It was, however, sometimes striking how, without any attempt to 'hug the audience', their single-minded concentration on, say, a solo Bach suite was as impactful as our Bach-with-sushi-made-and-served-by-us approach. We had been accustomed to saying that we didn't only want to play our pieces in the traditional way, but one of our guest artists reminded me one day that there is no 'only' about dedicating yourself to the study of an instrument and to the study of great music. In other words, he was reminding me that we needed to focus less on the container and more on the contents.

But what are the contents of a piece of music? What is music *about*, and is that the same thing? These are deep questions, to which listeners will have different answers according to how music strikes them and what role it plays in their mental life. If you put me on the spot and told me to come up with an immediate answer, I'd say that music is about transformation. What happens to the little cells of music, be they notes, short motifs or longer phrases, is a process akin to telling a story. It can't be more than 'akin', because there is no simple equivalent between a musical phrase and a sentence, nor is there a simple equivalent between a note and a word. (As Mendelssohn said, music is too definite for words and 'fills the soul with a thousand things better than words'.) But there is a *process*, in which things happen to the notes and phrases; they take various paths and move in various directions. What happens to them changes them, and those changes are expressed in alterations of harmony, rhythm and pace. They're expressed in journeys from simplicity to complexity and back. Music can often evoke memory's ability to unearth fragments and its sudden vivid recall of scenes from the past, scenes which sometimes turn out to be misremembered, but are sometimes recalled in their entirety with transcendent effect.

The transformations of music have a special character because they unfold in time – like theatre plays; but unlike theatre plays they are told in sounds alone, without words. When we go to the theatre we are in no doubt what the play is 'about' because it uses words, and we understand words because we use them every minute of our daily lives. If someone asks us what *Middlemarch* or *War and Peace* is about, we can easily pinpoint themes of personal relationships, regret, discovery, loss, difficult decisions and so on. But when we go to the symphony or the chamber music concert or the solo piano recital, we sometimes doubt our power to follow the narrative because, being expressed in musical sounds, it is at one remove from our everyday experience. Nobody says 'I do not understand words' but plenty of people say 'I am not musical.' Can that be true? Amusia (congenital or acquired) does exist, but is rare. We've learned that music comes before speech in human development, that babies respond to the rise and fall of their parents' voices and intuit their meaning from the music of their words before they understand the words themselves. I am always puzzled when I hear people claim that they are not musical, and I suppose they mean rather that they have never become familiar with music.

A good piece of classical music has a story it wants to tell. One can't press this analogy too far, because music and stories are not exact parallels, and music can famously express things which nobody has yet discovered how to put into words. Nevertheless, most of our favourite pieces of music have an internal structure and a developing argument or narrative – not a narrative in the sense of 'Once upon a time in a faraway land there was a princess', but in the sense that we are presented with musical units to which things happen, and we can follow the process because we know what change feels like. We instinctively understand what is turmoil and what is calm, or what is certainty and what is doubt. We also know how memory works, how it can reassure as well as deceive us. In Western classical music, the progress of the music is usually defined by harmonic and rhythmic changes which chart the twists and turns of the developing argument. These changes are signs from the composer which we are meant to be read, signs of a change of direction, or a change of activity or intensity. If a player simply ploughs through them without reading those signs and reacting to them, the music does not spring to life. In fact it's surprising how often you hear people ploughing through harmonic changes without instinctive adjustments of tempo, like a driver whose style and speed of driving doesn't change when they leave the motorway and turn off into rural lanes.

Sometimes the content is expressed as much by the structure of the music as by the particular themes placed within it. The proportions of a longer movement, such as a sonata movement, often have a beauty of their own and a way of occupying time which leaves an imprint on the imagination of the hearer. Just as one can perceive and admire the proportions of a piece of architecture, so one can sense the proportions of something expressed in the medium of time. Choice of tempo can change the proportions, but their relationship to one another is usually discernible.

It's a challenge to hear a piece of music afresh when a performing tradition has grown up over decades or longer. Now that we've had a century of recordings, we have also been deeply influenced by certain famous recordings which have enshrined the approach of the performers, not always in a helpful way. When I'm teaching, if I'm struck by something not sounding quite genuine I often ask the players why they're doing it that way, and their answer is often that 'it was like that on the recording'. This is a new problem; musicians in earlier centuries had no way of knowing how musicians of earlier generations sounded, so there was nothing to imitate or be intimidated by. The past was silent. But now we are influenced by 'Great Recordings' and by past performers whose possibly spur-of-the-moment decisions have become really quite prescriptive.

A good example in piano music might be Schubert's final piano sonata, the B-flat major Sonata D960. Because of the influence of certain recordings it has become traditional to approach the first movement in particular as the essence of profundity, a kind of statement 'ex cathedra'. Many pianists now tend to play it very slowly and portentously. Yet if you look at the score itself, there is no indication that Schubert intended this tempo, or had this kind of deeply serious and elder-statesman-like approach in mind. His marking is 'Molto moderato' – not a slow marking. There's nothing at all to indicate that Schubert imagined a grand, serious opening. The opening theme wanders very simply and quietly around a few notes, mostly confined within a major third (B-flat to D) and in a simple rhythm of crotchets and quavers. At the end of the first phrase comes the famous growling trill in the bass, which seems to bring a note of threat to the proceedings. After a pause, the simple melody resumes and develops.

It has become traditional to play the menacing trill very slowly and importantly, extending it beyond its written length, and slowing down even more towards the end. And it's traditional to bind the opening theme into this sorrowful atmosphere as though the menacing trill is known already, and the music is in a state of arrested development because of it. But it is not known already! When we hear the opening melody there is no hint of trouble to come. We forget that this is the music of a young man. It may have been one of Schubert's last works, but he was only thirty when he wrote it. Judging by his own markings and by the simplicity of the harmonic design in the opening pages, the score shows every sign of an innocent, flowing songfulness, with shadows (in the form of modulations to faraway keys) passing over it now and then. The content, it seems to me, is much more varied than we often hear it. And by playing the opening movement extremely slowly and tragically, the performer allows it to overbalance the other three movements in the sonata. The slow movement, where the musical pulse drops to its slowest (and that slowest point is still only andante sostenuto, nothing slower!), seems tedious if the first movement has already been so slow. The scherzo and finale can seem flippant after two very long, very slow movements. Many of these problems would vanish if pianists worked from the score without mindlessly swallowing preconceived ideas from pianists of earlier generations. Our assumption of 'the way we all play it' has become a label that we paste on the work without actually looking to see what the contents *are*.

Another surprising performance tradition is the one which has grown up around Elgar's 'Nimrod', one of his 'Enigma' Variations. Even in the composer's lifetime it was hijacked as ceremonial music, though he never intended this. Because of the association it now has with the Cenotaph and Remembrance Day, it has become traditional to play it extremely slowly and grandly; when 'Nimrod' strikes up, everyone knows it's the moment to get their hankies out and tremble with noble emotion. But Elgar did not write 'Nimrod' like that, as we know from his metronome marks and from his own performance on record. He was in the prime of life when he wrote it as a portrait of his friend Jaeger. Yes, the music is sincere, but it is manly and dignified, not a great imposing catafalque. It was a tribute to a man whose name, Jaeger, means 'hunter' in German. Nimrod in the Bible was a hunter, and so it was a playful pun on Jaeger's name. One would never guess this today from the way the piece is used. It has become a stock item at memorial services after tragic events, and was played tearfully by the National Radio Orchestra of Greece on the occasion of the orchestra's shut-down in June 2013. Have lots of people seen something in it that the composer himself failed to see? Or has it become 'a container'?

Friends of mine in an American string quartet laugh about a listener in Texas who visited their dressing-room immediately after their performance of Schubert's *Death and the Maiden* quartet. 'That was thoroughly dee-laht-ful!' he beamed. This struck the players as a ridiculous response to the content of the work. It seemed that all the listener had noticed was that he was at a pleasing event where four gifted players were in harmony. For him, this had far more prominence than the fact that they were playing something sad. But was it their fault or his that he hadn't 'got' the searching sadness of Schubert's music?

Confronted with music which revels in ambiguity, people can feel lost. The nuances and ambiguities of classical music sometimes seem to get on the nerves of people accustomed to short 'songs' whose character is plainly obvious. Given half an hour of late Beethoven or Schubert, people sometimes feel very unsure; even major keys cannot be relied upon to sound 'happy', nor minor keys to sound 'sad', and no sooner is a certain pulse established than it gives way to another. The mood is often very hard to pin down, and changes frequently. To the players, these ambiguities are sources of interest, seeds that we know are going to flower at some point in the music. We read them as messages from Beethoven that there are issues he wants to explore. But compared with, say, a pop song whose impact is instant and straightforward, this kind of long-breathed music seems to make many listeners feel that they're being bamboozled, perhaps blinded with science. We've grown so used to 'songs' being three minutes long that even seasoned musicians sometimes find it difficult to stay with the twists and turns of a Beethoven or Schubert sonata or quartet. So many things – Tweets, Facebook updates, emails, text messages, games – compete for our attention that it's a wonder there are many people still able to focus on a forty-minute symphony.

Many different kinds of music have their rituals, and these are tied up with what one might consider 'content' or 'container'. In pop, it may seem that spectacle is a distraction from the content, but when Lady Gaga steps out of a coffin on stage, the visual impact is designed to be as great as whatever she then goes on to sing. In many pop gigs, sheer decibel level is often one of the main points. 'We want to know about the loudest bands you've ever been deafened by!' coaxed Michael Hann in *The Guardian* in November 2012. 'I couldn't hear a thing – literally, nothing – for several days,' he recalled after a My Bloody Valentine gig. Their music was evidently not the most striking thing. At the opposite extreme, if you experience a jazz group or a folk group playing in a pub, their demeanour often seems to suggest they're making the point that there is *nothing to look at*, so much so that their audience often seems intimidated into not watching them.

Where on that spectrum do classical musicians lie? Some might say we don't take enough advantage of the possibilities offered by spectacle and amplification, but we really don't want to play that game. We hope our audiences are watching and listening, but 'show' is not the point. In an image-obsessed world, most of us feel that Sebök's advice 'not to play the container' has never been so necessary.

Temps perdu

In the last year or two I have started to notice concert reviews which mention that the performer brought an iPad or other electronic gadget on stage, put it on the music stand or on the music desk of the piano, and read from it during the performance. Because this possibility is so new it still seems to carry the cachet of technological novelty; people are fascinated by the fact that it can be done at all. I haven't detected a note of disapproval in the way such events are written about – rather the reverse. It's 'cool' to read the score from an iPad on the music desk, especially if it employs the very latest technology which enables the musician to turn the pages without actually touching the screen with their hands. It links classical musicians to the 'now' in a pleasing way and perhaps makes everyone feel that classical music is investing in its own future.

When I read about this kind of thing, I find myself wondering, 'Where has it gone, all the time I spent on memorising things for concert performance? Can I have it back?' – because memorising things has occupied a huge proportion of my private practice, as it does for most of my colleagues who do any kind of solo performing. When I read the admiring comments in the press about so-and-so having appeared at this or that festival with their iPad on the piano, I feel slightly aghast at the notion that 'playing from memory' may have been just a kind of passing fashion, not a requirement truly grounded in musical ethics.

The chequered history of playing from memory is linked to the rise in importance of The Composer in Western classical music. In many parts of the world, where music is part of the collective aural memory, passed on from one player or singer to another, there is no division into 'playing from the music' and 'playing from memory'. But we have suffered from that division. If music is largely improvised there is no place for written or printed sheets. In jazz performances, for example, you may see musicians with perhaps one sheet of paper to remind them of the chord changes in one particular tune, but most of what they play is improvised around the framework dictated by a song and its harmonies. There are many kinds of world music where certain longstanding formulas, treasuries of melodies or modes or chants, are used as the groundwork for elaboration. These underlying formulas are committed to memory during the musician's training and used to underpin complex improvisation throughout their musical lives. In Western societies, before the widespread use of printed music all musicians would have had a large repertoire of tunes and songs in their heads, but there was no requirement for these to be precisely the same in every detail whenever they were played. Musicians' memories were not taxed with the kind of micro-memory which modern soloists have to develop.

In classical music the situation is different because of the enormous repertoire of composed pieces which have come to have iconic status. Apart from some flexibility in adding ornaments, little cadential runs and cadenzas in music of the baroque and classical era, it is not permissible to play anything other than the notes written down by the composer – *and you must play all of the notes*. Those notes gradually came to have almost the authority of sacred texts. We know that Beethoven didn't like it when people came to play him his own piano sonatas and played them from memory. He felt that they would forget his detailed markings, his expression marks and his indications of legato and staccato and the lengths of phrases, and it displeased him to hear performances which left these things out. (From my own experience as a teacher I think he was probably right that most people, no matter how skilful they are at memorising, are not able to memorise all the 'little' markings.) Beethoven felt that his notated scores demanded respect.

For the same reason, Chopin was angry when he heard that other pianists were playing his works from memory. Mendelssohn had an excellent memory, but we know from a delightful anecdote that he didn't think it looked good to play from memory. On a visit to London he discovered that the piano part of his own D minor Trio was missing when he was due to perform it with two colleagues. He knew the piano part from memory, but he told his page-turner, 'Just put any piece of music on the piano and turn the pages from time to time while I'm playing, and then it need not look as if I'm playing from memory.' (*Need not look as if I'm playing from memory*! How things have changed.) At this period it was considered a mark of respect to the composer to use the score in public, even if you were the composer. Liszt, one of the first 'celebrity performers', who improvised in public and did play some of his repertoire from memory, used to play his own music from the score, to emphasise that there was nothing accidental about it. Many performers at that time would respectfully use the music of other people's compositions to show they were not pretending that *they* had composed it or were making it up on the spot. Playing from the score was thus an acknowledgement of the composer's 'intellectual property'.

But as the cult of the 'celebrity soloist' developed, by the early twentieth century, there was a change in fashion. It was part of the spectacle of a celebrity recital, an aspect of its theatricality, that the artist would perform from memory. The public came to expect it and, according to writers of the period, would feel a frisson of disapproval or anxiety should a soloist bring the scores on stage. Teachers started telling their students that it was obligatory to memorise their pieces for performance. Taking volumes of music on stage was considered sloppy, a sign of lack of preparation. When I was learning the piano, it was taken for granted that if I was to play a solo piece in public, I had to memorise it. There wasn't any discussion – my teacher took the view that playing from memory was expected by examiners at 'grade

exams', by adjudicators at music competitions, by critics reviewing
your concert, by fellow students and by the public. It was just part of
having a 'professional' attitude. Fortunately for me I found it fairly
easy to memorise, so I didn't particularly fight against the command-
ment, but even so the act of playing from memory *in public* added an
unanticipated element of strain.

Teachers maintained that playing from memory would make me
feel 'freer' and would foster better communication with the audience.
Whether this is true or not is still the subject of great debate amongst
fellow musicians whenever the subject of memorisation comes up.
Some people declare that they never feel so free as when they are
playing from memory. Others say they feel freer if the score is there
as a 'comfort blanket', even if they don't truly need it. Yet others
only feel free if they are frankly reading from the score. I suspect
that those who feel freer when playing from memory are those for
whom memorising has always come easily. I know lots of musicians
who find it hard to memorise and have forced themselves to do it, but
their reaction afterwards is usually, 'Phew! Glad that's over!', rather
than assent that they did actually find it liberating. There's an age
element to the question too, well documented by the many soloists
(such as Arthur Rubinstein, Clifford Curzon and Sviatoslav Richter)
who found it harder to memorise from middle age onwards and took
to using the score on stage. Perhaps 'harder' is not the right word – it
seems to be more a matter of losing confidence in one's powers of
memory, or more precisely in the reliability of those powers. I've
found, over the years, that I tend to devote longer and longer to the
task of memorising solo pieces.

There's another aspect to performing from memory that I haven't
seen much remarked on, and this is that concert performances usually
take place in the evening. For most people, the challenges of working
life take place during the day, when we are at our liveliest and our
brains are freshest. I suppose that most of us start the day with a store
of energy which gradually diminishes, leaving us depleted and ready
to relax in the evening. For anyone who has to perform in the evening,
the situation is very different. They have to be at their most alert at

a time when most people have wound down for the day. In other words, evening concerts make sense for the audience, but not always for the performers, except of course in the sense that performers need audiences. On the occasions when I've played in morning concerts, I've noticed that it's easier to be 'on the ball'; my reflexes are fast and my store of energy feels pleasantly full. Musicians vary a great deal, naturally; some musicians positively welcome the fact that they have until the evening to warm up, but for anyone whose body clock is set to optimum performance in the earlier part of the day, it can be quite challenging to keep on high alert throughout the evening, especially if the performance has been preceded by a long journey and a rehearsal, and very likely not enough food. Performing from memory is definitely helped by alertness, and I'd guess that memory retrieval probably varies along with individual biorhythms.

As a child I used to find that the process of learning the notes was pretty much identical with the process of memorising. It may still be the case, except that between then and now I have become increasingly aware of the fragility of memory under the pressure of public performance. I think I do still memorise easily, but to memorise entire solo recital programmes (for a two-hour concert) is a very big task. If I think about the period of time devoted to preparing a single recital programme, I could probably say that I'd be ready to perform it with the music several months before I feel ready to perform it *without* the music. This means that a big proportion of the entire time spent on preparation is spent on the consolidation of memory. Whether the resulting appreciation from the audience is worth it, I am not sure. I feel that if there was no expectation whatsoever to perform from memory, I could offer new works at a much earlier stage, because the point when I feel technically and artistically ready to play them arrives well before the point where I feel confident to play them without the music. You might suggest that between those two points there is an ongoing unconscious process of artistic maturing while I'm busy consolidating the memory side of things. Maybe there is, but when I look back on a solo recital I often have some regret about how long I spent on memorising it, and am not entirely sure why I felt I must.

I've often heard it said by performers that if they have a memory lapse in a concert, and have to stop and start again, the audience's reaction is one of ecstatic approval if they manage to get to the end without mishap second time round. I experienced this myself once when performing Schubert's late A major Piano Sonata. The final movement is a rondo, with a long theme followed by a set of episodes exploring the theme. I got to the end of the initial rondo section and blanked out completely. I simply couldn't remember what came next. It was silent inside my head (a scary feeling). After a few moments of all of us sitting there in silence (it felt endless but was probably only a few seconds), I turned to the audience, explained what had happened, apologised and said I was going to begin the movement again. I started again and this time, when I got to the moment in question, some kind of muscle memory kicked in and I sailed off into the first episode. At that moment I was aware of the whole audience breathing a collective sigh of relief and relaxing visibly. At the end, their applause and their smiles seemed particularly warm, and I remember being struck by how a memory lapse (which equalled 'disaster' in the eyes of my teachers) had actually turned out to be a bonding experience with the audience. Who knew?

But I was also slightly disheartened by the discovery, because it implied that something extra-musical, of 'human interest', was more meaningful to the audience than what I did musically, or to put it more grandly, my interpretation. Very natural, perhaps, but it made me wonder whether all the months of 'two-steps-forward-one-step-back' work spent on memorising a forty-minute sonata had actually been worthwhile if, in reality, a genuine memory lapse had more impact, or at any rate was more endearing. Since then, I've always wondered whether watching someone perform from memory is primarily a sort of sport, rather than something which truly enhances the musical experience. My teachers used to say that playing from memory would enable me to communicate better with the audience, but I saw it wasn't quite as simple as that: the audience might like me better if they had been allowed to witness and share in a little breakdown. However, I also realised that such bonding experiences have to happen naturally, and can't be contrived in advance.

In the world of music there seems to be a hierarchy of who's expected to be able to perform from memory and who isn't. It seems to follow the graph of how many musicians there are in the group. Orchestras almost never play from memory (just too risky when so many people are involved), though I have read of one or two remarkable exceptions, such as Hans von Bülow's Meiningen orchestra in the 1880s, who learned the occasional piece from memory, or the contemporary Italian-based orchestra Spira Mirabilis, whose projects focus on a single piece performed from memory. Chamber groups aren't expected to memorise, though a few string quartets have tried, notably the Kolisch Quartet in the 1920s and '30s who, remarkably, played most of their programmes from memory, including the fearsomely intellectual quartets by Arnold Schoenberg. More recently, the Zehetmair Quartet has performed from memory, learning one new programme a year. Chamber groups who work together part-time rarely attempt to play without the music, though I've been part of discussions about whether it should be attempted; but deciding to play from memory would obviously have to be a unanimous decision, and I've never known the motion be carried. My impression is that there are many individual chamber musicians who could play their core repertoire from memory, but don't.

Going down the size chart, duos (usually a string or wind player and a pianist) are not expected to play from memory, though one sometimes sees the single-line instrument (e.g. the violin, viola, cello, clarinet) play from memory while the pianist plays from the score. This is a custom I regret, and discourage when I have the chance, because I feel it gives a wrong message about the nature of the interaction between the two players, making it appear to innocent observers that the one who plays from memory must be the 'soloist', or is, at any rate, more important than their partner. It is easier to memorise a single line than it is to memorise a complicated piano part, but this practical fact should not, I believe, be seized upon by players of single-line instruments to distort the impression of an equal partnership with their pianist. In my view, either both should play from memory, or neither of them should.

It is the true soloist, such as the solo pianist, who is most subject to the perceived requirement to play from memory. Earlier I raised the question of whether watching someone perform from memory is a spectator sport, and I sometimes wonder whether the public's perception of soloists as 'celebrities' feeds into the desire to see them play from memory, almost as if it is the 'pound of flesh' the public exacts for the status they imagine the artist enjoys. Or it could be the other way round, that certain soloists have actively fostered the image of a lone artist communing directly with his muse, often gazing raptly upwards as though seeing Beethoven or Brahms floating in the air. It's a curious fact that the people most under pressure to play from memory are concerto soloists playing with orchestra. The orchestra is not, however, expected to play a concerto from memory, even though their part is musically substantial and they are playing for more of the time during the piece. Of course the 'point' of a concerto is to show off the virtuosic command of one instrumentalist pitted against an orchestra, so the theatrical element makes it easier to see why the soloist might be playing from memory while the orchestra isn't. Can one compare a soloist playing with an orchestra to a violinist playing with a piano in duo sonatas? I'd say no, because duo sonatas are more of a dialogue in which virtuoso display or dominance is not the point for either artist.

For pianists in particular, playing from memory is sometimes an appealing prospect because it means they don't have to have someone sitting at their side to turn their pages. It's often struck me as curious that something which is practised and prepared to the nth degree (such as a solo piano recital) should at the very last minute have a completely unknown ingredient added to it — a stranger sitting at the pianist's left elbow and standing up every minute or two throughout the concert to lean across the pianist and turn the page for them. Pianists do not take page-turners with them because it is too difficult logistically, let alone financially, so page-turners are usually supplied by the hall. Sometimes they are professionals, working on a team of page-turners employed by the hall, but much more often they are volunteers, or are volunteered (sometimes against their will) by a music society. Turning pages in a concert is an intricate task and hard to get right. The page-turner has to be able to rise from the chair and sit down again without making a noise; they have to be able to lean across the pianist without bumping into the pianist's left arm as they play or blocking their view of the score. They have to turn the page quickly and accurately, just before the pianist reaches the point, so that the pianist can see both the bottom of one page and the top of the next *as they read it in real time,* no easy task for a page-turner who has to ready themselves with the corner of the page grasped between finger and thumb, waiting for the precise moment to whip the page over as the music flows on.

Doing this well is an unsung art, and some page-turners are incredibly skilful. Some of them even manage to impart a sense of calm and moral support which is tremendously helpful. The best ones are often pianists themselves, attuned to the psychology of performance and to how much 'performing space' a pianist needs as their hands whizz about the keyboard. But pianists dread having a nervous or clumsy page-turner beside them. Even when they realise that the page-turner is a reluctant volunteer, doing it out of the goodness of their heart, it is still difficult to focus on the music if someone is fidgeting or breathing nervously at your side, and if you fear they're going to collide with your left arm every time they get up to turn the page. If they get really nervous, they may leap up and turn the page at the wrong moment, turn two pages at once, or even pull the music off the music desk and send it crashing onto the keyboard or the floor. Pianists quite often have to bat the page-turner away with their left arm in order to prevent them from turning the page too early. These are not fun things for either party to have to worry about. As I know from concerts I've attended as a listener, there can be a gruesome fascination in watching a hapless page-turner, and another kind of fascination if the page-turner is more interesting to look at, for whatever reason, than the pianist.

For all my chamber music concerts I have to build in time beforehand to go through the scores with the page-turner and explain any special requirements, like 'repeats', or places where they should take care to be particularly quiet because of what's happening in the music, or places where I want to turn the page myself, like at the end of each movement. As the page-turner is often a volunteer, a pianist can't require them to be present at the rehearsal, so this conference often takes place just minutes before the concert itself and is a slightly strange thing for the pianist to be doing at a moment when they might prefer to prepare their mind in quietness. Often the page-turner is nervous, and the pianist has to exert themselves to be reassuring while not being made nervous too. It's a curious position for both people to be placed in, and using an electronic gadget such as an iPad might well come to seem an attractive escape route (except of course that the pianist would then spend the evening worrying that the iPad was going to 'freeze' and decline to turn the next page). Playing from memory is the cleanest way of avoiding the whole set of potential problems.

Most people would agree that *knowing* something from memory and being able to *recall* that memory in stressful conditions are two different things. As is well known in physics, 'the addition of the observer to the thing observed' causes the outcome to be different than when the 'thing observed' is (for example) practising the piano in peaceful solitude. It's easy enough to remember when nobody is staring at you and you're not under time pressure. Imagine, for example, that you have just installed a burglar alarm in your house. In order to activate this alarm, you must turn off all the electric switches in your house in a particular sequence before you leave the house and within a certain time frame. Of course you know exactly where all the switches are – that's easy; it's part of your working knowledge of the house. But imagine if someone now composes a precise sequence for you to follow – upstairs light switch left, downstairs light switch back right, upstairs computer, hallway light, downstairs behind the television, kettle in the kitchen, reading lamp in study, electric blanket switch in bedroom, stairwell light, etc. You're told that you must remember things *in that sequence* and no other. There's no flexibility; you can't do things in a different order because you feel like it today, and moreover if it is not done in a predetermined length of time, the alarm will go off. No matter how easy you find it to visualise where all the switches are in your house, you would very likely be stressed by the requirement to recall them in a precise sequence under time pressure. You'd find yourself lying awake going over and over the pattern, trying to embed it in your conscious mind, worrying about whether you'd still remember it accurately next week, next month, in a year's time. In short, you'd have a glimpse into what it's like to be a classical musician playing from memory in public. For extra verisimilitude, add to the imagined scene a bunch of people sitting silently in your hallway and watching you perform the sequence.

The world of concert-going is currently confused about what it thinks of the requirement to play from memory. Memorising is often still specified for competitions and auditions, though sometimes there is discrimination among categories. Anthony Tommasini, writing in the *New York Times* in December 2012, pointed out that the Young Concert Artists scheme 'which presents exceptional emerging artists in concert, hews to standard practice for its competitive auditions. The requirements state: "Concertos and solo repertoire for all instruments and voice must be performed by memory. Scores may be used only in chamber music, sonatas with accompaniment and contemporary works."' Young Concert Artists is not unique in having these guidelines; one comes across them all the time in competitions. Such guidelines seem to reveal a hierarchy of who is expected to play from memory and who isn't, a hierarchy that clearly doesn't have much to do with music itself, but is more a set of assumptions about power and status. If it were truly the case that playing from memory freed everyone up and benefited the music, then surely everyone should do it. Conversely, if it makes people unduly nervous and detracts from a relaxed performance, nobody should be made to play from memory. I find it strange that Young Concert Artists, and other competitions, make a distinction between solo repertoire on the one hand and duos, chamber music and contemporary music on the other. Given that there is now a growing sense that the skill of playing from memory is not the same thing as the skill of interpreting music or the skill of communicating music to an audience, I'm surprised that aspiring musicians are still oppressed by such guidelines.

I had a couple of recent experiences where the memorisation requirement was shown to be quite silly. Both were in piano competitions where I was on the jury. In one, the competition had commissioned a new work which all the competitors had to learn and perform from memory. But the work, by Judith Weir, was called 'I turned the page ...'. It toyed with the notion that when the pianist turned each page there might be something surprising at the top of the next. The act of turning the pages and discovering what lay on the next page was integral to the conception of the piece, so it was nonsense to make people play it from memory. Competitors did so, because it was in the rules, but the audience would have been able to make nothing of the reason for the piece's title. And we on the jury, with copies of the score in front us, were bemused by seeing what was meant to be funny. The composer herself was present and I seem to remember her saying that nobody had asked her view on the matter before making it a requirement that the new work should be memorised.

The second experience concerned a competitor presenting a piece that had only just been completed by the American composer Elliott Carter. It was a fiendishly complex piece, and it was amazing that anyone had managed to master it in time for the competition. The pianist sent a note to the jury asking if he could be allowed to perform it from the score, as it was so new, both to him and to the world of music. But the organising committee (composed of non-musicians) was firm: an exception could not be made for one person when everyone else had laboured under the necessity of memorising their competition pieces. However, there were other voices raised in support of someone so enterprising. After a bit of debate, a lawyerly solution was hit upon: the competitor should be told he could play from the score in these special circumstances, *but he could not have a page-turner.* This solution was conveyed to the pianist, and a couple of days later we were treated to the extraordinary sight of him performing the work from huge individual pages which he swiped frantically off the music-desk and onto the floor as each page came to an end. Naturally we were all mesmerised by the ballet of the pages, and it was hard to focus on the music. By the time he had finished, the stage was littered with huge sheets of white paper, and I think we all felt suitably ashamed.

Many people may find that they have memorised music without even trying. In the chapter 'Giving people memories', I mentioned that if a piece of music appeals to you and, equally importantly, makes sense to you, it often stays with you, at least in narrative outline if not in detail. This is pure aural memory, very pleasing and perfectly sufficient for everyday life as a music-lover. But to play from memory in public, most musicians find that pure aural memory is not safe enough. They back it up with several other kinds of memorisation techniques: muscle memory, visual memory and analytical memory.

'Muscle memory' implies that the memory is in the muscles themselves. Memories are stored in the brain, but the brain can store a set of frequently repeated motor movements, and any musician will tell you that it feels as if the muscles themselves, or maybe the nerves in the hands and arms, have their own system of remembering. 'Frequently repeated' is key; this kind of memory develops through prolonged practice of something physical, and for many musicians it is perhaps the chief way in which they guide themselves through a performance without the score. It's a strange kind of memory to work with because it doesn't seem to be able to be hurried. Whenever I have to learn a completely new work from scratch, I'm aware of several stages in the process. As I look at the score, my fingers move around the keyboard in response to the notes I see on the score (I don't usually look at my hands during this process). Quite quickly I form a mental impression of how one might play these notes and what that would sound like. My intellectual grasp of the music at this stage is ahead of my physical ability to play those same notes. There's a stage, the duration of which I can't control, when I know exactly what notes I want to hear but have to concentrate consciously on making my hands play them. At this point I feel that my muscle memory is lagging behind my musical grasp of the piece, and I begin to feel annoyed by every wrong note I play, because it jars with what my eyes tell me I should be hearing.

I feel I should pay tribute to the usefulness of impatience. For me, impatience has been immensely valuable in my piano practice. It has driven me to keep as short as possible the period of time I have to spend moving between ignorance and knowledge of a new piece. I could put it more positively and say that I have a hunger to hear the piece being played properly, but perhaps it would be more honest to say that I can't tolerate things being wrong, especially if the source of the wrongness is me. When I'm teaching, I often feel that people are too content to dwell for a long time in that stage of half-knowing where they find their own mistakes all too forgivable. I feel they drag out the learning stage for longer than necessary and that it would be useful to inject a dose of impatience into the process, but of course it's often pointless to interfere in someone's way of learning something. All the same, I suspect that by unnecessarily prolonging the stage at which wrong notes, wrong chords and misreadings are acceptable, it's all too easy to commit those mistakes to memory. This is actually an occupational hazard for lots of musicians. If you passively repeat mistakes you may find that you've successfully fed those mistakes into your muscle memory, from where it will be hard to eradicate them. You may find, in fact, that you have successfully practised getting things wrong.

In *Beyond the Notes* I told the story of a fan who complimented the German pianist Wilhelm Backhaus by saying to him, 'Mr Backhaus, you never seem to play wrong notes in your recitals. How come?' And Backhaus's quiet answer: 'I only practise the right notes.' You might think that everyone 'only practises the right notes', but it's not so simple. I've realised that there is some kind of comfort in 'the learning stage', and often a subconscious urge to prolong it, perhaps because it keeps at arm's length that evil moment – which not everyone desires – where you might be required to get up on stage and play it in public. This is perhaps the opposite of perfectionism, or if not the opposite, then its shadow side: a desire to remain in the cosy half-light of imperfection. I often wonder about that when I'm visiting somewhere as a guest professor and students mention that they have been learning the same piece for a year now. Perhaps it is proof of the old saying that to travel hopefully is better than to arrive.

I hate hearing myself play wrong notes, and my irritation motivates me to press on to the point where my fingers can reliably play what my eyes read in the score, just so that I don't have to listen to wrong notes any more. Even after this, there's a stage when I'm no longer making silly mistakes but am still attending carefully to the task of moving my fingers around the keyboard in the required patterns. But then there comes a day when I seem to be able to move through these patterns of movement without so much conscious effort. This is not always strictly allied to the amount of time I have spent actually playing the piece. Sometimes one can take a break, go on holiday and come back to find that the tricky passages have mysteriously become second nature. It can occur between one day and another of normal practice, or at a less definable point when some stage of mental digestion has been reached. I imagine this stage corresponds to some neurological change in the brain, when a new connection between synapses has been made.

Once a muscle memory has been laid down, it seems to be remarkably stable. Musicians will know how hard it is, for example, to alter fingering laboriously memorised ages ago. Even if you hit upon a brilliant new fingering which makes your hand movement simpler, it's difficult to shift the original fingering from your memory, and the original one tends to spring back in conditions of stress, such as in performance. In everyday life one might notice the stability of muscle memory when something is changed in the house, leading to a slight alteration in an everyday physical task. For example, my family recently had a light switch moved up a few inches inside a tool cupboard. We were used to reaching round the door frame in the dark to switch on that light. Once the switch was moved, we all noticed that we were reaching into the cupboard to connect our fingers very accurately to the place where the switch wasn't any more. Weeks later we were still commenting that yet again we had reached into the cupboard to connect with the ghost of the switch. We had no idea we had formed this muscle memory so precisely. It was amazing how long it took everyone to adapt. And there are countless examples we all encounter in everyday life. Our lovely tortoiseshell cat died a year ago, but I'm still cautiously opening the front door every time I come home in case she's standing right behind it as she always used to.

Visual memory is crucial to many performers. By that I mean a kind of photographic recall of the pages of the score, perhaps not a perfectly detailed recall but a feeling for where you are 'on the page' as you play, to the extent that if you feel yourself faltering in performance you can 'look at' the imaginary page and get back on track. I've known musicians who claim they don't do this, but all the pianists I've spoken to about it have quite a strong visual recall of how the pages go by. I imagine this may be linked to the complexity of piano parts and the length of time that pianists have to spend with the score in front of them while they are learning the notes. Often one is unaware of having formed such an impression until something disturbs it.

For example, a while ago I decided that I had too much repertoire on my 'to do' list to attempt to memorise a particular piece, but I didn't want to have a page-turner sitting beside me on stage, because I wanted to create an atmosphere of calm and concentration. I took the score to the photocopy shop and made a tiny copy of each page. I then got a big piece of black card from an art shop, the biggest piece that would stand on the music desk of the piano without overbalancing, and I stuck a mosaic of tiny pages to this card. The mosaic had several rows. Pages 1–6 went across the top row from left to right, pages 7–12 across the second row, pages 13–18 across the third row down, and so on. I was pleased with this ingenious visual aid until I sat down at the piano, put it on the music desk and started to play. At which point I discovered that, based on the layout of my usual score, I had formed a very tenacious visual memory of where those pages 'were' in the space in front of me. With my new mosaic of tiny pages, everything was different. Page 1 was now a foot higher and inches to the left. Page 2 was to the right of page 1 – so far, so good – but page 3 was not 'on the left' again, but continued to the right of page 2! In short, it was a nightmare. I had started this experiment a couple of weeks before the performance I was focusing on, for safety, but in that fortnight I did not manage to re-learn the visual layout. It was supposed to be comforting to have the music in front of me, but I kept glancing up to the 'wrong' place, finding myself looking at page 27 when I wanted to 'read' page 5, or whatever. I had a vivid insight into what 'cognitive dissonance' might actually mean; it felt as if tiny gears were grinding horribly in my head. I did use my mosaic score in the concert, but it was almost as if I'd burdened myself with a new memorisation challenge – that of remembering the new location of the pages. Was it an advance on playing the concert from memory?

I have sometimes found that viewing the printed music in a different layout can be quite stimulating, though I prefer not to be surprised by this in a concert. I have no idea how it happens, but I have found that even seeing the music printed in a different 'font', or in a blacker ink, or with more spacious layout of the notes, can suggest a new way of viewing the notes and the relationship between them. Sometimes a new way of phrasing, a different kind of articulation, or even a different mood has been prompted by seeing a new edition where things simply 'look different', even if the notes are exactly the same notes. A new fingering may occur to me on seeing a group of notes disposed differently on the space of the page, or printed on a whiter page than I am used to. It can be surprisingly stimulating to see an 'Urtext' edition from which all the nineteenth-century, well-meaning editorial accretions have been removed; sometimes seeing the bare notes, minus the editorial layers, can spark sudden insights. If one has the chance to study an original manuscript, or a facsimile of one, it can sometimes be revelatory. I recently had a startling experience when I miniaturised a copy of a piece I hadn't memorised but wanted to play in concert without a page-turner by my side. When trying out the tiny version, I noticed for the first time ever a sentence printed at the bottom of one of the pages, explaining how to play the unusually printed 'ties' in a particular passage. Believe it or not, the matter of the ties was something that had puzzled me, but I never noticed the explanatory sentence of advice until it was half the size and barely legible. Which all goes to show that, as Margo says in *My Family and Other Animals*, 'a change is as good as a feast'.

Interpretative matters can seem to be clearer because of a layout change – goodness knows why. 'Aha!' I think on seeing a certain phrase on the bottom left of the page instead of the middle of the right-hand page. 'Of course!' I think on seeing the notes printed further apart from one another. Perhaps this is simply because of the shock of the new, like seeing a familiar face in an unexpected place and suddenly thinking how nice-looking it is. There must, I suppose, be a synaesthetic element to these rediscoveries of music through variation of layout, and I would say that it would be fascinating to hear the view of a neuroscientist on the matter, were it not for the fact that the press is currently full of reports that the human brain turns out to be far more complex than neuroscience can account for.

Another kind of memory I find very helpful is analytical memory of the structure of the music. Once I've understood the 'scheme' – the narrative of first theme, contrasting theme, section where the two are juggled together with various results, recapitulation where the themes come back in a new relation to one another (for example) – I find I can interlock that kind of structural understanding with the other kinds of memory. In fact, in performance I often find I seem to be using several different kinds of memory simultaneously, though I have no control over when one switches to another. There's simple 'ear' memory, muscle memory, visual memory and analytical memory. One moment I'm 'reading' from the score in my mind, the next I'm letting finger memory take over and move things forward without my conscious attention. Then, if I suddenly feel insecure, I can bring in 'analytical memory' to remind me that we're coming up to such-and-such a point now – another way of locating myself within the whole shape of the piece and reminding myself how far there is to go. In the background of all these is aural memory, which probably underlies them all. Sometimes you have the feeling of just sitting back and listening to yourself playing the music, a delightful feeling if you can hang on to it.

Of course, as well as doing meticulous preparation for a concert, you also have to be aware that sometimes it is more important to forget. This applies to performing with and without the music, but it is an important ingredient of the process of memorisation. You should know how *not* to recall all the calculations that march across your conscious mind every day when you are practising. One of my piano teachers used to say cheerily when I was going to play in public, 'And now: forget everything I've told you!' Easier said than done, but it was a helpful thought. Playing from memory in public is torture if your performance is a sequence of conscious thoughts about what to do next, be it a physical movement on the instrument or an expressive detail you've planned to include. You most definitely don't want to be providing the illustration of a mental lecture you're giving yourself. Although the myriad calculations were all useful at some point of your preparation, you have to reach a stage where as many conscious thoughts as possible can be dropped down to a subconscious level, leaving you free to move into a higher gear. But this stage is very hard to plan for, and can't be hurried. In fact, so much can it not be hurried that in some performances it never arrives. When the moment of 'trustful forgetting' actually happens, it makes all the difference between a performance which feels as if you're conscientiously tracing a blueprint and one which feels organic, as if the music is arising as you play.

So many composers have used structures like 'sonata form', variations, or rondo to play with the concept of things coming back in identical or in altered form. Often something that happens at the beginning of the piece will be referred to in the later stages, and the relationship between the main themes or motifs is altered by what the composer arranges to happen to them in the middle. We talk about the 'structure' of a piece of music, but a piece of music is not, in fact, like a piece of architecture. There is no 'form' we can apprehend very quickly as when a building, a sculpture or a painting stands in front of us in space (though even with those solid forms, an element of time is needed to walk around them and view them from all perspectives). What 'form' there is in music unfolds through time, and our apprehension of the form is built up gradually as we listen. The same is true even if you study a musical score without playing it: the medium of time is still essential, no matter how quickly you glance through the score. No impression of musical 'shape' can arise in a listener's mind unless they are capable of remembering what happened earlier, and what therefore is the significance of its happening again, or happening at intervals, or failing to happen again at the end. If you're not aware of any of that, music must simply seem to be a linear stream of sounds. It is memory that enables us to construct a sense of dynamic 'form' and to appreciate musical architecture.

The whole concept of 'recapitulation', an intimidating word for a beautiful event in music, is predicated on the listener recognising the return of something he heard earlier. Yes, music is a stream of notes, but that's not all that most composers intend to convey; it is also an attempt to create expectations, to play with those expectations and to satisfy them. It's a way of creating a parallel to our experience of daily life: the shape of a day, the start of a new day, days that seem to follow the same form, but not with the same content. Music is perhaps better than any of the other arts in representing to us this interplay of repetition and new content. But if we were like one of those unfortunate people who, after suffering brain damage, cannot form new memories and exist in an eternal present, we would be very limited in the emotional satisfaction we could get from these pieces of music which appeal to our memory and remind us that constant change is here to stay.

Music is often compared with a theatre play because of the way it tells a story, unfolding in time, transient in nature. But music is different from a theatre play in important ways. For example, in a theatre play, characters who are not speaking can nevertheless still be on stage. Their presence on stage is often crucial, because even when characters stand in silence and do nothing, the audience can see them witnessing the behaviour of other characters, overhearing things, being the motivation for other characters to speak or take action. All those romantic scenes in gardens and summerhouses where the drama is fuelled by someone else eavesdropping on the conversation in full view of the audience! There is nothing comparable in abstract music. Each musical theme or episode is the only thing that's happening while it's happening. There is no way that another theme can stand provocatively by in full view of the audience. If it's not being played, it is not 'there'. A composer can combine themes in counterpoint, of course, so that two characters are brought 'onto the stage' at the same time, but otherwise the only way that 'other characters' can be part of the ongoing musical action is if the listener is able to hold them in memory, to have a sense that they have not left the story and may return later on. Whether or not the overarching 'shape' is realised in the listener's mind is dependent on their ability to remember. The shape is formed not in physical space but in imaginative space built up through time. So it may well be that 'listening from memory' is at least as important as playing from memory.

Someone came up to me after a concert at which I'd made a few remarks about memorisation and said it might be interesting for me to know about the Jewish attitude towards sacred texts. She said that the holiness of a sacred text is considered to reside in its form as well as its content, so *the book itself* is an important part of prayers. Meaning is thought to be conveyed in every sign on the page, and there is meaning too in signs which have been left out. These signs and texts have been intensively studied for centuries, and there is always something new to be learned from them. Therefore the text is never spoken from memory, no matter how well it may be known, because that would be less of a learning experience than looking once more at the text itself. Reciting from memory would be a mere trick, never as valuable as having the book in front of you, paying close attention to it and acknowledging its superior wisdom. Reading from an old script, having those old words in front of your eyes, is a privilege, enabling you to be in touch with wisdom of long ago. As I listened I felt sure that Beethoven and composers like him would be nodding in agreement. Such an approach could cut through an awful lot of nonsense about for whose sake and why we should strive to play from memory in public concerts. But alas the element of 'performance' looms very large in music, focuses everyone's attention on 'how it looks', and will keep this debate alive a while longer.

Raw materials

Earlier this year our house was burgled. We had been at a funeral and came home late at night to find the kitchen window smashed and the contents of drawers and cupboards in piles on various floors, the thief having conducted what police later termed 'an untidy search'. It was a search of a kind they were familiar with, a search for cash and jewellery which could be quickly sold on for a few quid or melted down to be sold for 'gold weight'. We were told that the rocketing price of gold in recent years has inspired a lot of such burglaries, which was news to us.

I didn't have much gold, but what I had was gone, including a necklace I was given by my husband the year we got married and which I had worn for most of my concerts since. An antique gold bracelet I was given as a wedding present had gone too. Worst of all, the thief had taken the entire contents of a 'family heirloom' box containing, amongst other things, my late mother's engagement and wedding rings. On top of these rings I had placed a special handwritten card explaining to whom the jewellery had belonged, with their names and dates. The thief had thoughtfully placed the open box on my bed, empty except for this card.

The police explained to us that because reputable dealers will not touch stolen items, thieves generally go straight to 'dodgy' dealers who will give them cash on the spot – 'sadly, nothing like what the items are actually worth'. Failing that, thieves simply collect gold jewellery in polythene bags and post them off to gold dealers who weigh them, pay cash for the weight and melt the jewellery down. For a while I made myself look in the windows of local jewellery shops with 'vintage' sections to see if anything of mine would appear there, but I never saw anything.

I was tormented by the realisation that these things had just been melted down for cash. The raw material was the value, and that is only so because the commodities markets have pushed the price of gold so high. The historical value (to me) was neither here nor there, and nor were the goldsmith's skills, the design, the craft, the beauty of the object, which turned out to mean nothing compared with the value of a little lump of gold. To me, the value of the gold itself was nothing compared with the sentimental value, but I quickly realised that sentimental value has no monetary equivalent for an insurance company. I would have said that those things were priceless, but 'priceless' is a versatile word. In the art market, a 'priceless work of art' is one with an awfully high monetary value. But it can also mean that no price attaches to it, that it isn't worth anything.

I'm a musician and spend most of my time thinking about intangible things. After the burglary, I kept thinking about material things and their 'value' in several senses. I wondered about other valuable things which could easily be stolen. What about a stolen Stradivarius violin, for example? No thief would steal such a violin and chop it up, popping the fragments of wood in a padded envelope to send off to a wood dealer who would pay for a couple of hundred grams of wood weight. The value is not in the wood but in the skill of the maker, and in what a violinist can conjure from the finished product, the musical instrument. Of course the 'value' of a violin has become a complex matter now that the art market has taken an interest in old string instruments and pushed up their price to unheard-of levels. But of course every player of such instruments would agree that their chief value is the beauty and quality of tone which they make possible. If the violin is stolen it's not principally the monetary value that violinists weep about.

If a valuable pottery bowl is broken, its shards have no intrinsic value as raw material. Similarly, if a valuable painting were stolen, it would only retain its value if it remained in one piece, a testament to the artist's skill and imagination. No thief would scrape the flakes of paint off the canvas and collect them in a plastic bag to be weighed in a backstreet dealer's. The raw material of paint has very little value. Though if by some bizarre turn of events, commodities traders were to decide that paint itself were in short supply or could be hoarded in bank vaults in order to push the price up artificially, we might start to see art thieves targeting paintings for the value of the raw materials. Burglars wouldn't need to figure out how to remove paintings from their gallery settings; they could just bring a sharp knife and scrape the paint off Rembrandt self-portraits or Michelangelo frescoes in situ, leaving flayed canvases and plaques to remind us what was there.

When it comes to stealing things, music is a much more elusive commodity. What is the raw material of music? It wouldn't profit a burglar very much to steal my volumes of Mozart and Brahms, snip the pages into individual notes and see what they weighed. Nobody could go to a composer's hut and demand that they hand over all their As, Bs, Cs and so on, even though those notes may be as close as we can come to the raw material of music. It is impossible to steal music, because it doesn't exist as a physical object. You could steal the score of *The Marriage of Figaro*, but if you held it to your ear, it would be silent, as silent as a Stradivarius in untrained hands. The score is the blueprint for music, a representation of what the composer heard in his head, and a set of signs for other musicians to read, but until musicians come along and play it, arguably it does not yet exist as music.

Even when they do play it, causing particular sound waves to be present in the room and enabling listeners to form impressions in their brains of what those sound waves amount to, there is still nothing that you can grasp and put in a sack labelled 'swag'. People often say that the beauty of music is that it is fleeting, and indeed, no matter how experienced a musician you are, the transience of music remains a bit of a mystery. To play it requires intense physical effort, but what you make with your effort is nothing substantial or lasting. You try so hard to put the right ingredients into each particular note, but as soon as you've played it, it's gone. What you and your fellow musicians created together, no matter how long it took you, is not something you can put on a table at the end of the day and eat for dinner. The raw material of music will never be traded on the global market like coffee and sugar. People often ask whether musicians regret the fact that there's nothing to show for their work, and I in turn have wondered whether certain temperaments are drawn towards the 'spiritual' nature of music. Of course there are other lines of work whose products are not to be grasped – friends who are actors, psychoanalysts or priests have all mentioned the not-to-be-measured outcome of their efforts – but I think even musicians are not entirely sure what it is that passes through their hands.

Over time, the score itself may come to have historic value, and if the manuscript of, say, Beethoven's Ninth Symphony were to come up at auction it would doubtless fetch millions of euros. But nobody can buy the Ninth Symphony itself. If every copy of the score and every orchestral part were to be rounded up and destroyed, the Ninth Symphony would not disappear from the Earth, because it exists in many people's aural memories and imaginations, and could be reconstructed. Many people have played in it, sung in it, conducted it, listened to it, analysed it, recorded it, listened to those recordings. The knowledge of an iconic piece of music is shared between the minds of many people in the world. But nobody can reach into any of those minds and take it away.

It sometimes seems mystifying to me that those inanimate objects, bowls and paintings and jewellery and even musical scores, should be able to outlast their makers by so long. Our highly evolved species has learned to make incredible things which our fellow humans can take delight in, learn from and treasure. Yet we are not so highly evolved that we can remotely match those objects for longevity. We can hold one of Mozart's manuscripts in our hands and turn its pages, but he cannot. We can sit among Roman ruins admiring the builders' achievements, but we are haunted by the idea that these old clay bricks are still in robust health while the era in which they were made has melted away. We may be sitting on the Roman wall now, but what has happened to the time when the Romans made the wall and sat on it themselves? How can the wall still be here if the time is not?

When I was taking pottery lessons and had collected my first lumpy grey bowl from the kiln, my pottery teacher said in a no-nonsense manner, 'There you are! You've made something which will probably outlast you!' Maybe she meant it as encouragement, but I was horrified. This stupid clay bowl? What if an archaeologist came across it a thousand years from now and tried to deduce from it what sort of a person I was? They say that the part represents the whole, but in this case I devoutly hoped not. No archaeologist would have any way of knowing from my bowl that I loved music and was able to play it. What could be 'read' from my bowl, other than that the maker was ham-fisted with craft materials in such-and-such a year? Who would run an appraising eye over the contours and say, 'I reckon the person who made that must have had a lovely way with a Debussy prelude'? Suddenly it struck me as poignant that despite our sophistication and our creative skills, we ourselves can fade away, leaving behind things like spoons and shoes and pieces of paper.

'Interesting things happen when you deny people the consolation of technical excellence'

Last year, my friend Greg and I went to the Turner Prize Exhibition at Tate Britain in London. The Turner art prize always attracts attention and controversy because its shortlist generally focuses on artists who, in many cases, work with 'ideas' rather than traditional materials like paint or marble.

A while ago I took part in a festival where I was given accommodation in the same house as a young art historian doing research on conceptual art. She and I met at breakfast one day, and I must have said something 'old-fashioned' about an exhibition of paintings I had enjoyed. She said that there was probably nothing more to be expressed in paint, adding that thank goodness the days had gone when artists could lazily reach for the 'old medium' of paint instead of working with concepts. She said that the 'idea' was the important thing today; the materials, the technical skill and the product were of secondary importance, sometimes of no importance at all. It was not even important that the artist should make the work – an assistant could do the job just as well. A work of art could be simply the idea, communicated in a description or document without even going so far as to produce an exemplar of the idea. It was the 'idea' which lay behind such famous artworks as Tracy Emin's *My bed*, Damien Hirst's bisected, pickled or rotting animals in glass cases, or Martin Creed's *The lights going on and off.*

To the young art historian I said that the idea has always been the important thing behind a work of art, but that the idea *alone* is not enough to justify summoning people to an art gallery and charging them money to enter. I'm interested in modern art of all kinds, but I've become a little disillusioned with 'installations' and artworks whose significance is not apparent until you bend down to read the explanatory plaque on the wall. I have a self-imposed rule that I don't peer at the explanation unless the art itself is intriguing, but I don't generally manage to stick to the rule, because I'm often so curious to see what the artist thought they were doing. Often the explanation is complicated in inverse proportion to the effect of the installation itself. I hope I'm capable of enjoying a genuinely interesting idea, but it often seems to me that conceptual art demonstrates an impoverishment of ideas, while also encouraging a shocking increase in descriptive jargon. Even at my local artists' exhibitions in the neighbourhood, painters have taken to sticking 'mission statements' on the walls of their studios. 'Angela is passionate about colour. She believes that juxtapositions of red and blue can express the painful cognitive dissonance between the male and female aspects of her personality. She is pursuing a journey of self-realisation using paint and canvas as the weapons in her ongoing struggle to attain wholeness.' Such declarations might form an interesting counterpart to a compelling artwork, but if the mission statement is livelier than the work of art, then in my estimation the artist hasn't yet earned the right to make people give up their precious free time to come and stand in front of their work. As comedian Simon Munnery memorably remarked, 'Many are prepared to suffer for their art. Few are prepared to learn how to draw.'

A couple of years ago, in the Royal Academy of Art in London, I watched a group of schoolchildren being taken round an exhibition of contemporary art. One of the exhibits was a quartet of chairs arranged in a tapering pile, an orange office chair at the bottom and a child's formica chair at the top. An 'interpreter' was leading the schoolchildren in a discussion of this work. The explanatory plaque on the wall said, 'Four chairs are balanced on top of each other as they ascend towards the ceiling, asserting their defiance while struggling to avoid collapse.'

'What skills do you need to make this?' the interpreter was asking the children. There was a longish silence during which a bit of giggling and shoving took place. Someone said, 'Imagination?' 'Yes!' enthused the interpreter. 'Balance?' said a boy. 'Yes!' There was another longish pause. 'Cheek?' said someone. 'Yes, cheek! I think cheek is very important!' beamed the interpreter. 'This work is by a very famous artist, a famous *minimalist* artist,' he told them. 'What's minimalist?' one of the children asked. The interpreter smiled proudly. 'The artist is interested in how *little* you have to do to make art,' he replied. The children looked intrigued. This was not what teachers usually said in art lessons. 'What do you guess is the price of this work of art?' said the interpreter. Everyone knew this was probably a trick question, that they shouldn't be drawn into saying '50p', so they just giggled and whispered to each other. After a dramatic pause, the interpreter answered his own question: '£60,000!' he said triumphantly. 'What do you think of that?!' The children repeated this figure incredulously to one another, laughing as they all went off to make things from egg boxes and tissue paper. I felt sad as I watched them go. As far as I could see, the interpreter had merely succeeded in establishing in their minds that with a bit of cheek you could con people into paying outlandish sums of money for something trivial both in idea and execution. And yet this was not an explanation given by a cynic, a member of a local watercolour art group or an outraged reader of a conservative newspaper, spluttering as he writes to the editor to complain about some new-fangled nonsense. This was an interpretation offered from within the art establishment!

So there I was at the Turner Exhibition, trying to be open-minded. The shortlisted works included enormous black-and-white drawings of a town populated by turds, a video with a soundtrack so loud that we had to leave the room after a few seconds to protect our ears, and an empty white tent in which we and other visitors waited for a while until a group of people dressed in red Ku Klux Klan outfits came in with string puppets, made the puppets 'walk' jerkily across the front of the tent while music played and went away. We all waited for a bit in case enlightenment was forthcoming, but nothing else happened and nobody said anything, so everyone drifted away. As we came out of the tent, we glimpsed the puppeteers in their red pointy hats having coffee in an adjacent room.

Saying goodbye to Greg at the exit, I said that I couldn't help feeling a bit depressed about what I'd just seen. He considered this. Then he said, 'You're wrong to dismiss it, though, because interesting things happen when you deny people the consolation of technical excellence. Lots of artists are interested to see what happens when you provoke the viewer or wrong-foot them. Artists don't want people to file reverently in front of a painting just because it's famous, and then go away without having had any real moment of encounter with the work. They want to know what happens when you don't give the audience what they expect.'

With a painful shock I registered how remote such an art world is from my own. The music I love *demands* technical excellence, because its composers have been technically specific to the highest degree. With their pages of musical notes they have specified what's to happen during every millisecond of the time involved, and that in turn is because the complexity of thought involves intricate notation. The musician's task is to bring these notes to life, one after another. To do so requires real skill and control. There is no freedom to experiment with 'denying people the consolations of technical excellence'. Solid craftsmanship is our baseline, and it's important to realise that without it, there can be no 'real moment of encounter with the work.' When I play a concert, my contract is to play Mozart, not to Not Play Mozart. I felt some frustration, possibly mixed with envy, at the thought that conceptual artists could make their names and their fortunes with 'ideas' which required no craftsmanship and often seemed to me not particularly interesting. The fact that fortunes can be made with conceptual art is, of course, not the fault of the artists but a result of the art establishment's decision that such works have huge monetary value; to my way of thinking, that's where most of the immorality lies.

Mozart himself, who was very fond of a joke, loved to use humour in his music, but it's all expressed in terms of music itself. And of course composers since the dawn of time have made musical jokes. In the twentieth century, some composers had fun with the 'concept' and the 'situation' of musical performance, such as John Cage with his famous *4'33"*, where the pianist sits at the piano for four minutes and thirty-three seconds without playing anything, or La Monte Young's *Piano Piece for David Tudor #1*, where the pianist appears with a bale of hay and invites the piano to eat it. (There's now an app which enables you to download John Cage's *4'33"* of silence to your phone, and 'arrangements' of La Monte Young's piece where you can feed hay to other instruments instead.) But these experiments focus on the peripheral elements of a performance; there is no actual music. As soon as actual music begins, skill and fine judgement have to begin too. As a classical musician I don't have the option of walking on stage, placing a large stone on the floor, announcing to the audience that the stone is 'my concept' of Beethoven's final piano sonata and walking off again. Nor would I dare to claim that the resulting public outrage was planned by me as 'part of the artwork'. Even if I had the cheek to do it, I would not be paid £60,000 for it.

Plugged in

Like everyone else, I've wondered what it's doing to us all to be plugged in for so much of the time to our iPods, smartphones and other electronic gadgets. As a musician I can't help being aware that this is an awfully big change. Hearing music was, until quite recently, an unusual event in everyday life. Unless you sang or played music yourself, or someone made music in your presence, you wouldn't hear music; this was particularly true with instrumental music, obviously more unusual to come across than someone humming in your vicinity. The opportunity to attend a performance was something that people savoured and looked forward to, and wrote about afterwards in their diaries. Music was a spice of life, something to give a special flavour to the day, the month, the year; the visit of a renowned musician to your town would be a red-letter day, perhaps even a once-in-a-lifetime opportunity. If you weren't able to be present at such an artist's performance, you would only ever know how they played by hearsay, and that of course was the nature of most people's relationship to the famous musicians of the day.

Now, because of electronic devices, listening to music as we carry out everyday activities has become a commonplace thing. Perhaps 'commonplace' is an overstatement. The other day, when I complained to my hairdresser about his choice of music for the salon, he answered cheerfully, 'It's not meant to be listened to!'

Thanks to the internet, we have access to a vast repertoire of music from around the world, and with just a few clicks we can download enormous libraries of music to suit any mood. This is, of course, a tremendous resource for musicians. If I'm asked to learn something new, a piece I've never heard, it's easy to find a recording and often a video of a performance as well. If I'm seriously interested in the different ways a particular piece can be interpreted, I can spend the whole day in the comfort of my own home, listening to many different recordings in online libraries, and often for free (though obviously this has good and bad aspects as far as musicians are concerned). Compare this with the old days when my college record library might, if I was lucky, have one recording, which I could borrow if nobody else had already borrowed it! The richness of the internet, and the speed with which it has developed, is breath-taking.

There are downsides, though. The excitement of waiting for a special record to arrive in your local shop has been wiped away by the mechanical ease with which consumers can hoover up whole archives of 'songs', as all instrumental music now seems to be known. You don't even have to know what you want to order, if you take up many websites' offers to provide you with things 'similar to' the things you've shown an interest in in the past. When I was recently uploading some recordings of my own to a digital distributor, I was startled to be asked which three other artists my style of playing was 'similar to', so that their recordings could be sold on the back of my sale, or mine on the back of theirs. *Similar to*! After years of hoping to become unmistakably me, or at least a musician with a very personal sound, I was humiliated by this presumption of 'similarity' and had no idea how to answer the question. Fortunately I was able to override it, though not before spending some anxious moments wondering what my friends (or indeed enemies) might answer on my behalf.

Portable electronic gadgets are 'enablers' in many respects, but when you're merely watching other people use them, they can seem like a barrier between the user and the rest of the world. No-one need know what you are listening to as you nod your head in time with the music on your iPod. I imagine I'm not alone in feeling that the privacy of such listening can be used as a sort of weapon. I'm used to thinking of music as a *connective* thing. It's still a novel sight to see, for example, a London Tube train full of passengers each plugged in to their own personal library of music. People's heads move and their feet tap in time with rhythms that only they can hear, and if you're not listening to music yourself, this uncoordinated little ballet can look quite bizarre. Many people must have had the experience of asking someone to turn down the volume on their music device and being met with a hostile response. The 'right' of someone to listen to their choice of music at high volume has become at least as sacrosanct as the right of others not to be disturbed by noise.

Of course, this all began with mobile phones, the first of the electronic devices which became addictive almost before many of us had grasped the fact of their existence. We got used to the sight of teenagers glued to their phones. Motorists have had to develop an awareness of people crossing the road oblivious to traffic as they chat on their phones. All road users have to be alert to drivers using hand-held mobile phones, a custom quite common in the UK despite being illegal. Phones lie on the table at family mealtimes, even at romantic dinners. Family members often feel acutely aware that their chatter has no hope of competing with the maelstrom of social networking with its silent clamour of 'updates' and 'status changes'. This change in behaviour has happened incredibly fast, too fast for social etiquette to keep pace; people expect to be able to 'be connected' at all times and are intolerant of any breach of this entitlement. I wasn't allowed to read books at meals, but today it's practically a breach of some-one's human rights to tell them they can't have their phone beside their dinner-plate.

Mobile phones came to double as music devices; you could have a library of tracks on your phone too. There's now a host of gadgets on which we can both listen to music and connect to the rest of the world. When I catch myself feeling annoyed at the sight of teenagers glued to their iPods, phones and iPads, I wonder if I'm being hypocritical. Perhaps we have more in common than it seems. I seem to recall that when I was a teenager I was often only half-listening to what was being said around me, either because I was thinking about some book I was in the middle of reading, or because I was playing music in my head, probably going over the fingering of whatever piano piece I was learning. Into my musings filtered the distant reverberation of an exasperated voice saying, 'Susan, I'm talking to you!' Like most teenagers I had a sense of alienation from family routine and wanted an escape route – not a physical one (I wasn't that alienated), but a mental one during the longish period when I was fantasising about parallel existences, as most teenagers do. It felt important to have a way of tuning out. But my way of doing so was probably different from today's kind, because whether thinking about the book I was reading or playing music in my head, I was exercising my imagination actively to balance everyday reality with another world. I was not passively consuming some unchosen thing fed into my ears through cables. I was actively calling up music from my memory, trying to evoke its instrumental colour and mood. Summoning up an accurate memory of, for example, a Beethoven symphony is a pleasurable form of mental work, an active 'recreation' in more than one way. As there was nothing physically blocking my ears, I could still hear anyone who spoke to me while I was doing it.

I knew that the music I was listening to had been composed in the past, sometimes the long-ago past. Unlike today's young listeners I had no way of accessing music just composed by someone far away, and almost all the music I knew was old. Its 'pastness', and my ability to access it through an effort of the imagination, was part of its lovability. It made me feel, and still makes me feel, as if I could generate some mental energy by dwelling simultaneously in the past and the present, by feeling the gentle friction and the hint of conversation between the world of Mozart or Schumann and the world of today. But I knew it was in the past, I knew I was imagining it and I didn't confuse it with the present. I could choose to leave it at any time, knowing it would be there as I left it when I chose to return. Nothing more could be added to my favourite Mozart concertos; I would not come back to find them 'updated' or 'open for my interactive comments'.

This is rather different from being separated from your nearest and dearest by the tsunami of 'messages' on your phone. To be able to juxtapose your own present reality every minute of the day with present reality taking place somewhere else is a new experience for human beings, a development whose speed and uptake have left psychologists behind. What's it going to do to us? I've read research which suggests that the bond between young children and iPads is rewiring their neural circuitry, making them more comfortable with fast-changing input and less comfortable with things that require quiet focus. Our access to electronic data seems to put our own reality into a strange perspective, making whatever is actually happening to us seem tedious or negligible compared with what's going on right now in, say, the Middle East or Silicon Valley.

I once saw a newspaper photo of the scene in a London street after a teenager had been fatally stabbed. His friends had gathered to pay their respects. They sat on the wall or leaned against it. Almost all of them were on their phones, not focusing on the scene of the stabbing or on one another, but silently communicating with people who were not there, or with remote websites and games. It was a striking sight and seemed symbolic. Even at the scene of a tragedy there was 'no time to stand and stare'. I was struck by the thought that while their friend had gone, they were in a sense 'not there' either. It was hard to see in what way they were paying their respects by scrolling through text messages instead of standing quietly, thinking about what had happened, or talking to one another about it. Looking at that photo, and at many similar if more trivial scenes one can see every day on the street, I realised that there are almost no circumstances in which people would consider it appropriate to put their phones away. Marshall McLuhan was right about the medium being the message.

When I see that most of my fellow passengers on the London Tube are listening to music on earphones, I am not sure whether to feel part of their constituency or not. I've spent a large part of my life playing music, listening to it and imagining music in my head, but in all cases there was 'agency' on my part – I played the music, I went somewhere to listen to a concert, I made an effort to acquire a record I wanted to hear, I used mental effort to recall music. These were all tiny events in their ways, moments when I made a decision and called music into my life. Music was a special moment, a contrast to the majority of life, which happened without a soundtrack. Nobody I knew was passively addicted to music, but then how could we have been? The devices hadn't been invented that would have enabled us to listen to music as we sat on the bus, studied in the library, went jogging, drove to the supermarket, sorted the laundry, crossed the road in busy traffic. We can't take credit for not falling for a corrupting opportunity which was never put in our way. All the same, when I see how music is used today, I can't help feeling that it has been diminished. This is a strange thing to say, perhaps, when the availability of vast swathes of music has been very convenient for me whenever I wish to do online research or familiarise myself with something I'm going to teach. Digital music has given us a huge opportunity. I should rejoice that the same tides which sweep other people's music in to my shore must presumably be sweeping my recordings on to other people's shores. In a rational mood, I feel grateful that it's easy for someone in China or Russia to click on my tracks, for not long ago they'd never have come across my name. Shouldn't I feel glad that music has become ubiquitous? Music is not a rarity any more – just the opposite. In fact, music has become almost like the air we breathe – just something we need, something we can take for granted. Many would argue that music has never been more culturally important, nor more widely disseminated. Perhaps the truth of the matter is that it is I who feel diminished as I play the piano in my front room, watching people pass by in the street with their earphones in, not turning their heads towards me or noticing that live music is being played just a few yards away.

Fashion parade

What to wear for concerts is a constant challenge, especially if you are not bound by the consensus which dictates what members of an orchestra must wear. In the days with my chamber group Domus, we generally made a point of *not* wearing black, to prove we were independent thinkers and to scotch any notion that a chamber group is nothing more than a mini-orchestra. Nobody ever told us what to wear, so we could make up our own 'look', as colourful and unblack as we liked. Having said that, it was always hard to know exactly what clothes we should be looking for, partly because attitudes towards concert attire always seem to be shifting. There were no 'rules', no style guide handed down by management, but on the other hand there have always been strong feelings about the right sort of thing to wear for concerts. What I wore on the concert platform usually seemed to be out of step with the fashion available in high street stores, but in a subtle way. We never had any precise idea about the 'uniform' of a chamber group, except that we wanted to look as if we'd given the matter some thought, and coordinated our style with one another. There was general agreement about what kind of thing was 'appropriate', and it was often slightly anachronistic.

For a long time there was a feeling that women musicians should wear floor-length dresses of dignified appearance, preferably with demure sleeves covering the arms. I distinctly remember my mother and my piano teacher discussing the fact that bare muscly arms were 'not attractive' in a female performer, particularly a pianist in profile to the audience with the biceps of her right arm fully on display. Sleeves were essential, and even in the present era where the toned female arm is considered a thing of beauty (Michelle Obama being an inspiration), I confess I've never quite been able to banish the notion that bulging arm muscles are not something to flaunt.

'Long dresses' are sometimes specified in classical contracts. There have been times when floor-length dresses have been easy to obtain, when maxi-dresses happened to be in fashion, but also periods when long dresses were not at all easy to find because fashion had gone with shorter hemlines, plunge necklines and sleeveless designs. 'Cocktail dresses' were the most formal things you'd find in an off-the-peg store, but they seemed to be designed for people standing up and circulating at a party, not for sitting down and playing an instrument, especially on a high stage with the audience looking up at you. During those fashion phases it was more likely I'd find an 'evening dress' in a second-hand or vintage store; however, it was unlikely I'd find something in my size, and even when I did I sometimes found that I had misjudged the potential effect of a vintage garment. I was never any good as a dressmaker, and professional dressmakers were beyond my budget.

At the time of writing, maxi-dresses are back in fashion and so is glamour, even sequins, so it's easier to find concert wear than it has been for a while. You can find it in a local store instead of trailing around unfamiliar parts of the city. At the same time, I notice that many young musicians are moving away from that style of dress anyway. They are more likely to be wearing a sleeveless black top and smart black trousers with high-heeled shoes, a severe professional chic copied from female executives of the business world. When I'm on competition juries I have a good opportunity to see the range of current international concert wear. Currently there seem to be two interesting trends: women wearing 'men's attire' – black shirts and trousers, or plain black trouser suits of 'unisex' appearance – and a contrasting, super-feminine style one could call 'minimalist bling', tiny wisps of strapless shimmering gauze worn with sleek pony-tails and shoes so remarkably high that I have to fear for the safety of violins and cellos as their owners totter precariously across the platform with them. In my imagination I can often hear my piano teacher's sharp intake of breath. As for the demure sleeve, it now seems as outdated as the fashion for Victorian matriarchs to cover the shapely legs of the grand piano with little 'skirts', as I believe they did in some respectable households.

Lots of young women pianists clearly feel comfortable perform-ing in sleeveless and strapless outfits, and a good thing too, as the musicianly arm is (I have come to realise) a thing of beauty. Today's female musicians may confidently display more flesh than was once considered 'nice'. When you compare publicity shots of today's young pianists with, say, Clara Haskil in her austere, absolutely plain high-necked black dresses in the 1950s, or her black jackets and skirts worn with a high-necked buttoned white blouse, the contrast is striking.

What do musicians mean to signal when they wear formal dress? This question has raged in the musical world for a long time now. Symphony orchestras often still appear with the men wearing 'tails' and white tie, despite the fact that such outfits have all but disappeared from modern life. Even if they don't wear 'tails', orchestra members often wear dinner jackets. In fact, 'black tie' is a smart look that has been popular with many different kinds of musicians, not just clas-sical – jazz bands often wore black tie, and all the famous crooners of the Frank Sinatra/Bing Crosby era wore it. It's a look that has been remarkably enduring – even pop singer Robbie Williams wore it for his Sinatra tribute concerts. Nevertheless there's a feeling that if orchestras want to reach out to new audiences, they should not wear something that associates them with a previous era.

Many orchestras have experimented with more modern clothing – the black polo necks worn by the London Sinfonietta were a byword for innovation at one time – but I understand from orchestral friends that there is always fierce opposition to abandoning the more formal clothes of earlier times. Sometimes the opposition is on practical grounds, for many musicians feel that 'tails' are actually more comfortable to play in than, say, a suit jacket which tends to have a narrow, restricting sleeve. For orchestral women, long black dresses or long colourful dresses are still popular, and in some orchestras women are not permitted to wear trousers. Nobody has ever said that musicians should try to look like the ruling class of the Victorian era, a period when the status of classical music was high, but I've often wondered if this kind of thinking lies behind our manner of concert dress – in other words, nostalgia for a time when classical music was much respected.

The traditional formal concert wear for classical musicians is a curious hybrid, dictated neither by current fashion nor by trying to evoke a specific historical period. You can't usually take a classical musician dressed for a concert and say, 'I know what you're doing! You're trying to remind me of the eighteenth century!' or whatever. The look is evocative, but of a state of mind rather than a time period. It's intentionally outside the mainstream, in what musicians hope is a good way. Buying concert clothes has therefore always been a slightly alienating experience for me, because I felt I was looking for something that wasn't in fashion, and didn't know where to find it. You can't go to emporia specialising in 'musicians' uniforms'.

Cost was always a concern. As I discovered when I was a hard-up student, I was expected to 'look the part' when performing in a concert, even if there was no fee at all. How was this pressure communicated to me? I can't now recall, except for a general excitement amongst my friends about the event and what I'd be wearing, to which the correct answer was clearly not 'my everyday clothes'. The pressure increased when I became professional. Nobody ever furnished me or my colleagues with a 'uniform allowance', but even when the fee was small, there was always a definite expectation that we should wear something formal, glamorous, or smart – something far from ordinary, which would make audiences feel justified in having given up an evening and paid money to sit and watch us. For many audiences, the visual element of a concert is almost as interesting as the musical one, perhaps sometimes more interesting. I had one musician friend who went to live in Paris for a year, and during that year she won a competition which led to a high-profile concert in one of the city's most famous halls. She was interviewed by the press, but to her surprise what they principally wanted to know was what she was planning to wear and where in Paris she was going to look for her outfit.

Furthermore, as a woman working as a soloist or chamber musician, you feel pressure to wear something different at each concert, or when you appear again in front of the same audience. Nobody writes it into the contract that you mustn't return next season in the same frock, but the reaction of audience members makes it perfectly clear that they, especially the women, are taking a lively interest in what you wear on the platform and would be disappointed if it was the same thing you wore last time, which they can still describe. I have one or two female colleagues who go so far as to keep a note of what they wore in which venue, so that they don't make the mistake of going back in the same outfit. I don't do that, but when I'm returning to a venue I often try to visualise myself in that place last time, to see if I can remember what I wore.

Naturally, in a mixed chamber group of men and women this led to an unbalanced situation. Every New Year I trailed around the shops trying to acquire several new concert outfits in the January sales, while the men in my various groups continued to wear their usual suits on occasion after occasion. If I ever alluded to the fact that I was finding it expensive to add new outfits to my wardrobe, they would say, 'Well, don't. Just wear the same thing!' In theory I could have done, and certainly it would have saved an awful lot of time and money. I could have insisted on buying one smart black outfit and wearing it like a uniform at every concert, except that, as most female musicians will probably agree, women are subject to different expectations and cannot pretend otherwise. I play in a summer festival where all the concerts are in the same venue and in front of more or less the same audience. There has never been any edict about how varied our outfits must be, but every year, all the women musicians drag along huge suitcases of outfits because they feel they cannot appear day after day in the same frock, whereas the men wear their one colourful waistcoat at every concert. Once or twice some brave woman has brought a single outfit and worn it several times, but she has been exposed to what Oscar Wilde might have called 'comment on the platform' (and off it).

Let me digress for a moment to talk about the difficulty of getting changed for a concert if there's no proper dressing-room, as there often isn't because many concerts take place in venues other than purpose-built concert halls. A great many of my concerts were and are in churches or schools, not equipped with dressing-rooms and, in the case of ancient churches, sometimes not with running water or toilets either. My groups often travelled long distances to the concert venue and really needed somewhere to wash and change. But often, through no fault of the concert society, there was nowhere suitable. We were frequently given just one room to act as a general backstage dressing-room for all of us, men and women alike. I have never been insouciant enough to get changed in front of mixed company, so I always gathered up my clothes and crept off to get changed elsewhere – usually in the loo if there was one.

It takes some ingenuity to get changed into evening dress in the loo without dropping your clothes on the floor, but I became expert. I've quite often ended up getting changed in the back of my car. If there isn't any running water, things are difficult for people who need to put in contact lenses, as I do for concerts, because you must have clean hands. I've often put in my lenses at the staff-room sink in a school, or after washing my hands in the cooled water from a kettle in a church vestry. I often had to do my make-up and hair by looking at my reflection in a window, in a car mirror, or sometimes in the black shiny music desk of the grand piano before the doors open to the audience. When my groups became better known, one of the things I particularly relished, and still enjoy, was the privilege of having a dressing-room of my own. A room with a sink and clothes hooks and sometimes a shower, a sofa and even a piano – luxury indeed for someone who in the days of Domus used to get changed in the back of a van! I often think how surprised the audience would be to know from what unpromising backstage circumstances the artists arrive on the concert platform looking as lovely as they do.

It's difficult to know what to do with your valuables while you're on stage, especially if you are a woman. Evening dresses do not have pockets in them. So what are you to do with your handbag, your wallet, your phone and so on during the concert? You can't take them on stage with you and plonk them in a heap on the side of the piano. Rarely is there a locker, or a key for a dressing room, so women musicians have to come up with all sorts of schemes for the safekeeping of valuables, from asking someone to keep hold of them during the concert to stashing them somewhere backstage. When I'm onstage, I often have a distant descant running through my mind, which is, 'I hope my valuables are safe while I'm doing this.' I don't know any female musicians who have solved this problem entirely, and even for women who wear trousers on stage, the sort of pockets you get in smart trousers are never capacious enough to store wallet, keys, passport, phone and so on – quite apart from the fact that they ruin the outline. There is usually little alternative to leaving your valuables backstage. Even if you are handed a key for the dressing-room, there is nowhere to put the key in a concert frock, so you still have to think about where to leave the key while you're on stage. I won't reveal my solutions, out of solidarity with female colleagues grappling with the same problem.

When I think back over what I and my colleagues have worn at concerts, it seems to me that we were all flailing about in a sincere effort to live up to some image that all of us shared but none of us could really have defined. We wanted concerts to feel special, out of the ordinary, and our attempts to make them look special took various sartorial forms.

Exhibit A: the red Viyella dress I wore, aged eleven, to play in the London finals of the National Children's Piano-Playing Competition. The dress was made by my mother and was the grandest item of clothing I had ever had. It was cherry red, a soft wool, with a plain bodice, long sleeves (of course), a gathered knee-length skirt, and a restrained line of white lace around the cuffs and neckline. My piano teacher had said that a strong, warm colour would look best on the platform, but nothing garish or flamboyant. This led to a lively debate about which reds were 'flamboyant'. I hadn't worn red before and felt very good in my dress (this was before my mum and I started to have fights about hemlines). At the end of the competition a member of the audience gave me a little robin made out of wool, saying that my appearance on the platform had reminded her of a little robin, and she had bought me the robin as a memento. Another member of the audience bought me a box of Charbonnel et Walker chocolates, the pinnacle of my gourmet experience at that time. The robin and the empty chocolate box were displayed at home in a cabinet along with the special china for years afterwards.

Exhibit B: the midnight blue velvet 'empire line' evening dress which my sister made for me when I was asked to play Chopin's Second Piano Concerto with the college orchestra as a student. We had agreed that a long dark blue velvet dress with long sleeves was the acme of pianistic glamour. Unfortunately, my sister, making the dress at home 400 miles away in Scotland, had no opportunity to measure me or to try the dress on me as the process of making it went along. We had reckoned without the effect of a year of my subsisting on the celebrated student diet of chips with everything, buttered crumpets for tea, Chelsea buns from Fitzbillies' Cake Shop and half-pints of beer with the lads. When the midnight blue evening dress arrived, it was too tight, especially around the arms (my fault entirely). I did wear it for the concerto, but with a certain amount of uneasiness. I still have the dress and am hoping that one day, when the whirligig of time brings A-line velvet evening dresses back into fashion, I shall find a slim young musician who might wear it in tribute to all the trouble my sister went to.

Exhibit C: the floaty pale blue and white long dress I wore as a post-grad student for a big occasion when I played a concerto with the Royal Philharmonic Orchestra. The composer John Rutter, whom I knew at university, had written an orchestral piece with a big piano part and invited me to play the premiere with the RPO in Watford (I think). Being a student, I had no suitable clothes for such an event and no spare money either. I was in a quandary about what to wear and had nobody to advise me; I didn't even have a piano teacher at that time, as my course was academic and did not include instrumental tuition. Cambridge at the time was full of shops selling 'Indian'-style and vaguely Eastern clothing. I bought a long filmy cotton dress which looked delicate and pretty in the shop, but turned out to be virtually transparent under strong platform lights. Of course I didn't realise this until it was too late to do anything about it, and then I felt so self-conscious that I didn't enjoy the performance. In fact what I chiefly remember is my anxiety about the walk onto the platform and off again at the end. In my ears rang the advice of one of my early piano teachers, Mary Moore, who wisely said that you should never try out an outfit for the first time *in the concert itself.* I pensioned off that particular dress as nightwear.

Exhibit D: the white cotton dress I bought in the early 1980s when my group Domus took a crazy decision that we should all be clad in white for our first public concerts in our portable dome-shaped tent. The men bought white trousers and Elizabethan-looking white shirts with wide sleeves. The women bought floaty white summer dresses. Considering that all our work was outdoors and involved carrying boxes full of hubs, spanners and tubes around muddy fields, our all-white policy is hard to explain in retrospect, but it had something to do with our sense of being pioneering and incorruptible. It also had something to do with not wanting to look like traditional orchestral musicians, and white was symbolic of not being black. We frequently had nowhere proper to change for our concerts, and nowhere to wash either. We were subjected to the elements all day long, and it was usually raining when we had to put the dome up somewhere. Our white concert outfits were hanging in the back of the van or inside the tent, suspended from one of the aluminium tubes that formed the dome's skeleton. Often when we came to put them on, our clothes were actually damp, and I did occasionally wonder if I would get through a week of such concerts without coming down with flu. The sight of us all shivering in our white cotton outfits in the wind and rain made motherly audience members offer to bring us mugs of tea or blankets to put round our shoulders when we were offstage, a charming experience.

Exhibit E: the fuchsia-pink paisley-patterned long-sleeved Laura Ashley dress with a big flared skirt which I liked so much in the 1980s. The dress featured in some of Domus's publicity photographs and was recently included in an exhibition of archive photos of chamber musicians who took part in the International Musicians' Seminars in Prussia Cove. I thought my pink dress was perfect for concert wear until we started getting concerts in other European countries such as Germany, Spain and Italy where we quickly realised that the majority of the audience was more dressed-up than we were. It felt rather strange to be the focus of attention in a cotton dress when most of the women in the audience were in smart Chanel-type suits with lots of gold jewellery and beautifully coiffed hair. I think it was around this time I decided I should try a different look.

Exhibit F: the black-and-white second-hand 'couture' outfit I bought for a Wigmore Hall concert with my group Domus in the late 1980s. As usual, there was little money to upgrade our wardrobes. A singer friend told me about a shop in South Kensington where you could buy second-hand designer clothes for a fraction of the price. I went to have a look and found an extremely smart matching jacket and long skirt by an upmarket designer, perfect for a grand concert. The jacket and skirt were of heavy black watered silk. The fitted jacket had panels of vintage white lace overlaying it and buttons covered in lace, and the black skirt had an overskirt of this same vintage lace. Despite its second-hand price, it was by far the most expensive outfit I had ever bought and the first I ever had where I felt as if the clothes were wearing me, not the other way round. It was an interesting sensation and made me understand the remark quoted by Ralph Waldo Emerson who heard a lady declare that 'the sense of being perfectly well-dressed gives a feeling of inward tranquillity which religion is powerless to bestow'. I swanned onto the stage of the Wigmore Hall feeling like a celebrity. Our agent was in the audience with an important concert promoter as her guest. Afterwards she reported that he had said, 'Great playing. Awful clothes.' I put the outfit away at the back in my wardrobe until the lace had turned a delicate yellow, and then tried to sell it to a 'vintage' clothes shop where they offered me £10 for it. I ended up giving it to Oxfam.

Exhibit G: the red silk evening dress I bought at a boutique in Hampstead for a solo piano recital in the 1990s. It was floor-length silk with a heavy flared skirt and beautiful long sleeves ending in wide flounces which swirled gracefully around my hands as I moved about the keyboard. It felt like a grown-up version of my first concert dress, the red dress I had as an eleven-year-old. I wore the red silk evening dress for my special recital and then for a number of chamber music concerts with my group Domus in grander venues. The last time I wore it was when we went to France and played in a long-established concert series in, I think, Marseilles. Our concert was reviewed by a French critic, who wrote kindly about my playing but remarked that I was 'clad in the sort of dress that only a subject of Her Imperial Britannic Majesty would think to wear'. This was an unpleasant shock and I put the dress away until the feeling of shame had dissipated, which it didn't.

Exhibit H: the panoply of unisex Chinese jackets which I wore in the first decade of the twenty-first century when I had decided that it was safer to stop trying to choose 'evening dresses', which were increasingly hard to find in any case as such formal wear went out of fashion. It was difficult to find long dresses as hemlines rose and sleeveless dresses became de rigueur. I decided that as I was at that time playing in a trio with two men, I should not try to strike a definite note of feminine contrast and should instead just wear smart black trousers and a long colourful jacket. Chinese silk jackets had come into fashion and I found them very good for playing the piano, where you need something roomy so that your arms are not constricted. I was able to pick up a whole selection of Chinese jackets in beautiful colours: pearly grey, ivory, gold, black with a scarlet lining, and a lovely second-hand Shanghai Tang black velvet jacket with a lime green silk lining. I turned the sleeves back so that the lime green would show. With my burgeoning wardrobe of Chinese jackets and smart black trousers I felt I had hit upon an exotic yet practical outfit which made me look serious and purposeful without looking like 'one of the boys'.

Friends who belong to orchestras have told me many times over the years that the subject of concert clothes has caused some of their most heated discussions. For a whole orchestra to agree on a change of 'look' is a big thing, achievable only after long negotiation. Even groups specialising in contemporary music, who don't need to wear 'tails' or dinner suits, are in a bit of a quandary about what to wear, because there's always a feeling that performers should look somewhat different from members of the audience. Wearing black (e.g. black shirts and trousers) is a popular solution, just as it is in conventional orchestras. 'Unstructured' shirts worn loosely over black trousers is another popular look, for example in string quartets. Curiously, high glamour is favoured by young performers who can probably scarcely afford it. I'm sometimes amazed at the gorgeous figure-hugging creations worn by female students and young professionals in concerts at the end of masterclasses; the look seems more evocative of Hollywood Oscar ceremonies than the traditional classical concert. Often one feels that a really eye-catching outfit is chosen to distract from shortcomings of technique, though a few artists such as the young Chinese pianist Yuja Wang combine ultra-fashionable dress sense with superb mastery of their instrument.

In the past few years there have been some bold gestures by (male) solo musicians, such as violinist Nigel Kennedy or pianist James Rhodes, appearing on stage in moth-eaten t-shirts, sweatshirts with football logos, or outdoor clothing not associated with concerts: leather jackets, army greatcoats, woolly hats, camouflage jackets, chequered Palestinian scarves and so on. The 'inappropriateness' of such clothing is obviously the main point; it's a conscious attempt to remove classical music from the usual frame of reference and situate it somewhere new. I find this completely understandable, even if it seems to me that the clothing chosen instead is just as stereotypical of other groups and other attitudes.

There's certainly a desire for classical music to stop 'referencing' outdated historical fashions, and rightly so. The question is: what to wear instead? A friend of mine, playing in a musical project in Paris, had the opportunity to be dressed by a top couturier for the final concert. She found herself wearing a fantastic dress with green wings, which she said didn't feel as outlandish as you might expect. Wings seemed to evoke flights of imagination, soaring above the everyday, moving in an airy realm – one would hesitate to suggest them as routine concert wear, but it was a delight to hear that wearing wings to play Fauré felt surprisingly natural.

Concert clothes are still a puzzle. For no matter how much a musician may want to reassure the audience that they are 'all in it together', that a musician is just like they are, a regular guy who happens to be good at the violin or whatever, it isn't quite as simple as that. It's not an everyday thing we do. The music is something precious and rare; and if all goes as you hope, the moment of performance is equally so. Our brief appearance on the platform is the culmination of an awful lot of effort and dedication. Somehow it feels as if that should be reflected in the specialness of the clothes we wear, and perhaps it is even 'right' that the ideal concert clothes should be a little removed from mainstream fashion. We don't want to alienate anyone, but we don't want to understate the occasion either. After all, the music itself is something big, something of unusual stature. I think that's why we musicians have struggled continually to find the right look — because classical music isn't represented in anything you can buy off the peg. And sometimes you wish you didn't have to consider concert dress at all.

Enigma variations

A friend of mine, a member of a successful string quartet, once re-marked to me that classical music's best-kept secret is how often the members of a chamber group grow to hate one another.

Over the years I've repeated this remark to a number of non-musicians and they've all been shocked. They've seen films and read novels based on the notion that chamber music is one big group hug – or if not exactly a group hug, then at any rate an opportunity to put forward your best self. Isn't chamber music a metaphor for an ideal society, everyone listening and sharing respectfully, putting their skills and understanding at the service of the whole group? Doesn't it give you the magical combination of independence without isola-tion? How can it be that people voluntarily engaged in the delight-ful pursuit of shared and intimate music-making, playing the divine quartets of Haydn, Mozart and Beethoven, are anything other than friends? Chamber music at its most positive is a musical experience perhaps more touching than any other. So many works of chamber music feel as if they have been offered as insights into their composers' innermost thoughts. You feel privileged to hear such confidences, and to transmit them securely is a big but pleasing responsibility. When you have the opportunity to immerse yourself in these masterworks, together with really talented colleagues, you know you're communicating at a deep level. Because the music has so much soul, it calls for the musicians to put their souls on the line as well, and the experience can really bind people together. There's probably nothing to beat this kind of collaborative, 'more than the sum of the parts' music-making. It has given me my most cherished musical moments as well as some memorably telepathic ones. Almost every kind of professional musician enjoys playing chamber music and regards it as a 'pure' kind of music-making precisely because of the potential it offers to be free from egotism and directorial intervention. Amateur chamber groups adore their musical encounters.

The experience of being in a chamber group is especially intense, I believe, for musicians who have made a professional commitment to one another, rather than meeting on a one-off basis. Learning something together, figuring it out, building up your own approach, developing unanimity – these can raise your efforts to a point where the musicians move and turn together instinctively like a flock of birds. This kind of rapport, which is fuelled by music and can often transcend personal relationships, is a special experience. Many chamber groups at the start of their professional careers are emotionally close. So why do things change for many of them?

I've come to think of it as being like the 'larger theme' which Sir Edward Elgar claimed went 'through and over the whole set' of his famous 'Enigma' Variations, 'but is not played'. The unstated principal theme he referred to as 'a dark saying', but he never revealed what it was. The idea of an unstated theme which goes 'through and over the whole set' is a haunting one; the notion of the 'dark saying' has often been in my mind when I think about life as a professional chamber player.

A string quartet in particular has a wonderful image: the image of a conversation between like-minded friends. Illustrations of quartets usually show four people seriously engrossed in the effort to play beautiful music which is more than the sum of its parts. They never look like they're showing off; they look as though they're trying to push their egos aside for each other's sake. Each person has their special role to play, and everyone is equally important; it's an image of balance and democracy. Playing a string quartet seems to be an 'equal music', a microcosm of what every workplace or family should be like. Even better, the music they play is some of the best that has ever been written. Imagine the pleasure of devoting yourself for years on end to the intricate study of Haydn's, Mozart's, Beethoven's or Schubert's string quartets!

And yet, as the actor Philip Seymour Hoffman pointed out, 'Just because you like to do something doesn't mean you have fun doing it.' Within the music profession there are any number of stories about members of chamber groups who no longer speak to one another. There are infamous tales of world-renowned groups whose members won't travel on the same planes as one another, or stay in the same hotel. I was told a dreadful story about a quartet who ostracised one of its members and refused to speak to or look at them, even during concerts – a modern-day version of something I'd first read about in an anthropology book as a tribal punishment, a way of making someone give up and fade away.

As a young professional I took part in a festival in Israel where the artists had been allocated 'minders' to help them find their way about the city. A world-famous visiting quartet had been given a single minder who was driven to distraction trying to shepherd them around, for they wouldn't go anywhere together. So not only did she have to recommend restaurants, but she had to recommend places that she hadn't recommended to anyone else in the quartet, so that they wouldn't risk bumping into one another. She'd been told to eat with them if they wanted company, so she was running around from restaurant to restaurant, eating a main course with one person and dessert with another, and then trying to do the same at the next meal for the other two. They got separate taxis to the concert hall and, according to their minder, said virtually nothing to one another until they met on stage for their rehearsal, at which point they said what needed to be said about the music and then went their separate ways.

After hearing this, I went to one of their concerts and was most intrigued. Their entrance on stage from four different parts of the wings, two from stage left and two from stage right, looked symbolic; had I not been alerted to the situation I suppose it might have struck me as merely a cute bit of choreography. They didn't look or smile at one another, but that's not particularly unusual in the serious world of quartet playing, where it's sometimes a point of honour not to need to look. Despite the alleged *froideur* between them, their performance was polished and professional, impressively unanimous in many ways, and I marvelled at how music – at least for the time it takes to perform it – can unite people who no longer have much in common. It was obvious that they had long ago worked out their approach to their core repertoire, polished it and were able to stick to that game plan at each performance, putting on a show of cooperation. I remember shaking my head sadly and saying to my own colleagues afterwards, 'I could never make myself stay with a group if things had got like that.'

So why do groups stay together if things have got so bad? Perhaps each group would give a different answer, but there must be common elements. It takes an enormous amount of time and effort to learn the repertoire of a string quartet, an investment of years. First there are all the notes to learn, and then comes the work of developing a coordinated approach to tuning, the use of the bow, the approach to tone colour, articulation, degrees of 'attack', how exactly to start and end notes in the same way and at the same time. Then there is the matter of interpretation: digesting the music, building a shared approach to how the music works and what you want your listeners to understand when you play it. As these are generally long works of half an hour or so, each work divided into several movements, there are hundreds of 'junctions' in the music to be negotiated. Every transition, where one thing gives way to another, or is transformed into something else, needs to be handled unanimously. The whole choreography of where to speed up, slow down, take time, back off to give someone else more room to play, and the tapestry of moods and expressive nuances – all this takes long and patient work, the construction of a language particular to the group and shared only with your colleagues. It's absorbing work and comes to feel like your own secret: 'your brand', as some would say. You realise you are the guardians of your own interpretations.

Reputation takes a long time to establish. By the time you have done the work and established the reputation, you are more than committed to one another: you are tied together. To walk away from the group would be to waste a great deal of the work you have done together. Other groups may play the same repertoire, but will have their own approach to sonority, intonation, stylistic integrity, bow-strokes, tone colours and all those tiny decisions about musical 'give and take'. The knowledge you gain with one particular group is only partly transferable to another. You may be in the finest quartet in the world, but if you leave it, you cannot make a career as one-quarter of a quartet you don't belong to any more. Your interpretations are an intellectual property shared with particular co-creators. Everyone recognises that the invest-ment they have put into a group is not to be given up lightly. At the same time, the intensity of the work, and arguably the anxiety of the lifestyle, often seems to mean that people become hypersensitive to one another's foibles. They may even become allergic to one another's playing, a very difficult knot to untie. Observers sometimes say that differences between members of the group are intriguing to witness on stage, but what audi-ences witness on stage is just the tip of the iceberg; those same differ-ences can become thorns in the side of people who have to endure them day after day. Of course there are some groups who rub along together very well despite personality differences, but anecdotal evidence seems to indicate that they are the exception rather than the rule.

It is no secret in the pop world that groups break up acrimoniously – we read about their rows and dramas all the time in the press. Every-one understands that creative types are volatile, that egos clash and ambitions pull in different directions. But then everything about the pop world seems to be speeded up. Groups form quickly and disband quickly too. Their life together doesn't begin by the long slow climb up a mountain of existing repertoire. They often write their own material, generally composed of short songs. Many groups no doubt survive on little money, but success brings huge rewards very quickly. When pop groups split up, they are not often wasting many years of patient, intricate work together. For classical groups the situation is very different, not least because they are afraid to throw away their source of income. Even if players walk straight into another group, they will be in for a long haul.

Making a living from chamber music wasn't a profession until the twentieth century, and from some points of view isn't a profession even today. Playing chamber music has its roots in a European society where playing music at home was highly valued. True, it was done in one's spare time and for pleasure, but it was an important part of understanding and participating in a musical tradition so deeply embedded in culture that it was almost like an aspect of speaking the language. Playing chamber music, 'Hausmusik', was a widespread pastime in many European households in the eighteenth, nineteenth and even twentieth centuries, until World War II dispersed many of the participants (particularly in Germany and Austria), thus shattering old traditions. But it was only late in the nineteenth century that the idea of earning a living as a regular, professional chamber group developed – I believe the Bohemian Quartet was one of the first – and then more groups appeared as the circuit of concert societies and festivals widened, and the era of radio and recording and television made it possible to reach out to audiences all over the world.

To understand why young musicians of today might view chamber music as a viable way of earning a living, one has to realise that most of them have been heavily engaged in music since childhood. An awful lot is invested in their musical future, an investment of time, money, dedication and care. During their training many of them are encouraged to think of themselves as performers in the making, hopefully bringing glory to the family which has sacrificed so much to support them and buy their expensive instruments. As young musicians develop, they encounter different fields of music-making which seem to offer themselves as professional prospects. For instrumentalists, the core options are solo playing, chamber music and orchestral playing. All three areas have attracted the most eminent of players and are by no means mutually exclusive. Many soloists love to play chamber music, as do many orchestral musicians, so in this sense chamber music is the option on which everyone converges.

As young musicians build up their familiarity with recorded performances, they see how chamber groups of the past have become icons of the music world as a whole. Chamber groups are seen as idealists, as somehow 'pure'. Why would young players not want to follow in the footsteps of the Bohemian Quartet, the Amadeus, the Guarneri, the Alban Berg or the Beaux Arts Trio? For the chamber music enthusiast, it looks such a civilised way to be a professional musician. It offers the possibility of travelling the world without the loneliness which is famously the lot of the soloist. And when they look at other musical genres such as pop and rock, they see that small groups are clearly a recipe for success, so why wouldn't that be the case for classical music too?

My own introduction to chamber music playing came, as for so many young musicians, in my teenage years. When I was a junior student at the Royal Scottish Academy of Music, my piano teacher suggested I might like to try playing some piano trios. I was together with a violinist and a cellist. In some ways it was a bit like the famous scene in *The Wizard of Oz* where Dorothy's black-and-white house is picked up by the tornado and deposited in Munchkin-Land, and she emerges to discover that everything is suddenly in colour.

Until then, 99% of my piano playing had been done in a room on my own, facing a wall. It had never been possible before to have fun and chat during practice, to share jokes, talk about music, go for bacon rolls and mugs of tea in the canteen with 'my colleagues'. Nobody my own age had ever before said 'Wow!' when I managed a particularly virtuosic passage on the piano. The social element was new for me and proved a big attraction. And after years of solitary practice, listening to nobody but me, I discovered that I had an aptitude for listening to other people. Watching them, learning their ways, trying to guess what they were going to do were things that seemed to come naturally and seemed to enlarge the whole adventure.

In later years I was shocked to discover that some instrumentalists feel chamber music takes something away from the freedom and fullness of experience they have when playing as soloists; for me, playing chamber music positively *added* to the experience of music-making. I didn't feel diminished or constrained because I was part of a group. If anything, I felt that having more people involved made it more interesting, and I realised straight away the crucial role played by the pianist. The piano parts of the trios we learned were just as demanding pianistically as what I was playing on my own, so it never occurred to me that chamber music represented any kind of diminishment. And to my piano teachers' credit, they never gave me that impression either. I later learned that some piano teachers are suspicious of chamber music because they think it is 'a distraction' and will interfere with proper solo practice, so I feel I was lucky in having teachers who encouraged my chamber playing and let me bring my trio colleagues to my lessons if I wanted to. It seemed to make no difference whether we worked on a Beethoven solo piano sonata or a Beethoven trio – as long as it was music I was interested in.

My chamber playing got off to a good start when my student trio at the time won an important college prize with the first piece we learned (the Arensky Trio), and my enjoyment of chamber music continued through my university years at Cambridge with short-lived groups of various kinds, although for me piano trios always seemed to be the most satisfying format. After university, I went to the International Musicians' Seminar in Prussia Cove, first as a masterclass student and later to take part in 'Open Chamber Music', which brings together professional musicians of all generations and is one of the best environments in the UK (perhaps in the world) to meet potential chamber music partners. From that point on, my involvement in chamber music intensified. Suddenly I was in the company of kindred spirits who had also been waiting for the moment they could form serious chamber groups and were thrilled to find one another. We had all been practising our instruments since we were five, six, seven years old. It seemed to us as though plunging into the world of chamber music was eminently possible and desirable. So in we plunged.

Over the decades that followed, I have played in a whole variety of professional chamber groups. The two that dominated my life for a total of over thirty years were Domus, a piano quartet, and later the Florestan Trio. These were both small groups with a relatively stable membership (though there were some changes in membership over the years of Domus). Neither of these groups was ever full-time, though for most of the members, the group's earnings formed the majority of their income, especially in the early days. We found it was almost impossible to build up a dependably full-time career, at least one with an adequate income, and as time went on we accepted that there were good points about the variety we were forced to embrace. We had learned that the famous piano trio formed by Cortot, Thibaud and Casals was never remotely full-time – in fact, they usually met only for one month of the year, and in some years they didn't meet at all. The infrequency of their concerts didn't seem to harm their illustrious name, and the success of their individual activities actually enhanced the group's reputation. In the freelance music business, many musicians pursue solo as well as collaborative opportunities, to maximise their income as well as their work satisfaction. The fact that our groups were not full-time did not, however, mean that we were not devoted to them; our time together was intense, and we were all so deeply involved in trying to advance the group's cause that it did often feel like a full-time endeavour.

I have also played for many years in the Gaudier Ensemble, which began life as a Schubert Octet, drawn mostly from members of the Chamber Orchestra of Europe. Their membership has fluctuated over the years, though a core of founder members remains, and they play a wide range of repertoire, both with and without piano. I've played in many groups arising from the International Musicians' Seminars in Prussia Cove. I've played in many duos, made many appearances as a guest pianist with string quartets and given occasional concerts with various other kinds of ensembles. I have got to know countless chamber musicians in permanent and semi-permanent groups. And it seems clear that any group of people who work together, and rely on each other to earn their living, are bound to encounter difficulties in their relations with each other from time to time. But there is something special about making chamber music together at a professional level, and, perhaps unsurprisingly, the difficulties likely to arise are special too. Inevitably, the closer, smaller and more regular the group, the greater the intensity of the difficulties as well as the rewards.

One of the groups of enthusiastic young musicians that came together at Prussia Cove wanted to try creating a less formal atmosphere in classical concerts. We decided to form the ensemble which eventually became known as Domus. We began by giving concerts inside our own portable concert hall, a geodesic dome (the story is told in my book *Beyond the Notes*). It was a mad, enthralling start to life in a professional chamber group.

I was reminded of some of the reality of those days recently when I took part in a career advice seminar for young professional musicians. We asked them if there was anything that had come as a surprise to them about a career in music. Lots of hands shot up – they had had no idea how much time would be taken up in getting and administering their own concerts! There had been so much focus on the music itself when they were at college and on matters such as competitions and auditions and schemes which led to getting grants and having debut concerts funded. All well and good, but once they started getting those concerts, they found they were sadly unprepared for the amount of correspondence and arrangements that had to be made for each engagement. This was particularly true if the concert was for a group, with complicated individual travel and accommodation arrangements, especially as there is often one member of the group who does the admin on behalf of all the rest. Why was one person doing the work on behalf of the rest, you might wonder? In theory, such tasks could be shared, but they usually aren't. It seems to boil down to a question of personality; there is inevitably someone who can see what needs to be done and can't bear to see that it is not being done. When Domus began, I turned out to be that person. Even though I wasn't thrilled about doing admin, I was even less thrilled about seeing the consequences of its not being done: invitations not replied to, opportunities missed, people not thanked for helping us. I started amateurishly trying to do these tasks, and there seemed to be no end to them.

There are of course many non-musical roles to play within a music group and very valuable contributions to be made by, for example, the person who enjoys doing travel research, the person who understands accounts, the person who understands technology, the good cook, the steady driver, the sympathetic listener, the humorist and so on. But the person locked into everyday admin and correspondence with the rest of the world is never off duty.

At the seminar, one girl waited behind to ask me with some intensity whether it was normal to find yourself spending most of your day doing admin for the group. Her group did not have an agent, and she was doing all their admin on a voluntary basis. She had thought of herself as a viola player, but suddenly the viola was taking a back seat to being a glorified secretary. She was aghast at the amount of work involved in fixing rehearsals and travel for five people. She went on to give a long list of the issues that routinely had to be discussed and arranged, both with her colleagues and with concert organisers: parking, rehearsal at the venue, stage lighting, music stands, artists' biographies and photographs, the choice and order of the programme, guest tickets, piano tuning, page-turner, overnight accommodation, food before or after the concert and dietary requirements thereof, programme notes, thank-you letters. And then there was the whole issue of fee negotiation! Her alarm at this unexpected workload was fuelled by a suspicion that her efforts were not properly registered by the other players. She felt as if she had suddenly turned into 'their Mom', as she put it, and that they hardly noticed her devotion. To make things even more complicated, the members of her group, who had met at music college in London, actually hailed from several different countries. Sometimes a concert date would necessitate drawing together a number of people who were an international flight away. Was it realistic to continue like this?

I have an old file with hundreds of faint purple carbon copies of letters I wrote on behalf of my group Domus in the 1980s, at the point where we stopped using the dome and took to the ordinary concert circuit. Reading the file makes me feel quite sad. So many hopeful letters asking promoters to consider us! When a music club or a festival did express interest, there followed many letters discussing what we were going to play and when, and all the rest of it, a cascade of letters painstakingly typed out with the myriad practical details. Strangely enough, the advent of email and electronic communication of many different kinds has not alleviated the workload but merely changed it. I used to spend hours at my typewriter, and now spend hours at my computer instead. I used to spend an hour writing one letter, and now I write to lots of people in an hour. It may be possible to reach people more quickly, and to reach more people at once, but because of this we are taking on more tasks, communicating with more people, trying more initiatives, spreading information across more 'platforms', and feeling under more pressure to respond to questions immediately, whether we are 'on duty' or not. I now know lots of self-employed musicians who write work emails when they are wakeful in 'the wee small hours'.

As I listened to the young viola player at the seminar, and thought back to a similar stage in my own career, it struck me vividly that there has never been an easy or automatic way for any chamber group to obtain work. When we embarked on our professional lives, the way ahead seemed shrouded in mystery. Was there a trail to follow? We could not simply join a trade organisation, put a nameplate on the door and wait for people to ring the bell. We had no training in sales-manship, and ours was not the kind of skill necessarily in demand. We were not like accountants, nurses, architects or teachers who could be confident of being needed by their fellow townspeople. There were a few schemes which ran auditions and offered debut concerts to suc-cessful candidates, but apart from that, we were on our own. Maybe there were a few people in our town who wanted to hear us, but not every week or even every month, and definitely not enough to provide us with an income.

We knew that somewhere out there, probably scattered all over the world, were little pockets of people who loved chamber music and might love us, but whether or not they would ever get to know of our existence seemed unbelievably hit-and-miss. 'Networking' in the days before the internet was a much harder grind. I feel reverence for Mozart's father who somehow managed to arrange concert tours across Europe for his brilliant son in the mid-eighteenth century when presumably letters would take weeks to be answered! Every year we designed a brochure, got lots of copies printed and sat down to mail the brochures to as many music clubs as we could find out about, via directories published by the Arts Council and so on. Of all the letters and brochures we sent out, only a tiny fraction received any response, but it was enough to make us feel we were making headway.

In my old file there were letters to our bank manager trying to explain why the group's bank account was hovering perilously around the zero mark again. ('We have spent £900 on copies of our own records, to sell at concerts, but unfortunately at the present rate of sales, it will take us a while to recoup the costs.') There were many letters chasing up promises of concert offers 'next season'. ('Dear Concert Club Secretary, I have a letter on file in which you mention that your committee was hoping to book us next season, but we have not heard from you since.') There were letters to places we'd played months ago, asking when they were going to pay us and explaining in pathetic detail why the delay was a problem. There were letters to promoters asking if the fee could possibly be a bit larger if they were asking us to learn new repertoire especially because of some 'theme' around which they'd arranged their festival.

At the very beginning of Domus's career we had uniquely complicated administrative tasks because we were trying to set up something entirely new: giving concerts in our portable concert hall, seating 200. There was so much to do, and nobody to do it but us. What began as a lovely dream, the idea of giving informal concerts in a gorgeous hemispherical tent, had to be turned into a reality. Some of my colleagues threw themselves into the practical side of dome-building, a complex matter requiring resourcefulness, technical competence and advanced do-it-yourself skills, which they had in abundance. Since I was never gifted in those matters, I got busy with letter-writing, trying to let people know about our project and obtain permission to come and put up our tent in their park or field, on their hillside, at their festival or whatever. Our viola player Robin Ireland and I tackled many of the tasks together. Robin, in fact, straddled the twin tasks of admin and dealing with matters relating to the dome itself and its infrastructure – the PVC cover we had made for the dome, the stage and the lighting, the trailer we used to transport things. We were busy from morning to night with practical tasks and negotiations with landowners. Who knew that you had to get municipal permission to put up a tent like ours, or that there were all kinds of bye-laws that had to be complied with? Our idealistic dream felt as if it were crashing into one obstacle after another.

It was a steep learning curve. We had thought of ourselves as musicians, but playing music was often pushed to the bottom of the agenda; we seemed to have turned into arts administrators without having intended to do so. All this was for the sake of music, but music itself became a distant echo for longish periods in our daily lives. Because we were trying to interact with people who worked office hours, administration became literally our 'day job'. It was often evening before I had the time to sit down at the piano, or until Robin could take his viola out of its case, and by then we were too tired to practise.

The payoff was that we did manage to create opportunities that hadn't existed before, in places which hadn't had concerts before. We had actually been pioneering and made something happen! This was deeply satisfying. We had a memorable time playing concerts to audiences who were often quite excited by our presence and by our efforts to bring chamber music into their midst. Thirty years later I and my colleagues still occasionally get letters from people who say their love of chamber music really began then, when they sat close to us inside the dome and realised how much communication there was, between the musicians, between the players and the audience, and between the music and the audience. They hadn't realised that live music was so different from listening to records. We were proud of having been, shall I say, instrumental in their journey of discovery.

But we had painful discoveries of our own. In 1981, at the end of two weeks of concerts in Cheltenham with the dome, I wrote in my diary, 'On the way home we try to work out the finances of these two weeks. It's clear that if we allow £20 petrol for each of the cars, and X's train fare, it will leave us with about £100 in the bank. Out of this we have to pay seven players, and the bills for various things like spanners, work gloves, communal food and drink. We reckon this will leave each player with £10 or less for a fortnight of very hard work.' The members of the group were aghast when this was revealed. A few days later we had another meeting at which 'we abandon all previous policies of dividing the money in various subtle ways ... and opt simply for refunding Felix money he has spent on various technical things, repaying petrol expenses and dividing the remainder in seven.

This new way of calculating things leaves us with about £17 each for two weeks of work. It is shocking …'.

Indeed, it was shocking: £17 in 1981 would equate to around £61 at the time of writing in 2013 – out of which we each had to pay our rent for two weeks, not only in Cheltenham, but also in London where we lived the rest of the time and still had to pay rent while we were away. Not only was there no profit, but we were subsidising our own group, paying for the privilege of being in it, although none of us was affluent. Clearly this was not sustainable. But what else could we do? We had all spent years training for this moment. Not only that, in order to focus on a career in music, several of us had actually passed up chances (by leaving school early, for example) to obtain other qualifications. We had invested too much time and effort to turn away just because of what might be teething difficulties. As my mum used to say, 'As you make your bed, so must you lie in it.'

These experiences were the beginning of a hard-to-speak-about realisation that perhaps because of our idealism and, some might say, our naïveté, we were bound together in an unlucky financial enterprise. We thought that things would surely get better, little by little, if our hearts were in the right place and our motivation true. We knew we were attempting a great thing, bringing our beloved chamber music to new audiences and making those audiences feel comfortable and included. Fate would surely look kindly on us when it realised how valuable our project was. But no matter how attached we were to one another in human ways, and as musicians, we found we were also bound together by our collective lack of earning power. Having thought ourselves lucky to have one another, we became slowly aware of being liabilities to one another also. This was an unpleasant feeling. People sometimes ventured to utter the thought that if they had spent the time on promoting their own individual activities instead, they would have been financially a lot better off. The subject of income became an obsession. We all smiled with a mixture of recognition and pain when a senior banker told us a joke one day at a reception after a big concert. He said, 'Whenever I'm going to a dinner and I have the choice of sitting beside a banker or sitting beside a musician, I always choose the banker, because musicians only ever want to talk about money.'

It was normal for freelance musicians such as ourselves to try to juggle solo and collaborative opportunities, but we tried to stick to the principle that the group came first; our informal agreement was that if one of us was offered something which clashed with a group engagement, the group's concert would prevail. This was very idealistic, but we took it seriously; we couldn't envisage any other way that the group could flourish, or even survive. Naturally we were always afraid that if someone were suddenly to make unexpected headway in their individual career, they would abandon us. We felt that together we should have had more earning power than we did separately, but this was never the case, and still isn't for today's chamber groups. In classical music, concert promoters have always paid larger fees to well-known soloists than to chamber groups, even though there are obviously more people involved in a chamber group. Promoters say they take in more money at the box office when they put on a concert by a soloist. It remains a mystery why the situation is so utterly different to that of the pop world, where groups are a magnet for money and audiences.

You might imagine that the situation improves over the years, if you and your chamber group succeed in becoming well known. And it's true that if you have a long-established, respected chamber group, you can command slightly higher fees. But only slightly; the laws of supply and demand guarantee that. And there are two facts of life that remain generally fixed: agents' commission and the so-called 'global fee'.

In the early days of Domus, we didn't have an agent, and we didn't acquire one until we had done a lot of the spadework to establish ourselves on the concert circuit. It's never easy for a chamber group to find an agent, and it certainly wasn't in the days when there were very few competitions to catapult a young group into the public eye. Agencies are businesses, dependent on making money from the artists they promote, and they were never particularly interested in chamber groups because low fees meant less commission. They were also wary of the amount of admin involved. This extra work, set against the low fees, made little economic sense to many agents. Fortunately for us, some agents love chamber music and were personally motivated to have at least one chamber group on their books. However, because agents found it uneconomic to communicate with every person in the group individually about travel arrangements and so on, someone in the group had to liaise back and forth between the agency and the other musicians.

Meanwhile, the agents, however much they loved music, and however useful they might have been in finding more concerts, were rarely flexible about charging for their work. They charged 20%. But 20% of what? Not 20% of profits, of what actually ended up in our pockets, but 20% of the 'global fee', the gross fee offered by the concert promoter. Out of the 80% that was left we had to pay our rehearsal costs, travel expenses, hotel costs, restaurant bills, taxi fares to and from the concert hall and any other related costs (such as buying music) before we divided the remainder equally between us. Naturally, for a group of four this meant that the agent earned considerably more than any one of us did for each concert, even though the agent didn't have to practise, rehearse or travel far away to play the concert.

You might think that a well-established group would be in a position to ask for basic expenses to be paid on top of the fee, as is usual in many kinds of business. But in the low-finance world of chamber music, it is rare for a concert promoter to offer to pay expenses. It is much more usual for them to offer a single sum, out of which the musicians must pay all their expenses. Of course, for everyone but the musicians, the payment of a global fee makes life simple, because it is a fixed sum, which doesn't involve them in paying unknown quantities of travel and hotel costs. Agents prefer the global fee, because they usually take their commission 'off the top'. However, the musicians are faced with a number of unwelcome decisions, because they must decide how much of the global fee they spend on their own travel and accommodation. We never knew what we would earn until we had spent ages researching different travel options and having sometimes fractious meetings about the choices open to us.

I well remember that when Domus started getting offers of foreign engagements, they were usually single concerts, not tours. Before cheap airlines sprang into being, air fares had become very expensive. We were offered a concert in Spain for a global fee of something like £2000. There were four of us in the group, and one was a cellist. This meant that there were not four but five air tickets to buy. Cellos are too fragile and valuable to go in the hold, and too big to fit in overhead lockers, so airlines require them to be allocated their own seat. The cost of the cello ticket gets split between members of the group (though I do know of one ruthless pianist who refuses to allow this arrangement, on the grounds that a cello is the player's investment … and pension!). Strangely, although airlines sometimes offer price reductions to passengers, inanimate objects such as cellos don't qualify for special offers, which means that on occasion the cost of a cello ticket is considerably more than the cost of the cellist's.

I remember how horrified we were on the aforementioned occasion when we investigated the cost of flying to Spain and discovered that return tickets were £400 each, which meant that at a stroke we would have spent the entire fee, and that was before we'd paid commission. Moreover, had we stayed two nights in a Spanish hotel (the night before the concert and the night of the concert), we would have been *paying* hundreds of pounds to play the concert. Anyone with a bit of business sense will naturally think that going to Spain was therefore out of the question, but in fact we debated it long and hard. Being offered a concert abroad was exciting and seemed full of potential. We wondered, as many groups do, whether it was worth subsidising the concert ourselves because it would introduce us to a country which might like us and offer us lots of work in the future. But what if it didn't? We were horrified by the thought that our career was going to be scarred by similar situations on a regular basis. Fortunately, right around that time, several low-cost airlines came into being and gave us a lifeline.

But even when there is a more acceptable relationship between the fee and the cost of travel, the decisions you have to make are often divisive. There's usually someone who is prepared to economise by travelling cheaply at an 'anti-social' time of day, or minimising hotel costs by travelling out on the day of the concert. They're willing to go through a little discomfort to maximise the fee. Then there's someone else who thinks this is a ridiculous plan. How can people play their best if they're exhausted from having to get up at 4am to go to Stansted Airport? Instead, they propose going at a civilised time on the day before the concert, having a leisurely dinner and staying that night in a hotel. If everyone goes for that plan, however, there will only be a small amount of the fee left to split between the players. How to resolve the situation? Most groups try to arrive at a consensus, because it is much easier administratively if they all travel together, but this usually means either that someone is frustrated at having their fee reduced by 'unnecessarily high' travel expenses, or that someone else is cross about having to get up at dawn to catch a cheaper flight.

Sometimes we tried to keep costs to a minimum by flying out on the day of a concert rather than on the day before, thereby saving the cost of several hotel rooms. But after a few scary experiences where we very nearly missed, or did actually miss, a concert, we decided that we simply had to travel out on the day before and afford ourselves an extra night's accommodation. I remember one occasion when the Florestan Trio had a single concert in the Canary Islands. We got up in the middle of the night to catch a really early flight from London to Madrid and a connecting flight to Las Palmas. In theory it should have worked with hours to spare, as the concert was scheduled for late evening. But the first flight was delayed by several hours and we missed the connecting flight. We spent the whole day in a state of agitation, trying to figure out alternative routes and strategies (in the days before mobile phones, this wasn't easy). We did actually land in Las Palmas about an hour before the concert and just had time to rush to the hall, get changed and appear on stage, hearts still racing. The wear and tear on everyone's nerves was considerable, and we decided that the financial saving just wasn't worth it.

On occasion we tried to devise a complicated system whereby we calculated what each person's fee would be and left each person to book their own travel, as cheap or as luxurious as they wished. But such a system naturally resulted in people making such divergent plans that it was difficult to schedule rehearsals, let alone time to talk and plan (we often made use of journeys to address complicated issues). Individuals sometimes neglected to book their travel or passed the task to someone else, be it an agent or a member of the group, who ended up with an insane amount of record-keeping. When the fee was finally paid, three months after the concert, who would remember who'd done what, how much it cost and who owed what to whom?

If members of the group made unilateral decisions, there were all sorts of knock-on effects. Let's say two people decided to fly out peacefully on the day before the concert, but two decided to come out the following morning. There could be no rehearsal until everyone had arrived, so the two who had gone early would be compelled to wait around next day for the others, and then they'd have to rehearse in the afternoon of the concert – a situation they'd probably wished to avoid when they made the decision to travel out on the day before. Or perhaps the people travelling out on the day of the concert would miss their flight, thus making the whole journey pointless for those who'd flown out on the previous day!

On many occasions I've travelled somewhere to play a single concert with other musicians who converged on the city from various international destinations. In one recent example, the organiser explained that we should book our own travel and that after the concert he'd refund everyone's travel expenses before he divided up the remainder between us. Knowing this, I booked a low-cost airline. But after the concert, when the fee was divided up, I was amazed to find that several players (including those travelling from the same city as me) had bought expensive scheduled flights for hundreds of pounds each. Once they had been reimbursed, there was only a modest amount left to split between us.

The choice of hotels also arouses strong feelings. People have surprisingly firm views on whether they 'deserve' a modicum of luxury or not. There always seems to be someone who feels that they can't play their best unless they feel rested and a little pampered. Someone else will feel that luxury is unjustifiable. Both points of view are defensible, but how does one reconcile them, especially when the costs are coming out of the global fee?

People's lives become more complicated as they acquire partners and children, houses, elderly parents, health problems. Attitudes often diverge as the years go by and as outside commitments influence your feelings about how much you're prepared to spend on yourself. In a small group it can be very stressful if one person always tries to economise and eat a home-made sandwich while another carries around a copy of the *Good Food Guide* in order to search out the top restaurants. The result is that people may end up eating separately, or feeling constrained to eat in a place they didn't want to. My friends in orchestras have pointed out that in an orchestra of eighty people, there's always someone else who shares your wish to grab a sandwich, or conversely to splurge on the tasting menu at El Celler de Can Roca or Noma, so people are rarely left to dine alone, but in a small group there isn't much room for manoeuvre.

In chamber music, nobody is paid for rehearsals. This is probably the single biggest factor that makes it hard for young chamber musicians to get ahead financially. When we were building up our repertoire in Domus and the Florestan Trio, we devoted enormous amounts of time to rehearsal periods. Domus went so far as to go 'on retreat' to a friend's house in the countryside so that we could work in peace, cooking ourselves frugal pots of vegetable stew and going for walks to discuss matters of musical interpretation. With both groups, any concert fee had retrospectively to cover the period of time we spent preparing – hours and hours and hours of essentially unpaid time in every week, even though each of us was a full-time musician, and music *was* our day job – and it was never enough. We sometimes made ourselves really miserable by calculating how much we'd been paid for each hour of work – often pence rather than pounds. Now and then we had a little money from an arts organisation to help put on this or that project – much later, in the case of the trio, the Florestan Trust and our Friends' Organisation helped us to raise money for our annual festival and other specific events. But neither group had ongoing or underlying subsidy of any kind, and nor has any chamber group with which I've played.

As time went on, and our interpretations became well honed, we were able to cut down on rehearsal time, though only to a limited extent. But then things happened; in the case of Domus, people left the group and were replaced by new members who didn't know the repertoire, and we had to start again. We lamented once again the fact that all our rehearsal time was unpaid. It's true that when we became better known our concert fees were better than those of an orchestra member, but orchestral players are paid for rehearsals. When we calculated how much an orchestra member earned after adding on rehearsal fees and all the bits and pieces they are entitled to – porterage, overnight stay, *per diem* amounts for food – our chamber fees, after we'd paid commission, were much the same as their composite fees. Moreover, orchestras have their own management teams who decide programmes and guest artists, arrange tours, raise funding, do marketing and so on. The members of an orchestra do not have to worry about how to get concerts or what to play. On tour, they are handed detailed schedules and told that their suitcases will be collected from outside their rooms and that they should board the tour bus outside the hotel at a certain time.

Life as a chamber musician is nevertheless enjoyable if you and your colleagues are pulling in the same direction. I mentioned earlier that none of my groups was technically full-time; this was partly because there simply wasn't enough work to constitute a full-time career. We made a virtue of the fact that everyone was versatile and played in other things as well, bringing new ideas to the group and stopping us from becoming stale. However, no-one could control what rate of development would occur in those 'other things' we did as well. From time to time, individual members were offered opportunities which made them reassess their commitment to the group. It became increasingly hard to stick to the principle that the group came first. And once that principle was breached, there was no feeling of security. Domus and the Florestan Trio prided themselves on the fact that anyone who booked us could rely on getting exactly the people they thought they were getting. Our style and interpretation had grown up with us, developing organically and giving our performances an integrity unlikely to be offered by the ad hoc approach of larger, more randomly constituted ensembles. This was one of the core principles of the way we worked. So if someone in the group opted to accept a solo engagement which clashed with a chamber group event, it meant that the whole group missed out on a concert. Once or twice, someone plucked up courage to propose that one person's large solo fee might in all fairness be shared with the people who didn't get to earn anything on the day in question, but as they say, 'Life ain't like that.' We all hoped that our own turn would come. The idealism with which we started out was gradually modified into something more conditional. This was no doubt inevitable, but it was hard to live through, and painfully hard to discuss.

As the pianist, I was left high and dry when we had to turn down concerts. Those who played orchestral instruments were often able to find alternative work at short notice, because many orchestras use freelancers who just 'drop in'. Such an option wasn't available to me; I wasn't needed in an orchestra, and regular teaching jobs were incompatible with rehearsal periods and erratic concert dates, to say nothing of the campaign of letter-writing and 'networking' which is the lot of most would-be performers. I'd seen fellow pianists enter the teaching profession and rapidly conclude that they must abandon any serious performing ambitions of their own – and I was afraid of that happening to me. There wasn't really anything I could do to get work at short notice, except temping, which I did from time to time during fallow periods in the early years of Domus. My temporary employers would glance up with surprise the first time they heard me launch into the prestissimo typing of a letter. I'd catch the glance and explain, 'I'm a pianist – I'm used to keyboards.' Sometimes during these gaps I just got on with learning new repertoire – unpaid, of course. Life might have been simpler if the group had had flexible membership, but it didn't, and its ethos meant that it couldn't. I often wondered how many of our audience realised the sacrifices made for the sake of being able to keep an unchanging group going season after season.

The only chamber groups we knew who thrived financially were full-time groups – in fact almost always string quartets who managed to build up a busy concert diary or were able to back up their concert work with university residencies or state subsidies. Almost all the financially secure groups were in countries other than the UK . This is a curious irony about a country which contains London, one of the world's most important centres of classical music. Artists from all over the world converge on London in the hope of 'being in the melting-pot', and even if they do not live in London they make it a career goal to play there regularly, for to make it in London means a lot. Yet London itself is also a famously hard place for musicians to make a living, partly because there are so many musicians here. Britain ('Das Land ohne Musik' as a German critic called it) has always had a rather hands-off attitude to the arts, and we are often told by government policy-makers that 'the arts must pay for themselves'. If you ever read about state subsidies being paid to arts organisations the beneficiaries are almost invariably large ones, such as symphony orchestras or opera houses – I don't believe I have ever heard of a subsidy being given to a chamber group in the UK. There are countries which do support their chamber groups as a matter of national pride: I have known of such schemes in France, Germany, Denmark, Finland, Norway and the USA, and there may be others. It's a funny thing that in the UK, which has been so slow to adopt these ideas, there has long been a very active, indeed passionate, chamber music scene, one that is thriving in the artistic sense. But financially things have always been difficult, as I think today's young musicians would confirm. It is a rare chamber group that is able to make a living from the group alone. Everyone tries to supplement their income by freelance work or teaching. For groups such as ours, whose members had differing degrees of earning power, there were strong forces pulling the members apart from one another, and these forces grew more powerful as time went on.

When there are difficult decisions to be made, some groups seem to find it relatively easy to arrive at a consensus, whereas others have to debate every last motion. How to decide? I've come across various principles used by different groups. The groups I've worked with have always tended to go by majority vote. This is a standard voting method, but it has the drawback that someone with a minority view may be continually overruled, and this can have quite an impact on the feeling of camaraderie within the group. Take the issue of touring, for example. Concert tours are important for the group's profile and finances, but can also be hugely disruptive for the family of an individual who's away from home for two or three weeks. If one person in the group dislikes long tours, should that person be obliged to go on tour, just because of the operation of majority decision-making? Perhaps there could be a method of protecting the rights of those who may have good reasons for their minority view – should they, for example, have a right to prevail every so often, even if they are technically outvoted?

Other groups work on the opposite principle: everyone has to be happy about every decision. This is an 'all your eggs in one basket' approach, risky but admirable. I know a middle-European string quartet who stuck to the principle in big as well as small issues. For example, they were due to tour Japan shortly after the Fukushima nuclear power station accident, and most of them were looking forward to the trip, but one of the players felt that not enough was known about the possible health risks to people travelling through that area. The quartet had a meeting about whether or not to go to Japan. Three people voted yes and one voted no; therefore they didn't go, and they lost all the fees.

I remember wondering aloud whether allowing one person the power to cancel a whole foreign tour was advisable, but my friends in the quartet were amazingly philosophical: they shrugged and said, 'Well, how much fun would it have been to go to Japan with someone who was really unhappy about going? Can you imagine?' They also said, 'Someday it'll be me who doesn't want to do something, and then it'll be my turn to be happy that we have this system.' I was intrigued by this approach to decision-making, and quizzed them about how it worked. They agreed that they had to keep an eye on whether an individual was overusing their power of veto. In fact, this had never been the case, and interestingly, they claimed that because each person knew they *had* the power of veto, they generally didn't feel the need to use it. Both approaches have their dangers, of course. Majority voting in a group of four or five (or more), where alliances can shift continually and the outcome prove different with every vote, is very different from voting in a group of three.

There are other non-musical issues which can become very tense in small groups. For me, one such issue is timekeeping. I'm not sure which I dislike more, keeping other people waiting or being kept waiting myself. I was once staying in a Japanese hotel where I heard a Japanese guide instruct his English-speaking tour group thus: 'Our bus leaves hotel at 10am. Which means: you must be outside hotel by 9.50am to put luggage in bus. Which means: you must pay your bill by 9.45. Which means: you must leave your room by 9.30am because there will be queue at reception desk. Which means: you must finish breakfast by 9.15am. Which means: you should be in breakfast room by 8.30am because there will be queue at the buffet.' It was remarkably like hearing my own inner monologue uttered aloud by someone else.

Some of my chamber music colleagues also played in orchestras from time to time. Timekeeping is strictly enforced in big orchestras, usually by an orchestral manager who makes sure that sessions begin and end on time, that any overtime is agreed and negotiated, and that there are statutory breaks at pre-determined intervals; he also has the unpopular task of shooing people out of the coffee bar and back into the rehearsal at the end of the break. In a big orchestra it is not acceptable to be late for a rehearsal. To be habitually late would result in being fired, or at least put 'on notice'. This culture is accepted by all the members of the orchestra, who make great efforts to be on time accordingly.

However, released from the strict timekeeping and the sanctions of orchestras, my colleagues enjoyed the feeling that there was nobody official to scold them if they were late for a chamber rehearsal or meeting. They felt liberated by the absence of conductors and managers who could tell them off, humiliate them publicly or threaten not to book them again. Here we found ourselves at odds, because I experienced no such contrast. I've never belonged to a professional orchestra, and chamber music rehearsals have been at the heart of my working life. I made great efforts to be on time and found it difficult to accept that others allowed themselves so much leeway, especially when I knew that they would stir themselves to be on time for an orchestra rehearsal. Why did I continue to arrive on time? I don't really know, except that I felt agitated if I didn't. I even had some sort of holistic feeling that to tinker with my wish to be on time would somehow interfere with my musical ability to be *in tempo*.

Then there is the question of incompatible body-clocks. When you start touring with other musicians, you discover very quickly who wakes up early and likes to eat breakfast before 9am and who likes to prop up the bar last thing at night. You learn who needs to snooze in the afternoon before a concert and who cannot. One might imagine that touring is a very social activity, but not necessarily so. If your little group divides into early birds and night owls, or snoozers and non-snoozers, you may well wind up having most of your meals on your own. My unscientific straw poll has revealed that the prospect of dining alone worries women more than it does men, and for many women it is a real down-side to touring. Such differences in body-clock can play a big difference in work settings as well as socially. In rehearsals they may cause friction if one person is always raring to go, full of ideas and at their best at the beginning, while another warms up slowly and is firing on all cylinders towards the end. It makes life hard in a recording session where one person is all geared up to give it their best shot at 10am, while another relies on hours of playing to 'get into the groove' before they wish to be digitally immortalised. I've had some of my lowest moments in recording sessions when, after hours of playing, someone says, 'Well, obviously we can't use any of this morning's takes, because I feel I've only just woken up properly.'

Conflicting priorities, perceived imbalance or unfairness, different attitudes to behaviour and money are not unique to music. But outside music, not so many small groups try to organise themselves without arbitrators of one kind or another. In chamber music, which operates by consensus and has no institutional structure, non-musical frictions can be intense if individuals feel bereft of people to turn to when problems need to be resolved. Naturally one might expect that the individuals would turn to one another when there are things they need to get off their chest, but because the working environment is so intense, other members of the group are sometimes the last people you feel able to confide in. Instead, a 'speaking silence' often reigns. Playing beautiful music together at such times can feel like a cruel simulacrum of real communication.

Life might in some ways be easier with an external director or manager responsible for timekeeping and the like. I shudder to imagine such a person, but it's very hard for group members to police their own work schedules without rubbing each other up the wrong way. I have a friend, an orchestral player, whose orchestra recently got rid of its full-time music director/conductor and took up a policy of inviting guest conductors on an ever-changing rota. As soon as the full-time conductor had departed, the members of the orchestra started bickering among themselves. Individual players saw the opportunity to assert themselves and try to dictate terms which would suit them personally. Orchestral meetings got longer and longer, but the outcomes were less and less productive. The atmosphere became increasingly poisonous. One day my friend realised that all this had started when the members of the orchestra 'lost their common enemy', as he put it. In some ways I wonder if the difficulties experienced by chamber groups are simply examples of the tendency for people to fight amongst themselves when there's no figure of authority. Yet there's no solution, because the whole point of chamber music is that it's a little society of independent thinkers, with all the advantages and disadvantages of democracy.

To work honestly on great music requires self-disclosure to an unusual degree. You certainly don't want your fellow players to say (or think privately) that you haven't got it in you to convey the whole range of expression suggested by Beethoven, Mozart and Schubert etc. In order to delve deeply into music, chamber musicians must be willing to be vulnerable. Playing wonderful, mind-stretching music together, we experienced the emotion of it and were forced to grapple with a range of feelings which I dare say go far beyond what most people share with their co-workers. In the search for musical meaning, we revealed or were forced to reveal things which many people would probably find prudent to keep to themselves. Disclosing weakness could be painful, but revealing strengths was energising. We had to listen to what our subconscious minds were telling us as we played music, and use the suggestions in our interpretations. We tried to cajole and needle one another into going further, expressing more, playing better, supporting one another more actively. We spent all our rehearsals commenting on one another's way of playing things, and making requests and demands for things to be played differently.

Occasional visitors to our rehearsals would wonder aloud at how we put up with such an incessant barrage of commentary, not to say criticism, from one another. We did actually try quite hard to be tactful, but our comments still seemed surprising to people from 'outside'. (I remember an actor friend saying that actors would never put up with fellow actors telling them all day long that they'd expressed things inadequately.) They compared it with their own workplaces, where habitually inappropriate comments on colleagues' performance would result in a stern ticking-off from the human resources manager or a summons to arbitration. We had no such protection: nobody ever told us that in our handling of one another's sensibilities we had crossed a line and must cease forthwith. On the whole we were pleased to be able to say whatever we felt was needed for the sake of the music. There's a fine line, though, between persuading and *provoking* someone to change what they're doing. Every chamber group I've ever known has teetered constantly back and forth across this line. If they don't tackle the emotions which arise from great music, they're probably not much good as musicians or performers. Being willing to be vulnerable is a *sine qua non* of really successful chamber music playing, but being vulnerable on a daily basis is hard, hard work.

Many tears have been shed about how musicians can play divinely and then turn out to have shortcomings as people. The fact is that becoming extremely good at something so rarefied and demanding often means that some aspects of your character become overdeveloped while others are neglected, or develop strangely in reaction. In some families and some societies, the dreamy or self-centred musician is quite a cherished figure. In others, there is resistance to the artist who opts out of their share of everyday tasks. In my own native country, Scotland, there is a long tradition of scorn for anyone, artist or otherwise, who 'gets too big for their boots' and thinks they can escape the duties of childcare or grocery shopping. Retaining the common touch is very important, and the many excellent Scottish musicians I've known have all retained it. Yet, while I support the idea that even a gifted artist should take their turn at household chores and be a responsible citizen, it does sometimes lead to friction if you find yourself working with musicians from backgrounds which encourage or at least permit them to step aside and consider themselves 'special'.

The fact is that a good professional chamber group is a collection of very talented individuals who come together because of their shared love of the chamber music repertoire. I have known one or two groups who made a priority of getting on well together and being socially compatible, but the musical results were not always of the highest quality. Most of the artistically successful groups I've known have selected one another for their instrumental skill and musical judgement. They're certainly not in it because there's a good income to be made from it. I was discussing this lately with an old friend who said, 'Let's face it, chamber music isn't really a profession. Maybe it should just be played for pleasure, by people who earn their living in other ways.' But this cannot be the whole answer, because the chamber music repertoire contains some of music's most profound thoughts, and justice cannot be done to it unless players of great instrumental skill really commit to it and immerse themselves in it, which can't be done unless they do it professionally. That's not a moral stance on my part but simply an observation based on lots of listening. I'm convinced that just 'having a go' at it may be enjoyable, but is very unlikely to get all the way down through its layers. Once you've experienced performances which dig down through all the layers, you realise that they're very different from a quick reading. Having played chamber music in all sorts of settings, from the one-off fun play-through, to the part-time group and the long-term endeavour, I've found that the finest results come from seriously committed, long-standing groups. To be sure, many memorable performances spring from ad hoc meetings of talented people at music courses and festivals, but for consistent depth and quality it is difficult to better the dedicated ensemble.

Earning a living through chamber music is hard, and now more than ever I wonder whether it is responsible to encourage young chamber players to enter the fray. In some ways things are getting even harder as austerity bites into grants and funding, series close down for lack of support, and much of society looks the other way. Musicians find that their work is made freely available by 'sharing' websites and free downloads. Most classical musicians are already familiar with the situation of receiving no royalties for their recordings, so free downloads are merely more of the same, but players of all kinds find that increasingly they're being asked to do things for nothing. Suzanne Moore, writing in *The Guardian* (28 August 2013), referred to 'creatives' such as writers and musicians as 'the canaries in the mine', because they were among the first to find themselves being expected to work for free in the current climate, and others may soon find themselves in that position. David Byrne of Talking Heads has written about the way that 'streaming' websites are depriving musicians of income and about the way that technology is 'sucking all creative content' out of the world (*The Guardian*, 11 October 2013). Simon Morris at specialist violin dealers J&A Beare told *The Guardian* on 22 October 2013 that musicians are 'so underpaid that they have become the sponsors of music in this country'. For the purposes of research I signed up to receive jobs lists in the music field, and I notice on a daily basis that many such jobs are described as 'voluntary', 'unpaid', 'internship', or 'hourly paid' where there used to be a salary.

As my colleagues and I battled against the difficulties, I gradually came to see that one of the sources of our problems was that we were perceived as being in a weak position *because we wanted to play the concert*. Promoters seemed to assume that chamber music was not a business venture but a labour of love. We must be doing it because we were passionate about it, so at the end of the day we'd probably accept the situation and feel that we were lucky to be able to make any money at all from something that we *chose to do*. And of course we did choose to do it; as a friend of mine charmingly put it, we had all 'been hit with the music stick'. But we realised that playing chamber music was not perceived as 'a profession', no matter how exacting it was. We could not calmly present an enormous bill like lawyers or bankers do, regardless of how many hours of work had gone into the concert, because in the last analysis what we were supplying was *a treat* for our audiences – and, it seemed, ourselves. We could never itemise all our rehearsals and the time spent obtaining the concerts in the first place, and invoice our clients for £250 an hour, even though we have all had just as much highly specialised training as a lawyer or accountant or counsellor. Instead, we found ourselves arguing about how much discomfort we were prepared to put up with in order to salvage a meaningful chunk of the fee. To me it seems wrong that musicians should be put in this situation. If people were paid according to the quality of their work and the difficulty of the task, chamber musicians would be rich!

Chamber music is a blessing, and it's a pity that that should be compromised by the struggle to earn money from it, which should ideally have nothing to do with it. But if you love something and are really good at it, why shouldn't you try to make a living from it? Really there's only one explanation for why we persisted: it's a vocation. All my long-standing chamber colleagues have been passionate about our repertoire and committed to going into it as deeply as we could. We all realised it was a life's study, on the one hand to master our instruments to the point where we could express whatever we wanted to express in the music, and on the other to unlock the secrets of masterworks by the great composers who have saved some of their deepest reflections for chamber music. We were all spellbound by music, whatever we thought about the music profession. As time went by we all noticed that many of our non-musician friends were far from committed to their daily jobs. They had never felt a sense of *needing to do this*, a feeling that their day would be wasted without it. They put in the time in order to get the money, but obtained no particular satisfaction or pride from how they spent their days.

At least that was never the case for us; we had always put in the time if the work required it, whether or not we got money for it. We never felt that our chosen focus was trivial. Music remained a source of pleasure, consolation and satisfaction, and importantly, it remained independent of us. Its stature and interest were never diminished by what was going on in the group. Our *musical* selves somehow retained their own integrity, almost as if they were unaware of our interpersonal ups and downs. How was this possible? I can only think that music remained safely in its mysterious realm, above and beyond our struggles. We brought the music into being, but even as we played it, it lifted away from us and was untainted. As soon as we started playing, it was somehow possible to rise above our problems and genuinely work together in the mysterious task of making something more than the sum of the parts.

It's often remarked that being in a chamber group is a good deal like being in a marriage, and so it is, but with an important difference – that musicians choose each other on the basis of musical skills and compatibilities, rather than on the basis of romantic attraction or moral character. I think many musicians don't realise this sufficiently when committing to a group. It may well be the case that they all enjoy putting life, art and the cosmos to rights over a bottle of wine, but that is not the same as sharing expectations about task-sharing and fiscal responsibility. It's actually quite hard to sacrifice things and make compromises for the sake of people with whom you are *not* emotionally or romantically involved. You might think that being linked only by a shared love of music would make it simpler, but in practice it's very challenging to find yourself dependent on people whom you *didn't* choose for their personal qualities.

Making music is a very intimate thing, but being close to someone musically is not the same as being close to them personally, and when your day-to-day life choices are impacted by the ups and downs of the group and its earning power, it's hard to strike the right balance of commitment and detachment. In such an intense working relationship, people become painfully, almost forensically, sensitive to one another's behaviour. It's nobody's fault, but for many groups it's an energy-sapping reality. I've often thought that, before they commit to being in a long-term group together, would-be members of chamber groups should be made to fill in those internet dating questionnaires about long-range hopes and ambitions, attitudes to money, task-sharing, gender differences and childcare, how you'd feel if one of you suddenly acquired more earning power than the other, how well you function first thing in the morning or late at night, and so on. For a person's attitude to those things is rarely guessable from what they are like as a musician, and by the time you discover these incompatibilities, you are committed to an ongoing working relationship.

I gathered together these thoughts shortly before travelling to Munich to serve on the jury of the piano trio section of the ARD International Music Competition, one of the music world's most prestigious. A shortlist of twenty-four young piano trios had been admitted to the first round. Mostly in their twenties, they came from across the world, all of them already seasoned concert-givers, and many of them of a very high standard. The future for piano trios, and for chamber music, seemed bright. But during one interval, I found myself looking at a list of previous winners of the competition, which has been held every few years since 1961. Some of the trios I had never heard of, and some that were familiar to me had disbanded since winning the competition. Only one trio had achieved an international reputation and was still in existence, and even that one had changed its personnel since its early days. It seemed clear that professional piano trios were fragile organisms.

I was struck by the contrast between the immense dedication and discipline that had brought this year's crop of young musicians to this level of music-making and the prospects for their years ahead. We on the jury were sitting for hours making detailed notes on how these young musicians shaped phrases, defined musical characters and balanced inner parts, when really we should have been sharing with them our hard-won insights about how to tackle the task of *staying together*. Because further down the road that would become as important a goal as maintaining the excellence of their playing. There we were, scrutinising their grasp of structure or their palette of tone colour, when it might have been far more important to look them in the eye and tell them to be kind to one another when things get tough. How many of them had received any training in how to survive, how to negotiate, how to balance conflicting interests? Would their talent help or hinder them when it came to building healthy relationships with one another? A career in chamber music really is like a marriage: there is so much emphasis on establishing the relationship, on getting to the 'big day'. But it's after the big day that the real work begins.

Old people

I sometimes teach at ChamberStudio, a London scheme set up to provide high-level coaching for chamber groups who have finished their formal education and have therefore lost their automatic access to teachers. Typically they are in their twenties, and individually they are advanced instrumentalists. But often these chamber groups, who may not have started working together seriously until their post-graduate years or even later, haven't actually had much time to develop an authentic approach of their own. While they are doing so, they are glad to have coaching from people who've been there before and performed the repertoire the younger groups are now learning for the first time. I find the Chamber-Studio participants a particularly pleasing group to coach because they are idealistic and not so pressed for time that they are unwilling to try new approaches. They seem to find playing to more 'senior' musicians a good way of jumping quickly up the salmon ladder of ideas.

Playing devil's advocate, a provocative colleague of mine, a tutor on the ChamberStudio team, recently asked, 'Why do they want to learn from *old people*? They should be having their own ideas!' 'Yeah, good point!' I felt like replying. 'And why should they play *old music*? Why can't they make up their own music?'

It's a worthwhile question, however: why don't people just use their own ideas? For me, the answer is that there is hardly any idea which is entirely your own – how could there be? For ideas are formed from all sorts of information and all manner of observations of things and people around us, and no matter how original our synthesis of particles of information and insight may be, any 'idea' worth its salt is likely to have been inspired by something already in existence. I remember reading that the French poet Paul Valéry had once asked Albert Einstein whether he carried a notebook or a scrap of paper around with him to record all his original ideas. Einstein replied that original ideas come so rarely that one is not likely to forget them; therefore there is no need for a notebook, or even a scrap of paper.

As a veteran carrier of scraps of paper, I was mildly offended by Einstein's assertion, but when I thought about it I realised he must be right. Most of what feel like my own ideas are probably more like (re-)compositions of fragments of thought and experience, not truly deserving the label *original idea*. Even when you have what feels like a wholly new idea, it often turns out that others have had it too in a different time or place. Does that allow them to qualify as original ideas or not? I remember when I was about seven years old, learning about tones and semitones on the piano, it suddenly struck me that in theory there could be intervals smaller than semitones. Quarter-tones, eighth-tones – a new world of microtones! I was convinced I had had a brainwave until I tentatively put 'my idea' forward to my piano teacher and had to learn that quarter-tones and the like were known to the music of many ancient cultures, as well as to contemporary classical music. But I hadn't known that. As far as I know the idea was a 'light bulb moment' which came to me without input from anywhere else, so it was in its way an original idea. It certainly felt like it at the time. I suppose there must be many ideas, famous in their own time and place, that, unknown to the 'owner', had been thought in other times and places, often long ago.

Personally I have always enjoyed and looked forward to hearing the ideas of old people, especially if they are in dialogue with me rather than simply pontificating. For example, when I first went to the Open

Chamber Music Seminars in Prussia Cove in Cornwall, founded by the mighty Hungarian violinist Sándor Végh, there were a number of 'senior' musicians who came (unpaid) to play in chamber groups with people thirty, forty, fifty years younger than themselves. The cellist Tibor de Machula, the violinist Pina Carmirelli, the cellist Zara Nelsova, the pianist Lamar Crowson and Sándor Végh himself – these eminent players and teachers just joined in with the rest of us, debating the pros and cons of interpretative approaches as if they hadn't been doing so for half a century already. This was much appreciated by us young musicians, who regarded them as a kind of musical 'grandparents' and were well aware that they didn't have to put themselves through the strenuous rehearsals which were the norm in Prussia Cove. I think we felt that by working in chamber groups with them, a little of their wisdom would rub off on us. It was all part of that great 'chain of musicians' that Sándor Végh was always speaking about.

One of the positive things about the music world is the seamless way that young merges into old. The rules of retirement seem to pass by people who simply go on from one year to the next without thinking of themselves any differently. This must be partly a reflection of the non-cumulative nature of life in the arts. One 'season' follows another with the sense of September coming round again, and again, with nothing to remind you that everyone is growing older. This is both a curse and a blessing. The 'new season' mentality offers perpetual renewal, and also an unending series of opportunities to play Peter Pan, ever youthful, ever ready to fling yourself into the mêlée with musicians of all ages and stages, with no regard to seniority or rank. Most older players think of themselves not as senior members of their profession but more as long-serving juniors, or as co-evals with younger colleagues. This is good because nobody is treated with respect merely because they happen to be of a certain rank, as happens in so many professions. If you are a respected musician it's because people look up to you, rather than because you've got some job title or other. On the other hand, as time goes by, you sometimes crave a bit of structure, the automatic steps in status that come with an externally imposed hierarchy. But the world of players is not like that. It feels a bit like being in a revolving door where you hardly notice people entering or being flung out again because you're all so caught up with the thrill of revolving.

On the whole I've found musicians to be pleasantly un-ageist in their attitudes, though as in every other area of life, women seem to be more readily disparaged as 'old' than men are. There are many older men still active in concert life, but not so many older women, and it may be that older women get discouraged by comments about their appearance, the sort of comments which people feel free to make about women but would not think to make about men. Music is more and more an image-conscious profession, and the advantage is on the side of the young and the male.

A few years ago, I was on the jury of a competition in Graz where we were presented with a book of interviews with previous winners. In that book I was startled to read the comments of a prize-winning violinist. Asked if he had had the chance to speak to members of the jury and get their opinions on his playing, he replied that 'if you have an eighty-year-old violinist in front of you who could play these pieces maybe twenty-five years ago and who explains something to you: I find it presumptuous ["das finde ich ein wenig vermessen"]. To be on a par with them when one meets them, that is something concrete in my eyes.' I was very taken aback by the use of the word 'presumptuous' when applied to an eighty-year-old violinist. I checked the translation with some German friends who said that the word 'vermessen' could perhaps be rendered as 'out of order', but the meaning was clear: this young violinist considered it irrelevant to be given advice by old people. Let's hope his attitude was not typical of his generation's.

Personally I have always been grateful for feedback from people with vastly more experience than I've had. Such advice can help to shorten the period between going naively into a musical situation and having some idea of how to deal with it. Everything from philosophical nuggets to hard practical advice about what you'll find when you come to play this or that piece in a concert hall is welcome, and I like to be alerted to – for example – the danger that a particular passage will be inaudible, or that the tempo may need to be slowed for a bigger acoustic, or that the piano sounds better if it is further back on the stage of a certain hall. Equally important have been the reflections that older musicians have shared on life in a long-standing chamber group. In a London masterclass I attended recently where the American violinist Shmuel Ashkenazi was coaching string quartets, I was touched to hear him advise these young players about the wisdom of giving way to other colleagues in small and even medium-large interpretative matters, saving their combative moments for things that they really can't live with. With a wry smile, he said there aren't all that many of the latter, but when they do crop up, it's good to be able to call in a favour from the others on the grounds that you've often been tolerant of their requests. This kind of advice is hard to come by, and I know it could save young chamber groups an awful lot of heartache.

My first encounter with an older maestro was with Sándor Végh when he was teaching at Prussia Cove in the late 1970s and early '80s. He must have been in his late sixties, though at the time it was hard to establish the facts as his date of birth was given differently in different reference books (it is now agreed that he was born in 1912). He actually seemed somehow timeless, partly because of his energy, and partly because his physical largeness and roundness seemed to have plumped out the lines and wrinkles which mark a person as 'old'. To ask how old he was would have been as irrelevant as asking how old a snowman was meant to be; the shape was the thing that stuck in your mind. Végh had a passion for teaching and a temper to match. For many of us it was our first encounter with a style of central-European teaching which allowed the teacher to insult as well as praise. This was most intriguing for those of us who'd grown up in the educational school of 'If you can't say something nice, say nothing at all.' Our teachers had been careful to reward our efforts with praise and encouragement, and if they wanted to correct us they found tactful and neutral ways to phrase it. Sándor Végh on the other hand was immoderate both with praise and blame. I was in his class as a student, in a duo with violinist Krysia Osostowicz, and I had days when I was elated by Végh's compliments (some of these happy moments were captured in the BBC

TV documentary about Végh, *An Ideal Place*). But sometimes I played the piano for his violin students at short notice, and was taken aback when he mocked my occasional wrong notes: 'Why you play so blah-blah-blah-blah!?' he would shout, when he knew perfectly well I was sight-reading. Mocking students was heresy in the educational settings I was used to. It made everyone in Végh's class feel as if they were putting their head into the lion's mouth every time they had a lesson.

We put up with it because it was obvious that as well as the bluster and the shouting, we were being exposed to a radical and invigorating kind of thinking about how music communicates. Végh believed that music must always be dynamic, that a phrase has an organic shape created by the tensions and relaxations within it. I particularly enjoyed his ideas about things in music containing their opposites. For example, he would say that when we saw the word 'crescendo', meaning 'growing' or 'getting louder', we should take it as the low point from which something was going to grow, not the signal to start getting loud immediately. When we saw 'crescendo', he recommended that we should if anything respond by getting quieter, 'reculer pour mieux sauter' as the French say, in order to have a steeper expressive gradient ahead of us. 'Inside every forte is a piano' and 'Inside every piano is a forte' were likewise indications that musical moments could be multi-layered, that a soft passage might contain the germs of something much stronger, or that the climax of a piece might not 'just' be loud, but might be the last moment of strength and energy before something else claimed it and forced it to subside. When we saw an expressive instruction we were not just to respond like Pavlov's dog salivating at the sound of a bell: we should train ourselves to see the instruction as a stage in a dynamic process. This kind of 3-D approach to reading a musical score was far more 'organic' than anything we had come across before and made it much more interesting to debate what was actually *happening* in a piece of music, the currents which were driving it, the expressive forces acting on it. Végh believed that music could be made to 'speak', not by imitating actual human words, but by looking deeply into the composer's markings (such as staccato, legato, dots under a slur, rests) to understand what light and shade they could convey, as well as what texture they could bring to the surface.

Many of us had been trained to follow the composer's markings because it was 'the right thing to do', but not many of us had wholly understood that those same markings were clues to the inner life and communicative potential of the phrases. It was tremendous stuff, and like all the best teaching it didn't seem like an intellectual construct, but as if something perfectly obvious had been revealed, so that you found yourself thinking, 'Yes, of course! I always knew that really, but how good to have it pointed out!' Végh's temperament ensured that his insights were driven home by being endlessly repeated, and indeed it was remarkable how much energy and determination he had to say the same things over and over again to different students. I became aware of this when I started playing for the whole class of violinists and therefore had the opportunity to hear Végh tackle lesson after lesson with undiminished gusto. I felt that in his place I would have got bored with telling young musicians they were links in a vital chain that went back through him to his teacher Hubay, to Hubay's teacher Joseph Joachim, the great friend and interpreter of Brahms, and so on, but Végh never seemed to tire of it. I used to think this zeal for repetition must be a particular 'Hungarian' thing, but it wasn't, as I discovered later when working with other Hungarian maestros such as György Sebök who espoused a quite different style of saying something once in a quiet voice and never referring to it again. Végh had a passion for stamping his belief in music's 'speaking power' on us all, and it was lucky he did, because a whole generation of young Prussia Cove musicians went away with his voice ringing loudly in our ears. We used to imitate some of the speeches we had heard him make so often, because his 'mashup' of Hungarian and English was so tasty ('I feel me like a fish on the dry', 'Look me what I do!'). Not so very long afterwards, it seemed, we were recalling his words in a more sober spirit of passing them on to our own students. We began to understand why it was important to say things over and over again. And there came a point when we realised that his speech about 'knowing you were a link in a chain going back to Brahms' was not just amusing but actually true.

After a long break from going to Prussia Cove, I went back in 2012 to join in with Open Chamber Music. It was the fifteenth anniversary of Végh's death. On the last evening of the week, Hilary Behrens (who co-founded the seminars along with Végh) asked me if I would say a few words about Végh after dinner, recalling what he said in his lessons for the benefit of the younger participants who never heard him. Hilary explained that he would have liked to say something himself, but found it difficult to speak in public on a topic so emotional. I said that it surely wasn't necessary, in Prussia Cove of all places, to specify what it was that Végh had talked about when he taught there. But Hilary said he had lately had the feeling that some of the more recent participants didn't actually know all that much about what Végh stood for. I wasn't sure he could be right about this – why did they come to Prussia Cove if it wasn't because of Végh's legacy? After all, even if they didn't hear Végh themselves, a lot of them had studied with people who studied with Végh or played in his orchestras or his chamber groups – but I agreed to say something after supper.

I stood on a step at one end of the candlelit dining-room and tried to describe some of the characteristic things that Sándor said in his lessons: how he often invoked the movement of the wind and waves, which we could all see out of the windows in Prussia Cove, to illuminate the type of movement inside a piece of music. How he explained that great music mirrors not only the beautiful emotions of life, but also the dark, strange and ugly ones – music was a reflection of life, all of it. How therefore we had all to develop a huge expressive range so that we could find a tone and a colour appropriate to what was being expressed, be it something uplifting or something frightening, something regretful, something gorgeous, or something thin and sad. How we should be very suspicious of the trend towards favouring a big, glossy sound, designed to fill the world's large concert halls but no longer able to speak to the human heart. As I spoke, I became aware of the looks on the faces of some of the younger musicians in the room. I realised that this *was* new to them. I felt encouraged and went on a bit more than I had planned to. Afterwards, when I had sat down again, people kept coming up to me and saying that they were glad to have heard those tales about Végh's lessons, because all they had really known about him was that he was held in great regard, but they had not really known what his ideas *were* specifically, or what he sounded like as he enlarged upon them. They said they knew Prussia Cove had gained its reputation because of Végh's classes, but what he actually *said* had never been passed on to them, and it hadn't even occurred to them that they could know it. They liked the anecdotes which older players sometimes told in rehearsal, but these titbits were really all they had of the original feast. I was thunderstruck by the realisation that even in the very place where someone had made a huge impact, it was possible within a fairly short time (fifteen years in this case) of their final disappearance for the specifics of their teaching to fade away gradually like the Cheshire Cat in *Alice in Wonderland*, leaving only a grin behind. Or in Végh's case, a belly-laugh. 'Ha, ha, ha! You understand me? You agree with me?'

That evening was a wake-up call for me, because I discovered that what I'd thought was a shared body of knowledge was less fully shared than I realised. For me, Végh's insights were woven into the sights and sounds of Prussia Cove – the waves, the wind, the storms – and I couldn't help but recall them as I trudged up and down the coastal paths, but they were not part of the landscape for people who had never heard him. It seemed obvious when you thought about it. I had not really considered what it must be like to go to a place associated with a teacher who had died before you even picked up a musical instrument for the first time; how much of his influence can you really feel? I realised too that even recordings are of limited help. Many people had told me how unimpressed they were by hearing Sándor Végh recorded in the later-life period when his playing was often scratchy, tonally thin and out of tune. I had heard those recordings too, but for me the interpretative spirit remained bright; I had no difficulty in overlaying them with the knowledge of what he was 'about'. I realised, however, that minus that knowledge those recordings might be quite hard to like. Even the earlier recordings, such as his celebrated Beethoven quartet cycle with the Végh Quartet, might not speak to people in quite the way I imagined. Times change, and tastes change with them. A style of playing found very expressive and compelling in an earlier decade or era might not strike a modern audience in the same way.

I remember attending a lecture on sound recordings of famous actors of the past century, recordings held in the National Sound Archive in London. Before playing us each recording, the lecturer read out some admiring contemporary descriptions of the actor concerned, referring to such things as his or her natural way of speaking, avoidance of artificiality, light touch with rhetoric and so on. When we heard the recordings, though, our natural impulse was to burst out laughing. The actors sounded stilted and ridiculously contrived, their upper-class accents frozen in time, their use of vocal pitch laughably 'ham' to modern ears. How could this kind of thing ever have been admired for being 'natural'? It seemed all too dated. When we had finished laughing, we fell silent. We felt chastened. The obvious next thought was: well, what about the people we think are shining examples of good playing today? Will there come a time when they too seem amusingly obsolete?

In fact it's not unusual for gifted teachers to be somewhat unconvincing as players. I've seen this enough times to accept that one can have a clever head without necessarily having equally clever hands, though it's kind of hard to know how nature can allow a person to have one but not the other. If it is true that the hands are the servants of the brain, then having a good brain should be enough, but it doesn't always seem to be. Mastering a musical instrument is something for which you need good hands, and sometimes the hands seem to 'know' things by themselves. The sheer craft and technique involved in playing an instrument sometimes seems to run in a channel of its own, not much to do with how articulate a person is when they speak, how good their musical ear is, or how much wisdom they possess. The world of music is full of talented players not noted for their wisdom and steadiness in other aspects of their lives. I know lots of people who have a caressing way with an instrument but couldn't tell you what form or key the piece is in, when it was written, or anything else about it. The converse is also true. I know people who understand music deeply and love it passionately, but have never managed to become particularly skilful on any musical instrument, no matter how much they would like to be.

It's certainly possible for someone to be a marvellous teacher without being able to jump on a platform and wow the audience with their own performances of the music they teach so persuasively. For example, György Sebök gave the most stunning demonstrations during piano lessons, but even his most devoted pupils felt that his public concerts didn't necessarily hold the same magic. Therefore when I see a video clip or hear a sound recording of someone who was an inspiring teacher, I'm sometimes uncomfortably aware that the recording alone may not convey what was so compelling about their teaching. In the case of Sándor Végh, I never heard him play until he was in his late sixties and well into his 'scratchy' phase. There was still a tremendous communicative spirit in his playing, shown in his control of phrasing and timing as well as his body language and facial expressions, but as for his sheer control of violin sound, I had to take it on trust that it was terrific in his earlier days. I didn't find that difficult to imagine because his intent to *convey* music was still so vividly alive. His ability to 'speak' the music with his violin bow was intact. But these days when I see the odd YouTube clip of his playing, I wonder what someone would make of Végh if that was all they had to go on. By the time I knew him, I think it is fair to say that his teaching was more expressive than his playing.

How then to preserve someone's teaching? It's hard, particularly if the teacher was from an age when 'methods' and 'outcomes' and 'impacts' were not considered in need of measurement like they are now. Film can capture a teaching session pretty well, if the participants are not made too self-conscious by the filming process, but the few attempts I've seen to pin down a great musician's teaching style in words haven't been all that successful, and appear not to be widely read by musicians themselves. There is just so much information missing, and perhaps this is inevitable. There have been books of György Sebök's aphorisms noted down by people who heard him say them in piano lessons. These aphorisms are horribly tantalising to read, because they hint at a whole philosophy which you have to guess at. Minus the music itself, and minus the context in which those remarks were made, they often seem gnomic, not in a good way. I have pages of my own notes from when I was sitting in Sebök's classes, and I find now that if I can't recall the context of his remarks, the phrases I scribbled down sometimes seem like runes.

I read a review of an attempt to 'capture the master's style' by literature students of the Argentinian writer Jorge Luis Borges. They had collected the notes they made while listening to him lecture and published them in a book. It was evident from those notes that the consciousness binding those remarks together had slipped away, leaving behind a series of isolated remarks evocative mostly to those who had actually met him or heard him speak.

My experience of talking for ten minutes about Sándor Végh to a roomful of people who'd never met him was instructive for me. Obviously I knew that major figures of history slip away from us, but now I actually saw it happening 'in real time', as they say, to someone I knew. In my own family circle I had seen how knowledge of members of the older generation became diluted as time went on, but Végh was a public figure, someone who not only influenced but was determined to influence as many up-and-coming musicians as possible. Twenty years before, all my Prussia Cove friends had known exactly what Sándor Végh was all about. We didn't need to reconstruct his approach, because it was part of our daily musical practice. Now it seemed that lots of younger musicians didn't have much of a clue about him. Their wish to come to Prussia Cove, the place where he taught, was certainly a kind of homage, but how could it be more than that, since they never even saw him or heard him teach?

Not for the first time I was struck with the wish that I could pass some of my own Prussia Cove memories to them by osmosis. I couldn't quite imagine how it must be for new visitors to wander a landscape empty of associations. I wanted to be able to sit in the Great Room where Végh taught and make them see him in his 'throne', the big handsome carved armchair he liked, looking out to sea, tracing the curve of the waves with the tip of his violin bow as he spoke to us about the ebb and flow of music. My little speech about Végh at least set lots of conversations going – next morning a whole bunch of us sat around talking intensely from breakfast until after lunch without getting up from the table. Kitchen helpers cleared plates around us and re-set the table a few hours later, quietly reaching around us in order not to disturb our conversation. We vowed to make sure that Sándor's musical ideas were transmitted onwards to those new 'links in the chain'. After we had dispersed back to our various homes around the world, we continued to remind one another to keep those ideas alive in our rehearsals and teaching. For a long while afterwards I had the feeling that an imaginary globe was criss-crossed with illuminated lines connecting us, glowing in the dark.

What is interpretation?

'I think you should write about what interpretation is,' said a musician friend of mine, an orchestral player, 'because lots of people wonder. I wonder myself,' he added.

'But you do it all day long!' I said. 'You spend your life carrying out different conductors' interpretations! You know more about it than most musicians.' 'No, I don't,' he said. 'Different conductors just come along and stand in front of us and say "Louder here", or "Make it drier", or "More from the brass". Or even, "Just listen to one another! This should feel like chamber music." Sometimes conductors don't say much at all, just indicate faster and slower, or louder and softer. The next one comes along, says something different, and we all rub out the old pencil markings and put new ones in. Is that interpretation?'

This kind of sentiment has been expressed in my hearing by lots of orchestral musicians, though of course I must offset it at once by paying tribute to the small number of truly inspiring conductors whose effect on even jaded orchestras can be electrifying. It's always striking to hear orchestral players recalling the moment when a wonderful conductor stood in front of them; all of a sudden they remembered what it was that had drawn them into music in the first place, and found themselves falling in love again with the very works they thought had lost their savour. A friend of mine played in the Bayerischer Rundfunk when Carlos Kleiber used occasionally to accept engagements with them, and she told me that members of the orchestra actually used to change their holiday entitlement so that they could be 'on duty' when Kleiber was due to conduct. This, as she pointed out, was rather different to their more usual practice of trying to be unavoidably called away elsewhere when certain conductors stopped by.

Almost all my interpretative work has been done without a conductor, either on my own or with small numbers of colleagues. Once we had left our study days behind us, nobody ever told us how to find the right tempo and character, when to play louder and softer, who should take the lead at any given moment, or when we'd done enough. We felt responsible for what happened in our performances, and, after receiving some excellent masterclasses in student years, we were conscious that we shouldn't waste people's time by playing without thinking. We wanted to solve as many problems as we could before we exposed people to our answers. This process of thinking about music – interpretation – is hard mental work which, once you set it going, seems to continue in off-duty hours and in the small hours of the night. Moreover, it continues (off and on) for years and years.

Composers often declare that they stop thinking about a piece the minute they've finished it and moved on to another, but performers do *not* stop thinking about those same pieces. It feels as if they pass into our hands for the next stage, and almost as if we become their curators. None of us took this lightly. We worked out our interpretations for ourselves, and amongst ourselves, by some mysterious process of 'entrainment' whereby we played and tried to sense things, played again and tried to grope (verbally or without speaking) towards a shared understanding of what was happening in the music. In this quest we felt supported by the awareness of a long tradition of respect and veneration for great composers, so in that sense we were not alone, and we knew that others before us had found it a fulfilling task. We drew on knowledge they had applied to the task, and also on knowledge of what their results had been.

Had we not done any work of 'interpretation', would the outcome have been much different? Could we just have played what we saw in front of us and trusted that the musical message would come across as the composer wanted? My answer would be to refer you to performances where musicians just play the notes without having digested them. Something may come across, but such a performance usually falls well short of making the music live and breathe, and can be a dispiriting experience for the listener. To my mind, it's akin to going to a restaurant, ordering a delicious dish, and being served the raw ingredients with no attempt having been made to cook them. Music and cooking have quite a lot in common; that's shown by all the food and cooking metaphors used in rehearsal, not only in the classical field. Just as food can't cook itself, music can't play itself and depends on having someone play it. But there's a very big difference between just playing the notes and filtering those notes through the musicians' intellectual, emotional and historical understanding. Some of those skills can be taught and you have to work out others for yourself, in the same way that you have to work out for yourself what's happening to you in life, a parallel sort of interpretation. In other words, the work of interpreting music is similar to the work of 'the examined life'.

Probably there is no such thing as 'no interpretation'. Since music has to be created each time a piece is played, players have to make all sorts of decisions each time they put bow to string, finger to key, or reed to lip. They cannot do nothing, for if they do nothing there will be no sound. So you might say that whatever they do is already a choice, and a choice is already an interpretation of sorts. It may be an inadequate interpretation, but one can't deny that there are choices being made all the way along the line. A friend of mine, after hearing me talk about the importance of interpretation, got very excited about the subject and tried to persuade me to start a concert series in which, each evening, a single piece of music would be played first of all *without interpretation* and, after the interval, *with interpretation*. He thought this would demonstrate the difference between the two, to everyone's instant enlightenment. I thought it was a striking idea too, until I considered it more closely and realised that it is not possible to sit down and play something *without interpretation*, because even to make the very first sound would require choices of one kind or another. Even if they are bad choices, or choices which fail to reveal the inner voice of the music, they are still choices on the part of the player. So there is always some sort of interpretation going on; the task is to raise the bar so that the intensity of the interpretation matches the intensity of the music.

It often seems to me that what we do is the equivalent of what art teachers do when they tell their pupils not to start by drawing the outline of the object, but to start with a bit of shading in the middle, and then something contrasting with the shaded area, and to work gradually outwards, adding shaded and unshaded areas until they get to the edge, without considering how big the final drawing will be. In that way, starting from somewhere in the middle, they have a chance of being able to represent each area fully, rather than committing themselves to an outline (as I always did in school art classes) and then striving to cram all the detail inside that shape, with unsatisfactory results. In our rehearsals we often tried to start from some passage we felt expressed the kernel of the matter – some typical gesture of the composer's, or something that seemed central to what the piece was about – and treated that as the 'shaded area' from which we'd begin to work outwards without preconceived ideas of the ultimate dimensions. This is a good way to work because it seems to result in things being bigger than they might otherwise be.

We felt our way towards a moment when music seemed to lift off the page and become 'more than the sum of the parts'. This is a well-used phrase, but it accurately describes something that all good musicians experience. We felt we had a duty towards the piece which went beyond simply playing the notes accurately and with technical command. To us that didn't amount to interpretation; it was merely execution. We tried to read beyond the notes to sense the state of mind or emotion which had produced them, and to see beyond the composer's often minimal expressive instructions, though they were obviously signposts on the way. The way towards what? Towards a collective understanding of a piece of music as a living, breathing organism, if that doesn't sound too pretentious. Well, no matter if it does, because that's what all my best musical companions have thought they were doing.

As I found when talking to an academic audience about 'the contents' and 'the container', academics are resistant to the idea of music having 'a meaning' which exists independently of the musicians who decide what meaning they're going to give it. Can a performance of music be anything other than a collection of decisions taken by instrumentally skilled people with historical and stylistic understanding? Whatever the audience hears has been put there by the musicians, and that's the end of it, surely? But that's not the way that we looked at it. The task, as we saw it, was to 'listen in' and hear what the music was trying to say. We were generally dealing with long, complex works of music lasting roughly half an hour, often somewhat more. They were usually constructed in several movements with interrelated material and cross-references between movements. So much could be worked out from studying the score. What was harder to work out was what would happen once we started playing and thereby added the medium of sound and the dimension of time. And that seems to be where practising musicians and academics part company about what is really *going on.*

I've long thought it is a great pity that academics and performers speak such different languages – in fact, not just different but often mutually exclusive languages. I've had to learn to use both languages at different times, and during my university years I had to switch back and forth between them like a bilingual speaker. In very broad terms, academic musicians are careful to use objective language, to study things they can measure, and not to claim anything they cannot prove, while performers tend to use highly subjective, often synaesthetic language which mirrors their poetical and emotional response to music. Speakers of each language harbour doubts about the ability of the other to say anything useful. Having been exposed to both ways of talking about music, I have to say that for me the way that players talk to one another is more illuminating. Though it's undoubtedly subjective, it is also much more evocative, and as we are dealing with something as alchemical as music, poetical language seems more able to match our deep experience. Player-speak is quite a hidden world, because players usually feel too self-conscious to use such language to 'outsiders'.

I was once on the advisory panel of a project where academics wanted to sit in on chamber rehearsals and study how the players were talking to each other about the music, but of course the players stopped behaving naturally the minute they realised a researcher was trying to pin down their improvised metaphors on paper like exotic butterflies in a collection. Players who haven't been down the academic route often form a dim view of academia when they encounter it in the form of programme notes or pre-concert talks, the latter usually given by someone who has not met the musicians or spoken to them about the music and who doesn't stay to hear the concert either. I have a friend who organises a concert series where music is juxtaposed with a presentation about the context of the music or its artistic influences, and she told me that she had stopped inviting academics to give these talks 'because they are so bad at putting their points across to ordinary concert-goers'. Many programme notes are regarded by players as dry, remote and largely beside the point. There are honourable exceptions, but on the whole the literature of programme notes is not a compelling genre.

I don't know if my experience is typical, but I'd say most players don't even bother to read programme notes, or if they do, it's usually to mock them by reading out bits they find ridiculous. And there is some justification for this view, though some concert halls and festivals are gradually changing things by commissioning writers more in touch with performance practice and enquiry. Even today, however, one still often comes across programme notes which describe music like this: 'The first subject is couched in the minor mode and utilises phrases of regular length. A transitional passage gives way to a secondary theme with some dotted rhythms. After a codetta, the development section moves into the subdominant. From there, it moves through several chromatic keys, incorporating a fugal passage with some stretti. The recapitulation follows a standard formula.' It's a pity, because programme notes are obviously meant to provide a bridge between the listener and the music, but I suspect that in many cases they serve to confirm people's view that you don't have much chance of understanding this kind of music without prior training. It is better if the players themselves speak to the audience about the music, but many don't like doing so because it distracts them or makes them nervous; they find they are shaking when they sit down afterwards and pick up their instrument to play.

It is of course terribly hard to write about music. It makes me think of the old story of the woman who lost her wedding ring one night and was discovered searching for it under a lamp-post. When asked if that was where she lost her ring, she said, 'No, but there's more light here.' Writers of programme notes often seem to feel that there is 'more light' in collateral anecdotes. Side-stepping the task of writing about music, they explain instead that, for example, Brahms was holidaying beside such-and-such a lake when he wrote this piece, or that Mozart had terrible money worries and a bad cough when he wrote this or that, or that Beethoven was having horrible rows with his landlords about the state of his rooms and pestering aristocratic women who were afraid of him. Such anecdotes provide diversion, though they don't often throw a very useful light on the piece of music you're hearing.

Visual art has its own distinctive 'programme-note' style. In January 2013 *The Guardian* published an article by Andy Beckett about the growth of 'International Art English'. He gave an example from an exhibition hand-out at a Mayfair gallery: 'The artist brings the viewer face to face with their own preconceived hierarchy of cultural values and assumptions of artistic worth. ... Each mirror imaginatively propels its viewer forward into the seemingly infinite progression of possible reproductions that the artist's practice engenders, whilst simultaneously pulling them backwards in a quest for the "original" source or referent that underlines X's oeuvre.' Such a style is widely used despite the fact that many visitors to galleries find it induces 'bafflement, exhaustion or irritation'. It's a slightly different approach from the one used by writers about music: more focused on the visual artist's motive and interior drama, less on the surface structure of the work. In visual art you don't tend to find the equivalent of programme notes about music: 'The painting begins with a red square in the top left-hand corner and juxtaposes this with a large area of white. There is a black stripe under the red square running from left to right. Below the black stripe is a larger area of blue.' And so on. The difference may be accounted for partly by the fact that a painting can be seen pretty much in a single glance – its surface need not be described step by step – whereas music unfolds in time, cannot be glimpsed in a single moment, and sometimes benefits from having its sequence of steps laid out like the pattern on a carpet.

Both music and art seem to struggle to find descriptive words that won't alienate the public, though it sometimes seems as though they actually quite like using alienating language. I have some sympathy with this because writing about the arts is not the same as writing, say, an official report, and it's probably a mistake to think that you can be utterly straightforward in your language while still conveying the strange and poetical thinking behind a work of art. It feels rather as if you need to twist away a little from the straight path in order to be true. George Orwell said that we should find the clearest, most straightforward way to say what we mean, but Einstein said things should be 'as simple as possible, but not simpler'. Writing about art in a 'simple' way is not a straightforward task because the effect of art is not simple, even if the means are. It must sometimes be tempting to abandon all high-flying language and just state prosaically that there will be 'a theme of four bars' length', but on the other hand I can also see why you might feel there's nothing for it but to allege 'the Jungian interrogation of blue'.

Explaining art is now regarded as a kind of interpretation – indeed, a profession – of its own. Museums and galleries advertise for interpreters, by which they mean not artists, but people who will explain works of art to visitors. I've seen some of those interpreters at work, and have enjoyed the sight of a group of laughing, fascinated children in front of a famous painting. It looked a whole lot more fun than my school outings to galleries. At first I was startled when I came across the word 'interpreter' in that context, because in music it is used to mean the musician. I have not yet seen the word applied, for example, to the writer of programme notes or the person giving a pre-concert talk, though such a usage would be in line with the way the term is used by art galleries. I recall a frisson of annoyance at seeing the word 'interpreter' on a badge pinned to the jumper of someone asking school kids whether they would fancy trying on the costumes worn by the young ballet dancers in a Degas painting, when to me interpreting means a long, intense process of digesting music and working out how to realise your understanding in sound. My dictionary doesn't include this newly coined use of interpreter for someone working in a museum or heritage site, but it does define an interpreter as 'a person who translates orally for the benefit of two or more parties speaking different languages', and I acknowledge that this is a good description of what those people in the Royal Academy of Arts were doing.

Gallery interpreters speak about the work of art but do not themselves *perform* it or call it into existence. Musicians have a much more primary role; they actually summon music from silence into sound, or from theory into action, and are its indispensable medium. They are much more closely bound to the material of the music, which wouldn't exist without their efforts. I don't doubt that a great deal of skill is required to explain Raphael or Picasso entertainingly to an audience of school children, but the interpreter in that case is not actually painting the picture. It has been painted already. The same is not true of music, where all that has been 'painted' already is the musical score, and nobody ever held a musical score up to their ears and exclaimed at its effect on their nervous system. Even the instruments we use to make music are silent until we play them. I remember once seeing a violinist complimented on the wonderful sound of his violin. He held the violin up to his ear, pretended to listen to it, and then said, 'I don't hear anything' (a gambit famously used by violinist Fritz Kreisler). The person who'd delivered the compliment was a bit offended, but the violinist was making an important point: even the finest instrument is silent until someone plays it, just as the most masterful composition remains latent until musicians come along and play it. The role of musicians in the *reality* of music is far more central than the role of a museum interpreter in a Monet water-lily painting. Anyone who has ever sat in a concert audience and found tears coming into their eyes at the sheer *sound* of beautiful music must have realised that the sound waves were being made by the real live musicians in front of them, not by the composer.

Musicians' indispensable role in bringing a musical score to life gives them a different relationship to the 'source material' than most other interpreters have. Perhaps a literary translator comes closest, for in making available a text in a new language, they have to pull the text through their own consciousness and into their native language, making millions of creative decisions based on how people speak that language today. Their decisions are not only supplementary to the original author's decisions, but in a way they're new decisions about a new text, because a change of language brings a change of language use, and language use is evolving all the time. Anyone who has read a parallel-text translation, with the original on one page and the translation on the opposite page, will have realised that in many cases there is no exactly equivalent way of saying something in another language. It seems that the language you speak determines to some extent the thoughts you think, and it is not always possible to transfer thoughts across from one language to another. The word order of the original, the sound of the words, the grammatical structure – all these play their part in how the original text makes its impact on readers, and if the text is to be translated, there will be different solutions for every new language, not only depending on which language but also on when the translation is made. An ancient classic text like the *Aeneid*, which you might think had been definitively translated or at any rate translated 'enough', is in fact appearing every year in new translations.

At first glance this may seem surprising. But as language changes, past translations start to seem dated, stilted and consequently stiff and opaque to the modern reader. Many of us have been put off reading 'the classics' because of fusty old translations in outdated idioms. If the *Aeneid* was vivid and enthralling to its original audience, then new translations into a modern idiom are necessary if the modern reader is to have a chance of recapturing the original freshness. Musicians tread a similar path, taking old musical texts and filtering them through a modern consciousness in the hope of making them seem as natural and idiomatic now as they did when Mozart or Schubert wrote them. This is really the answer to those people who say, 'Surely there are enough recordings of Beethoven's string quartets now? Why do we need a new one?' Because even though there are plenty of good recordings made in this or that decade, playing style is always changing, and older recordings may already seem to 'speak' in the tones of not-now.

Actors are engaged in a similar work of interpreting the text. Although some actors try to think of themselves as a blank canvas until the director tells them what this or that line 'means', good actors do much of the interpreting themselves. There are many parallels with what goes on in music. As with music, the original text is a given, though arguably an actor has more leeway because perhaps fewer of the parameters are fixed – for example, a playwright does not notate precisely when in time the next words should be spoken, or in what rhythm and with what rests between the 'notes'. A playwright also does not specify the exact instrument, so a high voice may be as appropriate as a low one. As theatre-goers we must all have realised that the same role inhabited by different actors can have astonishingly different effects. Some actors may seem wooden, some will seem ham, whereas others will make you feel that King Lear is standing in front of you. Just as with performances of music, some actors make you feel you've heard the text itself come to life, whereas with others you can never shake off the sense that you're watching acting. I have no experience of acting beyond schooldays, but I imagine that a great deal of the work for an actor is in trying to listen with great sensitivity to the intonation and nuance of spoken lines, so that anything distracting or extraneous to the meaning is weeded out and the intonation matches the inner content – no easy task, obviously, but you know it when you hear it.

I can't resist mentioning a marvellous story told by someone who worked in the BBC Sound Archive. The archive had been given several historical recordings which might or might not have been of Mr Gladstone, the Victorian prime minister. They wanted to verify which of the recordings might be of Mr Gladstone speaking by playing them to someone who knew him. Having discovered that Mr Gladstone's butler was still alive, they went down to the country to visit him, taking the recordings with them. The old butler was sitting in his armchair. They played him the first recording. He listened to it carefully, shook his head and said, 'It could be. I'm not sure. It does sound a bit like him, right enough.' They played him the second recording, and again he thought it was possible. 'It could be him. I'm sorry, I can't be certain. It was a long time ago, you see.' Then they played him the third recording, and at the sound of the voice, the old butler rose from his chair and stood to attention. No analysis was needed. I've always thought this a perfect illustration of the importance of intonation.

Some ethnomusicologists have taken a hard line on whether there is meaning in a musical score or whether all the meaning is a property of the musicians. Christopher Small, for example, used the word 'Musicking' as the title of one of his books because he wanted to draw attention to the fact that music is a process, an activity, something you *do*. He didn't believe that music should be a *thing*, like a score or a recording. At the other end of the spectrum are historians and analysts who believe that the score is 'das Ding an sich', the thing as it is in itself, and any performance just an imperfect and temporary perception of it. I know academics who don't go to many concerts because for them that's not where the importance lies; their real work is done in a silent library with a score in front of them. Most musicians' attitudes are somewhere in between. I and most of my colleagues have always believed that we are searching for meaning in the text (the score) and uncovering that meaning, revealing it, bringing it alive for today's listeners. We recognise also that whatever meaning we dig out of the score has to be filtered through our consciousness. When you are engaged in this work, it may come to feel as if there is some kind of interpenetration between music and mind, with influence flowing in both directions. It has to be a partnership because – if you accept that music involves actual sound – without us the score would not exist *as music*; we are its route to the surface. Despite this partnership, I think I would be correct in saying that most musicians think of the primary meaning as being located in the score. I don't think we conceive of ourselves as ventriloquists, pretending to make the inanimate score speak while actually doing all the speaking ourselves.

Occasionally I bump into scholars and semioticians who tell me this is not so. Meaning, they say, is created at the point of reception, so it is the musician, reading from the score, who creates what meaning there may be. Obviously it must be true that an animate being, such as a musician, is the one who actively takes meaning from an inanimate object such as a score, but to say that meaning is created at the point of reception implies that the only meaning a musician can bring to a score is one they are capable of extracting from their own limited experience. Does the score actively communicate meaning? Clearly the ink-on-paper score cannot do so, but the composer actively sought to communicate meaning when he took his pen and ink and wrote down those notes. I'm indebted to my husband Robert Philip for the delightful image of a musical score being analogous to a batch of dried peas or beans, inedible in their current state, but needing only the addition of water to swell up and return to their former glory. The musician supplies the water in the form of their care and attention, but the meaning was there already. Robert has pointed out that it's not a perfect analogy because anyone – even a machine – can add the water to a batch of dried peas, but I still think the image is helpful. What we musicians like so much about the masterworks of Bach, Mozart, Schubert and so on is that their music suggests a wider horizon, a stretching of emotional or existential experience beyond that which may have happened to fall into our path, and which it asks us to respond to, or at least grapple with. Rather than shrinking the music to fit one's domestic world, it feels as if one has to jump over one's domestic boundaries and attempt to grow to the stature of the music.

If I claim that meaning resides in the score and has only to be picked up by the musician's antennae, I must, however, also admit that not every musician picks up the same meaning from the same score, and the amount of meaning they pick up also varies, as every concert-goer will have realised. So what does that indicate about the ability of the score to communicate meaning? Does it indeed all depend on the 'receiving' ability of the musician? Anyone with experience of teaching will know that it is possible for students to learn a piece without realising much of its meaning, yet when the meaning is suggested to them, they happily agree and incorporate this into their understanding of the music. So who created the meaning? There is no easy answer to such questions, and probably never will be, but for me it has always been helpful to think of myself as an open ear for what the composer has said in those ink manuscripts. I don't think of myself as the one who donates the meaning; it could only be *my* meaning if I was also the one who made up the notes.

If I play an angry tumultuous passage in a sonata movement by Schubert, I don't feel I am portraying *my* anger; I feel it is *his*. I am not angry, nor do I have to imagine that I am. You might say that I can only portray the anger that I personally am capable of feeling, or that I can only represent the spiritual heights that I personally have been able to reach, but this is one of the good things about great music – it works on you, opening wider vistas which you are able to add, by proxy at least, to your own mental landscape. I don't think that working on great music would hold as much interest for me as it does if I thought it was inert and I was merely lending it *my* grasp of things.

Even after years of performing certain late works of Beethoven, for example, there are still many passages I don't truly understand. Often these are places where surprising things are juxtaposed without the links being made clear. I've sometimes tried to 'find the logic' in them, so that I can play them in a way which seems comprehensible, but the danger in that approach is that it may end up reducing the music to a smaller scale. After trying this and that over the years I've come to feel it's probably a mistake to attempt to resolve these mysteries by inventing connections between things which may not have connections, or at least not ones immediately apparent. Sometimes there's a sense that the composer is making larger connections which he could see, even if the players can't. Or one may have a sense that the lack of audible connection is an important metaphor of its own. There may be nothing for it but to play exactly what is written and trust that there is meaning inherent in the notes, a meaning which, even if it eludes the performer, may mysteriously come across to the listener. I'm sure most musicians would agree that they have experienced something like this with great music, which is why it may be 'simpler than possible' to assert that meaning is only created by the performer.

Some aspects of interpretation are easier if you know things about the form of the piece and its historical background, about the style and the instruments of the time, and if possible about how the composers themselves performed their music. This will save you from committing errors like using the pedal too much in Bach, Haydn and Mozart, or too little in Chopin, Liszt and Rachmaninov. It will help you to consider what composers of several hundred years ago meant by 'loud' or 'fast', and whether those words might mean something different today. I've had some interesting discussions with students about what an eighteenth-century person might have meant by 'very fast', for example. Would they calibrate their sense of speed from things they had seen with their own eyes, like a running man or a galloping horse? Or would they easily have been able to imagine things faster than any they had witnessed, and if so, is that surreal speed what they had in mind when they indicated that their music should be played presto? What about us – do we derive our sense of very fast from modern things like cars, planes and rockets? If we emulate the pace of a galloping horse, will that still seem very fast to a twenty-first-century listener? Or is it rather the case that, despite everyone's sense that life is speeding up all the time, there's actually something stable and dependable about musical tempi? Do tempi relate more to things like walking speed, breathing rates, dancing steps, heartbeats – things that can't have changed very much between Bach's time and ours?

A friend told me that in his (now defunct) string quartet, discussion of tempo was often left until the end, after they had practised everything else. 'Then finally we'd say, "Now – how fast should we play it, then?"' I found this surprising. The tempo and character of the music are inseparable, two sides of the same coin. In my experience you can't sort out how you're going to play the other elements of the music and then stick a tempo on afterwards as if it were a garnish. For me, tempo should be a *result*. It doesn't exist in isolation. By changing the tempo, you will change the character, and vice versa. You can try this out yourself by singing any favourite song to yourself at different speeds and noticing what it does to the character of the music. Or you can do it the other way round and sing a tune to yourself in a soothing way, followed by an energetic way, followed by an angry way, and so on. You'll probably find that as you alter the character, you instinctively alter the tempo. You'll notice that certain tempi and characters seem to support one another in a harmonious way, and this will be 'your' tempo of that particular song. When you hear performances that strike you as too fast or too slow it's usually because there is a mismatch between tempo and character.

When you're playing an instrument you're very aware of the physical consequences of an alteration in tempo, because you will have to modify tone and articulation (how you 'pronounce' the notes) accordingly. If you play something a lot slower than usual, you'll have to amplify the tone of individual notes to adapt them to their newly extended duration, using a slower bow, a heavier arm weight, a deeper breath or whatever. The character of the notes will change as the tempo changes. If you use the same density of tone you were using at the original tempo – i.e. the same pressure and speed of bow, the same weight and touch on the keys – the musical material will seem thin and attenuated, not well adapted to its new slow context. (I must mention here a stimulating moment in a lesson I heard in György Sebők's summer masterclasses when he said to a viola player, 'You don't play long notes. You just play short notes and hold them.') Conversely, if you play something a lot faster than usual, the amplitude of tone will have to be modified too. You have to focus on the character of rhythm and articulation in order to make the music fit its new tempo. If you don't make these alterations (often instinctive for musicians) then it will seem as if you're playing a slow thing speeded-up or a quick thing slowed down; more generally it will feel as if the music does not 'sit well' – and indeed one does have exactly that impression in unconvincing performances.

Finding the relationship between tempo, tone and character is a very subtle business. I am still not entirely sure whether it varies for each person or whether there are absolutes all music-lovers would agree upon. When I'm working on a piece, experimentally shifting different coordinates of character, tone and tempo, there is often a moment when they click together in a way which feels absolute. When this happens, I feel that I am now hearing 'it' rather than 'a plausible version of it'. However, I have occasionally found that for some people my tempi are on the fast side, especially in slow movements. They comment that my tempi are always 'flowing' and that in their view this may sometimes be at the cost of what they call 'profundity'. Perhaps indeed it is true that a sense of musical flow is a top priority for me, but in slow movements I never have the feeling that I am playing too fast, only that I have found the spot on the coordinates where it seems to me that what the music is trying to say and the way this message is conveyed in terms of tone and timing are working in harness perfectly. Therefore I'm sometimes surprised if a reviewer comments on the lack of slowness in a slow movement, or rather on my preference for a sense of forward movement. Maybe this 'preference' is in turn linked to the way my nervous system operates. It is true that other people's performances of music at very slow tempi often strike me as too slow in an absolute sense. When my attention is overly drawn to individual notes in a phrase, and when these notes have a 'presence' that prevents me from understanding the shape of the whole phrase, then it seems to me that one of the elements is out of balance, and therefore the chosen tempo is too slow. Yet at the same time I accept that a musician who chooses to play like that must be convinced by his or her own tempo, unless they are striving for a kind of *theatrical effect* of slowness, which I confess I sometimes think they are.

The slowest 'performance' I ever heard part of was in Bach's church in Eisenach in Germany where, by way of 'homage', an organ had been electronically rigged up to play one of his melodies extremely slowly, one note at a time. In fact each note was made to last for hours or days at a time if I remember rightly (I realised later that the idea was probably taken from John Cage's organ piece *As Slow as Possible*). The idea was, I think, to pay tribute to Bach's enduring significance, using extreme slowness as a mark of respect and eternal verity, but as far as

I was concerned the tribute was devoid of musical meaning. In fact, the memory of one single loud organ note resounding implacably in the church all the time I was looking round it has stayed with me as a misconceived tribute to a great musician.

I've often felt that people equate extreme slowness with profundity, but that's not a link that has ever made much sense to me. In my ears, profundity can be achieved at all sorts of tempi and in all sorts of moods. A flowing andante or adagio, if it matches the unfolding of the musical material, is more likely to move me than one where I feel the performer is exerting their willpower to slow everything down to fit a preconceived notion of importance. The profundity of something graceful, or blissful, or accepting is for me as touching as the profundity of sadness. Furthermore, for me sadness is sometimes more touching if it is not laboured and if it is worn lightly rather than signposted with huge gestures. I'm willing to grant that there may be a cultural aspect to my response. I'm not from a demonstrative nation, and tragedy writ large has always left me rather cold. A performance which confides in me is more likely to win my heart than one which batters me into submission.

There are enormous armouries of weapons available to performers who want to dramatise music, but it doesn't always seem to me that the use of these weapons is suggested by the music itself. In this era of putting a high value on image, there's a lot of hair-tossing and swaying on the concert platform, a lot of grimacing, leaning back from the piano stool and gazing heavenward. There's a lot of bringing in the backstory from the performer's personal life too, and some artists have publicised things like nervous breakdowns and mental health issues in order to win the sympathy of the audience and make everyone feel tremendous relief if the concert turns out smoothly. Sometimes the backstory is woven into the artist's behaviour on the platform; a well-publicised story such as a struggle with depression will be manifested in the performance by unusual tempi, very fast or very slow, which the audience will 'read' as biographical information. I feel uncomfortable if I suspect that drama in a performance is a calculated application of an idea external to the music. I'm even more uncomfortable when

I sense that such wilful use of drama is a big hit with the audience, but that is another story. It's not my way of working at music, for good or ill. What interests me is finding the perfect balancing-point between idea and utterance, and fortunately it often seems to be possible. However, I often find that resolving these matters takes time and has to be worked out not only at the instrument but away from it, testing out different tempi by matching them to (for example) the pace of my footsteps, or the rhythm of my breathing. Again I find myself wondering whether one's sense of tempo is inextricably linked to the way one's nervous system operates. But that's how it is: you are the material you have to work with.

Historical awareness, based on literature about how people played in different centuries and in different contexts, will help you to determine how much rubato you can use in music of different kinds and to understand the character of music which would have sounded very different on, say, a nineteenth-century piano with a lighter touch than today's. It is sometimes useful to know what size rooms were used for concerts or what kind of people were in the audience and how they behaved during the performance. Reading descriptions of how composers played will prevent you from thinking, for example, that Chopin's piano music needs to be played loudly. It may help to know that composers took liberties and didn't always follow their own instructions when they performed their own music, even when they had given specific tempo markings. It may be liberating to hear from their recordings that composers fluffed their own music and got things wrong, no matter how stern and exacting the instructions may be in their scores. All these are important tools for the study of music and the preparation of a performance, and play a part in what you can talk about in rehearsal.

Important as they are, however, they don't feel like the meat of the matter. Even taken altogether, they don't quite seem to add up to what I and my fellow musicians thought we were doing when we 'listened in' to a great piece of music. There's something more, more than the sum of the parts, a kind of identification with the whole piece which gives you, the performer, the feeling that you know it like you know a friend – maybe even better than you know a friend. It means watching and observing and learning the low points and the high points, the times of energy and the times of repose, the simple bits and the complex, the times when it is settled and when it wants to move on and when it has moved too far away. You need to get a feel for how it turns corners and how it gets across the junctions between different themes or episodes. You need to know what is 'a play within a play'.

All of these are things which can be read through the signals given in the score, and reading them enables you to build up a conception of the piece which feels organic and almost breathing. I've debated this with friends who study reception theory in other linguistic fields. They have tried to convince me that *I'm* the one doing the work, not that I am (as I imagine) putting my ear trumpet to the score and hearing it speak wise things to me in its tiny old voice. But it doesn't *feel* as if I am the only one doing the work. Maybe that's an illusion, used unconsciously by musicians to make them feel they are harnessing themselves to a power larger than themselves. It feels necessary to believe that we are listening to the score, absorbing what it has to say and relaying it to the audience. To cut out the first part of that process, and to think that the transaction is simply between musician and audience, would be to cut the whole experience down to a smaller size, and I believe it would cut it down for the audience too.

When I was reading about the history of interpretation I came across the word 'hermeneutics', the theory of text interpretation. Hermeneutics is named after the Greek god Hermes, the messenger. As well as mediating between gods and mortals, Hermes was the god of transitions and boundaries, a protector of travellers across those borders. Hermeneutics is therefore the art and study of transitions. Without attempting to draw too close a parallel, this sounds to me a pretty good description of what musicians try to do when they 'interpret' music. I even like the idea that someone who interprets a text is a hermeneut, though it's probably wise to suppress that thought before I'm tempted to describe myself thus on my passport and make people even warier than they are when they see 'classical musician'. I love the idea that musicians are guardians of boundaries, protectors of travellers across the border between music and the rest of life. That's often what it feels like when you are performing to an audience. When listeners enter imaginatively into a work of music they are, in a way, travelling into a distant land, with the musicians holding up lanterns for them.

When people immerse themselves in music they willingly suspend some of their normal senses and amplify others. Coleridge wrote in 1817 about the 'suspension of disbelief' which a good writer can make a reader feel, so that even a fantastical storyline can be accepted and relished. In performances of music, similarly, listeners consent to leave everyday reality and sink into the alternative world proposed by music. They have to sink in, and they have to emerge again afterwards. Most people will recognise the sense of having to shake themselves back to reality at the end of a wonderful concert. I've occasionally received letters from people describing how long a performance had lingered with them, making them reluctant to accept that the poetry of that moment had gone. There's definitely some kind of border between the everyday world and the realm of music in which people can become 'all ears', and musicians are aware of standing on the border between the two.

I've heard lots of people talk inspiringly about interpretation, and I've realised there are many different views on what is actually going on. For me, the task of interpretation is focused on a wish to extract understanding from the essence of the musical material – not from my thoughts about it, and not only from knowledge about it, but *from the essence itself*. Once I feel I have understood this essence, my work is concentrated on trying to clear away anything extraneous which might get in the way of it. This sounds like a simple formula, but that clearing away of anything extraneous is a long and meticulous task which involves self-observation as well as factual knowledge. I have often been inspired by the memory of a long-ago newspaper cartoon in the B.C. series drawn by the American cartoonist Johnny Hart, depicting episodes in the life of a Stone Age caveman. I haven't seen it for many years and haven't been able to verify exactly what it said, but my recollection is that it showed the caveman, B.C., admiring the handiwork of a sculptor who had chiselled out of a block of marble an incredible likeness of his friend Johnny. The statue and Johnny were side by side in the studio and B.C. was looking from one to the other, dumbfounded. 'How did you make it so like him?' he asks. The sculptor replies, 'Easy. I just took away all the bits that didn't look like Johnny.'

Bullfrogs

In the programme of Scottish National Orchestra concerts to which my Mum and I used to go on Friday nights, there was a courteous announcement about coughing. It explained that an 'unmuffled' cough in the concert hall had been found to be about as loud as a note played mezzo-forte on the French horn. Audiences were politely requested to use a handkerchief to muffle the sound of a cough. The sucking of boiled sweets was recommended as a way to avoid coughing in the concert.

I remember reading research from the Common Cold Centre some years later which measured a cough at an average of 70–90 decibels, described as 'like a noisy radio or the sound of a tube train'. This image was somewhat more arresting than 'a note played mezzo-forte on the French horn'. The loudest cough they'd measured was, it turned out, not much quieter than a pneumatic drill. Coughs were said to be 'like a football crowd roar'. All these comparisons are, of course, slightly misleading because they bring to mind a continuous sound event, whereas a cough is usually an explosive single moment. But it's useful to make people aware of how disturbing a cough can be.

In the British Isles, with our damp climate and unpredictable weather, coughs and colds are a feature of life, particularly in winter. They are also an occupational hazard for musicians. I sometimes feel as if I've spent years listening to people coughing in concerts. For some reason, when I'm practising at home, trying to imagine myself playing a particular piece in public, I never imagine the sound of coughing superimposed on my performance – when it happens in reality, it always startles me. When I'm in the audience myself, I know how uncomfortable it can be if you suddenly get the urge to cough. In fact, it can be excruciating. I've had a few moments where I thought the effort of suppressing a cough might cause me to go purple and expire there and then on the floor of the Upper Circle – either that or I was going to have to cause a sensation by ploughing my way to the exit past enraged fellow listeners, spluttering as I went.

Funnily enough it is not this kind of cough that really disturbs me when I hear it from the stage. Even a performer in the heat of battle can recognise a 'necessary' cough, a cough which cannot be helped and which the sufferer is trying to keep as quiet as possible. Such a cough may be disturbing, but you also feel sorry for the poor person. It is not nearly as annoying as the uninhibited bark of a cough ringing out from the stalls like a gunshot. If you're deep in trying to create a beautifully quiet musical atmosphere, such a cough is like being slapped on the ear. It can nearly make you fall off the piano stool. Everyone is sympathetic towards a 'medical' cough which cannot be helped, but it's hard to feel sympathetic towards an uncovered recreational cough, particularly if the same person persists in repeating it throughout the evening. They probably imagine they are the only person who's coughing, but on stage you can hear coughs ringing out from all over the hall, upstairs and downstairs, like one of these auditory tests of how good your depth perception is. Bark: back row of the stalls! Bark: up in the balcony! Bark: left aisle near the side door! As I once wrote on my blog, the noise sometimes sounds like bullfrogs calling to one another at night from different parts of the swamp.

It's a very curious thing that the coughing rarely comes from performers on the platform. Naturally we are as vulnerable as everyone else to the coughs and colds of winter, but there seems to be some mechanism which prevents musicians (and actors too, I believe) from coughing and sneezing on stage. I've been told it has something to do with the effect of adrenalin on the nervous system. Whatever the reason, it's a remarkable thing that you can go on stage suffering from a nasty cold and then realise that you haven't coughed or sneezed once while you were playing. Sure enough, back in the dressing-room your nose may run and you may give way to a volley of sneezing, but mercifully the urge to cough and sneeze while performing is quite rare. Not totally absent, of course – in the grip of a nasty cough I've occasionally had to turn aside between movements of a piece and just cough as much as I need to, but in general it's amazing how the excitement of performance seems to keep coughing at bay.

In one's excitingly cough-free state, one's all the more aware of people coughing in the audience. Don't get me wrong: I know sometimes people really can't help it. However, there's a type of cough I might call the Cough Rampant. Listening to it you can just tell that the cougher is completely unembarrassed and is making not the slightest attempt to muffle it. This type of cough is unfortunately the one most commonly encountered in the concert hall. There's also the Cough Demonstrative, which seems to hold a note of apology, but an apology you're meant to hear: 'Excuse me! I really have to do this, but I do know I'm doing it, so that's fine, isn't it!' The Common Cold Centre's comparison with the noise of a pneumatic drill is apposite, because a loud cough can really break apart a moment of shared concentration. I wonder that it doesn't occur to coughers that musicians may be disturbed by their coughing. Perhaps they think we won't hear it over the noise of the music? But in fact it is all too audible, and it catches our attention in a dramatic way. One of my colleagues used to say, as we came off stage after listening to a bout of coughing, 'They think we're on the telly!' We suspected that audiences didn't quite believe we were real people, sharing the same acoustic space with them, hearing the same things they heard, making music 'live' right in front of them. Surely they wouldn't cough so loudly if they thought we could hear them? And even if they thought the performers were incapable of hearing them, surely they would be reluctant to disturb their fellow listeners? Yet they don't seem to be.

Coughing in concerts is not a new phenomenon, and performers have always been aware of it. In 1931, Sergei Rachmaninov wrote to his friend Nikolai Medtner who was about to perform Rachmaninov's *Variations on a Theme of Corelli*, 'I've played the *Variations* about fifteen times, but of these fifteen performances only one was good. The others were sloppy. I can't play my own compositions! And it's so boring! Not once have I played these all in continuity. I was guided by the coughing of the audience. Whenever the coughing would increase, I would skip the next variation. Whenever there was no coughing, I would play them in proper order. In one concert, I don't remember where – some small town – the coughing was so violent that I played only ten variations [out of 20]. My best record was set in New York, where I played 18 variations.' It is all very well for the composer to omit bits of his own composition, but no pianist today would feel at liberty to abridge the music in response to coughing, and certainly not in New York.

I recently listened back to the recordings of several of my duo concerts with violinist Erich Höbarth, recorded live. I was making notes on which works were suitable for transfer to an album, so I needed to find recordings where there wasn't too much audience noise. As I listened, I became super-aware of the audience's coughing and where it occurred. I had to rule out whole movements for album purposes because of the quantity of coughing; when you're sitting in a concert, the moment passes and is forgotten, but you really don't want to have all that coughing immortalised on a recording you might listen to time and time again. Interestingly, I discovered that whenever there was a sudden loud bark of a cough from someone in the front rows, one or other of the performers made a tiny mistake a second afterwards. It was clear that a loud cough triggered a mini-lapse in concentration. It was perhaps 'princess and pea' stuff, tiny errors that only another musician would notice, but sometimes a sudden cough from the audience seemed to provoke a wrong note from me or a miss-hit from Erich's bow.

Musicians don't want their listeners to feel excluded from the concert in any way, but on the other hand they are desperate for a canvas of quiet on which to paint. Most practice is done in quiet rooms with nothing to break the concentration. Performers get used to the background of silence against which they can gradually build up their familiarity with the piece and their sense of security with it. Always in their mind's eye is the receptive audience, hanging on their every note. They imagine themselves performing in ideal circumstances, their music the focus of everyone's interest. After months of private practice, therefore, it can be a shock to arrive at the actual concert venue and discover that there are all sorts of unexpected noises to contend with – from sounds as subtle as the hum of electric lighting or air conditioning to more startling noises made by the audience: coughing, talking, bending down and rummaging in bags for things, unwrapping sweets, coming in and out of the room, doors banging, seats clonking. Coughing from the audience has come to feel like a gauntlet that has to be run. There's often a counterpoint of 'live audience' noise which feels like its own performance and is overlaid on what the musicians are trying to do. Of course it is unrealistic to imagine that you'll be able to play your programme entirely without distractions – though it does happen – and it's natural for the audience to produce its own tapestry of noises at a live event, but there is often an uneasy (and occasionally it feels competitive) interaction between the 'intended' performance of the musicians and the 'unintended' performance of the audience.

I've sometimes felt that people save up their coughs for quiet moments in the music. This is something I find hard to understand. If I'm in the audience myself and feel I need to cough, I try to wait until there's a loud bit of music, and then cough when the decibel level will give me cover. But I've often had the distinct impression that people save up their coughs for the stillest, most intimate moments of the music. Do they feel, perhaps, that the quietest moments are the most relaxed, the ones where there's 'not much happening', therefore they can also relax and cough now? I hardly dare think so, because for me those quiet moments are often the most intense of the piece. I don't like to think that there are those who don't feel the same way, but experience seems to show that people feel freer to cough in quiet passages than in loud ones. They often seem to cough immediately after the final note in a quiet slow movement, so that the beautiful silence into which the music should fade is ruined. For the musicians it's as if those people had stuck their hands in the air and shouted, 'I didn't get the point!'

Part of the problem may be that in the last couple of decades, people have got used to music being amplified. There are plenty of concerts (of music other than classical) where a cough would pass completely unnoticed by the performers because the prevailing noise level is so loud, and I wonder whether people have come to regard that as the default setting. Quite apart from amplification, people have also got used to listening to music on headphones, turning the volume up as high as they like. If they cough when listening to music on headphones, there are no live performers to startle. I suspect that this may not be a trivial point. The majority of people's listening is now done to recorded music, in settings other than concert halls. Music has become much more of a commodity than it was, and musicians more taken for granted. It's possible that audiences are starting to forget that musicians are real people, disturbed by unexpected noise. I've heard more than one person comment that when they go to a classical concert they are surprised by how quiet the 'acoustic' instruments are. Of course, these instruments are not quiet in an absolute sense: they are quiet only in comparison with amplified or recorded music. They seem quiet only if you're at the back of a big modern concert hall.

It may be that our attention span has decreased. The majority of albums today consist of a string of songs of three or four minutes' duration. This has become the norm for chunks of music; in contrast, classical pieces are usually quite a bit longer than that. In my repertoire, thirty minutes (divided into three or four movements) is standard for a trio or quartet, and it could be forty (Beethoven's 'Archduke' Trio, Dvořák's F minor Piano Trio), forty-five (Brahms' G minor Piano Quartet) or even fifty (Schubert's E-flat Piano Trio). These leisurely musical ruminations, which must once have seemed natural, now seem notably extended. Even when you are used to performing them, your attention is sometimes drawn (by fidget-ing and rustling) to the fact that they require long periods of still-ness and quietness from an audience more used to having breaks and leg-stretching and chatting opportunities every few minutes. I never used to consider these works long, but in some mysteri-ous way, as people's listening habits have changed around me, I have developed a slightly different perspective on these Romantic works. They don't yet strike me as 'too long', but in some indefin-able way they now strike even me as 'long', whereas I used to think that's just the way they were. Now I feel I detect the beginnings of dissatisfaction in some audiences when the music sails way past the four-minute mark. I don't know what can be done about this until music-lovers develop a collective desire for longer immer-sion in music. I think it's not impossible that people will eventu-ally feel a need for 'long-form' music, because I can't believe that they're going to be satisfied forever with bite-sized chunks. In the meantime, I feel that the stately length of some classical works is a factor in the restlessness of the audience and its impulse to break up proceedings by coughing.

A few months ago I was asked to join a discussion on BBC Radio 4's *Today* programme about coughing at classical concerts. New re-search had been published in Germany by Professor Andreas Wagener who found that people cough 'excessively' in a concert, more times on average than they would in a normal day. Why? There are several possible practical reasons. The air may be dry or stale in a concert hall. Air conditioning may irritate people's throats. The typical classi-cal audience may be older than other types of audience, more prone to respiratory ailments. But these explanations did not account for the discovery that people cough more in quiet passages of music. They also did not explain why, when distinguished performers lost their tempers and turned to the audience to implore them not to cough so much, the coughing ceased. Clearly the coughing was not strictly speaking of the 'necessary' variety.

Professor Wagener also found the coughing was 'non-random' and tended to occur during unfamiliar or complex pieces. He conjectured that there might be an element of protest about coughing in concerts. This seemed to bear out what I'd thought privately over the years. Could it be that because people feel constrained by the quiet, respectful atmosphere of the concert hall, they unconsciously wish to rebel against it? Does there come a moment when they get fed up with sitting absolutely still and suddenly wish to draw attention to themselves, to document their presence by shouting out, 'I'm also here! Don't think it's all about you!!' Obviously one could never prove it, but enough has been written about the so-called 'intimidating atmosphere' of classical concerts to suggest that there may be an element of passive-aggressive behaviour about the Cough Demonstrative. I remember hearing the American choreographer Mark Morris, in a question-and-answer session at Sadler's Wells, describing how he'd been in the audience at a classical concert where he uncrossed his legs during a quiet passage, making a tiny susurration with the corduroy of his trousers, and the man in front of him whirled round and gave him the Evil Eye. Everyone laughed at the anecdote, but I felt sad that this view of 'stuffy' classical audiences is becoming a cliché, because the urge to rebel will come to seem all too understandable.

The conductor Sir Colin Davis suggested that audiences cough out of boredom. This too seems plausible; I have read that cinema audiences cough more in the 'boring bits' of movies. We are moving further and further away in time from the eras in which the great works of classical music were composed. Their musical language is not exactly our vernacular. For musicians, it's a language they instinctively like, have learned and feel entirely comfortable with, but it may that for some of the audience the musical language is now at one remove. It may be no more than opening a novel which begins, 'It is a truth universally acknowledged' rather than, 'Everyone knows'. Of course you know what Jane Austen's phrase means, but her choice of words seems to necessitate a tiny adjustment to the reader's synapses. There may be something comparable going on in music. Clearly audiences sometimes feel a touch alienated by older language, and perhaps their coughing is an unconscious way of indicating their discomfort.

I thought it was very interesting that audiences who had been admonished by someone like pianist Alfred Brendel or baritone Thomas Quasthoff would pipe down and keep quiet afterwards. It seemed to indicate that they could have kept quiet beforehand too, had they wished to. Perhaps it was important that the performer had grown exasperated enough to break the convention of staying silent on the platform. It must have been a shock for people to hear a personal plea from a great performer, whom they must suddenly have realised could hear every noise they made and was capable of feeling unhappy about it. Perhaps this in turn indicates that for reasons connected with changing listening habits and social customs, it's important for classical performers to find ways of interacting with the audience, not necessarily by speaking from the platform, if that is nerve-racking for the musician, but by somehow diluting the remoteness associated with the classical performer for a century now. Everyone needs to be made aware of the fact that the performers are not 'on the telly' but are in fact flesh-and-blood creatures summoning up all their faculties of stamina and concentration to produce a good performance there and then.

It's a remarkable fact that in some concert halls, despite the respiratory infections of winter, the audience remains utterly silent – not because they are terrified, but because they are rapt. Luckily for me I've experienced this in all sorts of settings, and I'm always grateful for it. In London's Wigmore Hall, for example, where there's a long tradition of chamber music, solo recitals and song, and an audience which supports the tradition, it's sometimes hard to remember that there are actually 500 people in the hall, so quiet are they. I heard the same silence recently in the Prinzregententheater in Munich, where 800 people seemed to have suspended their breathing. A week later I heard it in a tiny old village church in Cornwall for a concert of chamber music. Such an audience is an inspiring thing for the performer to encounter. It seems to prove that if people are there because they want to be there, the urge for individuals to document their presence by coughing does not really arise. On the contrary, it feels as if they sink gratefully into a collective concentration and actively hope that nothing will break the surface. When performing to listeners like that, it seems to me that just as coughing can ripple through an audience, silence can ripple through an audience as well.

The iceberg

Sometimes, when I'm playing the piano at home, it occurs to me that the vast majority of my playing has not been done for listeners. Obviously some of my practising has been heard by family members, whether or not they wanted to listen. Our late lamented tortoiseshell cat is the only creature who has actually sat in on my practice sessions for longish periods of time, and even she had a discouraging way of getting up with a sigh, going to sit by the door and scratching forlornly at the paintwork until I let her out. But although I have played lots of concerts, the amount of time I have spent playing to audiences is only a fraction of the time I have spent playing to nobody. At a rough calculation, 90% – maybe more – of my piano playing has only been heard by me. When I think about this situation in the abstract, it feels as if we musicians are constantly shooting arrows into the dark, without an audience to provide the target.

I imagine that the 'classical music' of many cultures requires a comparable degree of private preparation. The majority of our playing is unobserved and unattended. Much of our time is spent in getting things into a reliable state for the benefit of future listeners (as well as for the benefit of our own professional reputations). Some musicians genuinely enjoy their practice time, but for many it's a necessary discipline. They need it to develop and maintain their knowledge of their instrument, their understanding of their own physique and their intellectual grasp of the music they'll one day be performing for an audience. They need it to build up stamina, both of muscle and memory. They work out in great detail how they want to play things, what timing makes most sense, how to balance melody against harmony and why. Speaking for myself, I'd say that a lot of practice is designed to shore me up against the depredations of adrenalin when it surges in during a performance. I forget which musician was alleged to have said that you have to be 150% secure at home in order to be 100% secure on the platform, but he was certainly right. Even after years of concert experience I am still surprised how little control one has over nerves. Sometimes it seems one has learned to master them, and then all of a sudden, without warning, they leap out of hiding and ambush you. For me, as for many players, the only defence against them is to be really well prepared.

At various times I've shared a house with other musicians, mostly string players, and have heard them practising day after day. Often their practice centred on short sections and fragments, 'difficult bits' played over and over again. The door was closed between the practiser and the rest of us, and nothing was said about the practice session when the player came out of the room, neither by them nor by the rest of us. We all understood that it was not designed to be overheard, and like the butler in Oscar Wilde's *Importance of Being Earnest*, we 'didn't think it polite to listen'. Indeed, we all understood that whoever was practising should be able to feel that they were unobserved. Nevertheless I often had the impression that the practising was like a black cloud hovering over the household. A cloud of bees, perhaps, angrily buzzing. Frustration with oneself was a common ingredient, and bad-tempered practising often brought to my mind the image of a child crayoning furiously over the outlines of a drawing.

It can't be denied, of course, that the process of mastering an instrument is engrossing in its own right. As with other lengthy training (such as in ballet) which demands constant upkeep all through professional life, the very discipline becomes a valuable way of structuring your day. Even if you have no audience to feel responsible to, practising a musical instrument can be very instructive. You can learn a lot about yourself and apply the knowledge elsewhere. I often felt that practising made my perceptions finer, or at the very least gave them an enthralling forum.

Sometimes all this 'playing for nobody' seems a colossal waste. After all, what is music for? To energise, to soothe, to divert; for dancing, for singing, for dreaming. It seems mad that these purposes are lost in the professional musician's search for accuracy and security. Practice is necessary, because the music we play is complex and technically demanding. We know that people will pay money to come and hear us, and knowing that those hours and minutes upon the stage are the proof of the pudding, we prepare assiduously. Yet it often seems to me that those moments in front of the public are just the tip of the iceberg in a musician's life. Beneath the water line is a huge dark bulk of time spent practising, stopping and starting, trying things out with minute increments of change, wearing grooves in one's memory, repeating things over and over again to make sure that success can be repeated and relied upon. Sometimes, when they're on stage I think I can see on musicians' heavy, preoccupied faces the effects of spending that much time below the waterline.

How many other lines of work require 90% of preparation for 10% of time spent in the presence of one's 'customers'? Most people train until they know how to do something, and then immediately begin doing it for money. There may be refresher courses and up-dating days, but basically there's no more training or private practice. People turn professional, get up in the morning and go straight out to do the job. They're paid for every hour they spend at work. When they come home, they can shut the door on that subject until it's time to go out and do the next job. Life is different in the arts, especially the performing arts. Actors spend long periods learning their lines, and long periods of time in rehearsal, developing their understanding of the characters they play. Dancers spend far more time in class and in rehearsal than they do in actual performance. Perhaps the cases of writers and composers are not quite comparable, because although they labour alone for long periods, as do painters and sculptors, their finished creations leave their hands and take on an existence of their own. They pass into the hands of individual readers and performers, or are displayed in galleries and public places for anyone to look at when they choose. Though the composer, author or painter may anxiously follow what happens to their creations, there's nothing quite analogous to the moment when the musician has to step onto the stage under the platform lights and do it all *for real*. The audience knows nothing of the time spent alone beforehand. All they respond to is what happens in the moment of performance.

I now realise that some of my best playing hasn't been heard by anyone but me – and the same must go for many musicians. When your practice has matured enough to be able to play whole works in one continuous flow, you do play to an imaginary audience, and you try to give your performance as you would wish it to be on the platform. Of course, you can't know what the actual presence of an audience will do to you. As I said in an earlier chapter, the addition of the observer changes the behaviour of the thing observed. Sometimes a real audience can be a tremendous stimulus, pushing you to heights you didn't know you were capable of. Sometimes the nerves you feel in front of an audience can diminish your performance. Some performers rise to meet the audience's expectations while others feel crushed by them, and this is probably more a matter of temperament than of musicianship. Good musicians live in a world of imagination, and the access to that world may sometimes be barred by a roomful of strangers.

In fact, freed from the weird things that can happen to you in public (such as when your hands are clammy, your heart rate goes up, your breathing patterns are altered, or you're startled by noises off), your unobserved performances in a peaceful practice studio may be the best you'll ever play those pieces. Sometimes you even feel you've managed to achieve the 150% at home which is said to guarantee 100% on the platform. Now and then there are thrilling moments when you feel (as many musicians probably do) that you may just have played something better, more purely, more truthfully than it has ever been played before by anybody. Hard on the heels of this elation comes the suspicion that it was probably engendered by the intense sharpening of perception that accompanies deep absorption in one's practice, combined perhaps with a lack of oxygen in the room, the fact that you'd had too much coffee, or some other mind-altering factor. But what if it were true? What if luck, focus and the prevailing winds had actually combined to produce a supreme musical expression? At such times it seems a terrible waste that not a single other person was there to cherish the experience of hearing the music fly free, and you at your unburdened best. But in a corner of your mind you also know that had listeners been there, their very presence might have chased you from that solitary paradise.

Starting and beginning

Last summer I was teaching on a European Chamber Music Academy course along with ECMA's artistic director, Austrian violist Hatto Beyerle, co-founder of the Alban Berg Quartet. One lunch-break, I wandered down to his teaching room to see how he was getting on. His students had gone for lunch and he was sitting alone in the hall, ruminating on the morning's class. 'I constantly find myself thinking', he said to me sadly in English, 'that so many musicians today don't know how to begin. They start, but they don't *begin*.'

I particularly love these kinds of observations which might, or might not, arise from an imperfect use of another language. Or is it actually a more sensitive use of language than a native speaker's? In any case, it woke me up. 'They start, but they don't begin.' What could be the difference? In English, 'starting' and 'beginning' are used more or less interchangeably. It reminded me of Mr Habib in the film *Father of the Bride* who buys Steve Martin's family home and then orders a wrecking crew to demolish it. 'Commence to start!' he yells at the crew. We laugh because commencing and starting are the same thing in English – as are starting and beginning, you might have thought.

But Hatto enlightened me by explaining what he meant. He said that many performers struck him as 'starting from cold', selecting a merely random moment to play, and then giving the music a colour and shape once it was going on. He rarely felt, he said, that players were *waiting for the music to come towards them* in the silence that preceded the first note, waiting for that mysterious moment when it felt inevitable to leap into the musical current. With graceful hand movements and eloquent words he described the movement of the music towards the player, and the antennae which the player must develop in order to sense the 'beginning' of the music. To 'start' was a merely mechanical procedure. To 'begin' was to tune into an imaginative realm. The idea of music coming towards you was a beautiful metaphor, one which I wished the students could have heard. It described the difference, well known to all experienced performers, between you making the decision and the mysterious feeling of 'it' deciding.

Of course one might immediately counter that there is no music unless someone plays it, and therefore there can be no music 'preceding' the players' first notes. However, the quality of those first notes can be profoundly influenced by what the musicians imagine as they prepare to play. I often say to students that *intention* must precede the notes. They shouldn't simply clunk down the opening notes like someone slapping a lump of dough onto a work surface. They should first imagine the atmosphere they want to conjure up, the sound they want to hear; they should switch on a musical current which will carry them irresistibly into the opening phrase. As the pianist Artur Schnabel advised, 'Hear first, then play.' This effort of the imagination is a kind of mental lubrication which allows music to glide into being. When students have grasped this idea it makes all the difference to the sound they produce.

As well as helping the music to 'begin', it's also beneficial to have something to focus on during that strange limbo at the start of a performance, during which many self-conscious players wrestle with a tangle of thoughts often peripheral to the music itself. How consoling, then, to put your effort instead into imagining that a wave of music is coming towards you, and that when the crest of the wave arrives, you will be swept along on it. Then silence can be a beautiful upbeat to music.

Light and heavy

I was recently inspired by reading that scientists have shown it's possible for sound waves to counteract the effects of gravity. Yes, they did mean something very specific under experimental conditions, but why ignore a wonderful opportunity for an analogy? I took the opportunity to imagine sound waves counteracting gravity, making light music.

Light music has always been an important part of my musical life. My family was keen on light music of the dance band variety (Victor Sylvester), the American crooners (Bing Crosby) or the Saturday night light-entertainment television programmes (Russ Conway, Mrs Mills, Billy Cotton, the Black and White Minstrels, Eric and Ernie's songs). My father liked Victorian music hall and had an extensive repertoire of comic and sentimental music hall songs which he sang to us at bedtime. I've tried to import the composers of the American Songbook (Gershwin, Cole Porter, Irving Berlin, Jerome Kern, Lorenz Hart, Duke Ellington) into piano recitals as encores. I've done improvisations on songs by Edith Piaf, The Beatles, Billy Joel, Stevie Wonder in concerts. I've played in Astor Piazzolla evenings. I've done stints in cocktail bars. I've recorded Billy Mayerl's delightful salon music from the 1920s.

I love jazz and listen to it most evenings when I'm at home. Not that I consider it light music; I'm well aware of its potential seriousness. Early in my career I took some time off to study jazz, spending a semester at the New England Conservatory and having lessons with Jaki Byard, a wonderful African-American jazz pianist. When the Greater London Arts Association had a Young Jazz Musician of the Year competition in the early 1980s, I was one of the winners. I probably would have taken jazz further, except that I couldn't quite find my footing in the jazz world of the time. Some combination of my classical training, university background, 'Protestant work ethic' and the fact that I'm a woman seemed to put me outside the fold. To my disappointment I didn't seem to fit in, at least in the circles I tried to join. Other women jazz players have said the same thing – the marvellous saxophonist Barbara Thompson, in an interview for the Open University, spoke of her sense of 'not fitting in' to the jazz scene. Around that time I also tried to get into the session world in London (because playing for adverts, jingles, TV and film music was much more lucrative than classical music), but the small coterie of sought-after session pianists at the time were men and seemed determined to keep it that way.

I mention all this just to show that I have nothing against popular or light music, and might have taken that career path had circumstances been different. In fact, I esteem light music very highly indeed. 'Light' is not really the right word for something so graceful and touching. Nor is it helpful to imply a comparison with 'heavy' music, the classical music in counterpoint to which 'light' music was so named. If I had to choose which experience I was most pleased to have been able to offer listeners, the profundity of Beethoven or the delight of Billy Mayerl, I would choose Beethoven, but it's a close-run thing – not because of which music I think is 'better', but because of people's responses. It's still the case, I think, that I've had more letters about Billy Mayerl's music than on any other single topic. The way people describe what it means to them makes it clear that although it's 'light', it can also be balm to their souls in a way they appreciate because it is so clearly unpatronising.

I've often had a feeling that when classical music and popular music began their disastrous split at the start of the twentieth century, when Schoenberg and the Second Viennese School led the way into 'modern music', a certain vein of composing went, as it were, to the left while

Schoenberg & Co. went to the right. When I listen to the beautifully constructed, harmonically and rhythmically subtle songs of writers like Porter, Kern, Gershwin and Hart, I feel that they are really the people who represent the continuous line from late-Romantic music. They were the ones who remained interested in being friends with their listeners. I can understand why violinist Fritz Kreisler once allegedly said that if he had his career over again, he would devote himself to light music. People's reaction to light music is so pleasant and straightforwardly appreciative, whereas the reaction to classical music is always more complex. And it's not true that light music is trivial. It can express subtle emotions, and people choose it to express their feelings on many apparently 'serious' occasions.

I enjoyed all my early encounters with light music. However, once I started coming across pieces of classical music, in the form of a Readers' Digest LP box set of 'your favourite classical music', I felt that this kind of music offered something more, and I grasped at it. In a way it was like going from reading a comic to reading a fine novel. I became aware that music could tell a longer story, contain more layers, map out a more varied landscape, take you with it on a journey you couldn't predict. It was music which seemed to set itself a more difficult task and to live up to the task. I felt my horizons expanding.

This change had nothing to do with any social component. I liked the music and the skill of the playing. I had no idea of what kind of lives the composers led, or where in society they stood. I made no association between classical music and social class, for I knew nothing about such links, if indeed there were any. At that point I'd never been to a classical concert or met a classical musician, and nor had anyone else in my household. It was quite a long time before I came across the notion that classical music is 'elitist', and I admit that it always puzzled me. For me as a music-loving child it was nothing to do with that. We didn't have a piano in our house, and a piano was only acquired in response to suggestions made by the parents of my school-friends, in whose houses I'd been trying to play the piano. I don't remember this myself, but my interest must have been striking enough for my parents to decide to be brave and buy a piano.

My first piano lessons were with a neighbourhood piano teacher who lived down the road in a bungalow like ours. His front room had an upright piano in it, as ours did. When I went for my lessons, nothing whispered to me, 'Aren't you getting above your station?' Perhaps my most important childhood piano teacher, Mary Moore, represented (with her Blüthner and Bechstein grand pianos) a more cultured lifestyle than any I had come into contact with before, but I didn't associate her lifestyle with the music I was learning – it just seemed something to do with her, not with *the music* as such. When I had progressed enough to be asked to perform piano pieces at school, and was praised by my teacher, I did notice the tone of my classmates' comments: 'You think you're so posh, just because you can *play the piano*', one or two of them would say with a sneer. 'Snobby classical music.' At the time I had no real idea of what they were talking about, and neither did they, probably; they must have been echoing something that had been said at home. Why would I think I was 'posh' because I could play the piano? It didn't make sense. I wasn't from a posh background and they knew it. It felt as if there was a subtext to playing the piano, or at least to playing classical piano music, which had never been explained to me.

When I was nearing my teenage years, The Beatles burst onto the scene. In our house we didn't buy pop records, but I heard The Beatles on television. I liked their music, which was melodious, cheery and cheeky, and easy to relate to. It struck me as a cross between George Formby and Elvis, with a distinctively British twist. It was easy to memorise by ear and play on the piano. Their songs had amusing lyrics, sweet harmony changes and fun instrumentation, with instruments borrowed from the symphony orchestra. The Beatles' cute Liverpool accents made an exciting change from the measured voices we usually heard on TV and radio. I remember staying up late to hear 'Penny Lane' and 'Strawberry Fields' being discussed on a culture programme. So far, so good; I welcomed The Beatles into my musical world. Where I couldn't quite follow, however, was when young womanhood began screaming and fainting at their concerts. This too I watched with some amazement on television. Vast crowds of swooning girls not much older than me were screaming, wailing and sobbing so loudly that the Fab Four were more or less inaudible. I saw a look in the girls' eyes that I had never seen on the faces of any other crowd. My mother (a trained nurse) saw it too and was appalled. Medical personnel were carting away those who had actually passed out with excitement. What was going on? Clearly the response was not really about the music, because you couldn't hear the music above the screaming.

Even had it been audible, it seemed to me that the music itself did not justify this type of response. I couldn't feel the connection between the fairly straightforward music and the passionate response. Yes, it was very likeable – I liked it too – but why were people's eyes rolling back into their heads? Of course The Beatles had tapped into a hitherto unknown potential for mass ecstasy among British teenagers; it was everyone's first glimpse of 'teen power', perhaps surprising even The Beatles as they strummed their way to being 'more popular than Jesus', as Lennon joked in 1966. It was the beginning of a change in culture. And before long my classmates were dividing up into those who liked John, those who liked Paul, those who liked George and those who liked Ringo. We wrote the appropriate name on our pencil cases and on the covers of our textbooks. We were little tribes of John or Paul supporters. I was proud to buy Lennon's slim volumes of poetry, savour his dry humour and think of myself as 'groovy'.

From The Beatles I moved on to liking other melodious popular music such as Bob Dylan, Simon and Garfunkel, the Beach Boys, Carole King, James Taylor, Stevie Wonder, Nina Simone, Janis Joplin. I liked traditional jazz, 'gypsy' jazz, popular jazz and Broadway; Louis Armstrong, Sinatra and Ella Fitzgerald, Duke Ellington, Erroll Garner, Art Tatum, Oscar Peterson, Django Reinhardt and the Hot Club de France. I loved MGM musicals and played their songs endlessly on the piano, singing along. I loved *The Sound of Music, Mary Poppins, West Side Story* and the Sondheim musicals. I was a fan of Jacques Loussier and his jazzed-up versions of Bach. I was fond of the Swingle Singers and close-harmony groups; of Nana Mouskouri and Georges Moustaki. Later on I developed a taste for groups like Pink Floyd, Weather Report and Queen. I could 'do' the whole of

'Bohemian Rhapsody' with the best of them. I bought Joni Mitchell's dreamy folk-rock albums as they came out and played them endlessly on the LP record player I'd borrowed from the college library. For me there was no contradiction between liking classical music and liking this 'lighter' stuff. The music was inventive and satisfying, and it was clear that tremendous skill was involved in performing it. It may not have moved me as much as classical music did at its best, but it gave me a lot of what I hoped for from music. And it was a plus point that liking it didn't have to be justified to anyone. All your friends were interested in pop music too. You never saw That Look which you witnessed on their faces when friendship obliged them to come and hear classical concerts.

So why didn't I find light music as deeply satisfying as classical music? Most of the popular music I liked was based on 'the song', a tightly constructed piece of three or four minutes, designed for dancing to, as an entertaining interlude, or as a lyrical moment within a spoken narrative. As such, these songs had limited opportunity to unfold. In fact, their aim was the opposite: to give an intense hit of emotion and sweetness. They packed an amazing amount into a short span, but it was not their goal to contemplate in a leisurely manner, to mull over the musical material and let it wander into distant regions from which it might return having been changed by its experiences. It was just a different sort of thing. I found that short songs could easily arouse my interest and entertain me for a few minutes, but then they let me go and vanished. The music I was learning in my piano lessons was more like a long poem or a good book. Its duration alone offered opportunities which were not really part of popular music's ambitions, even though there were some artists and groups who developed extended pieces on their albums. I enjoyed what seemed to me the greater range and depth of classical pieces. Perhaps this was largely a matter of temperament: a girl who liked to stare into space and ponder things was set up by nature to appreciate the 'long-form' meditations of classical music. It was also a matter of instrumentation. The piano was my instrument, but it didn't figure much in the new popular music I collected, and indeed lots of amplified electric-guitar-and-drums music sounded a bit silly when I tried to play it on the piano. In classical music, on the other hand, the piano had been king for a long time. Acres of wonderful music had been written specifically for it.

Being immersed in serious music (classical or jazz, notated or improvised) has trained me to love the way that music can unfold in time, illuminating a process of thinking, of transforming cells of musical material. As a musician you can enter into this process and 'think along' with it. This is an important opportunity for anyone with an enquiring mind. Everyday life contains many set-piece transactions which people pass through almost on automatic pilot, using long-agreed etiquette guidelines to indicate what should be said and when. New thoughts or responses to those situations are surplus to requirements, so people with lots of new thoughts will often find there's not much outlet for them. Interpreting and performing great music, on the other hand, requires active and detailed engagement as well as a well-developed sense of perspective which helps you to give each phrase its proper context within the whole. There is plenty to think about and ample reason to think about it. Equally importantly, you have to learn how to feel as well as think the musical material, because it speaks to heart as well as head. In many ways it's actually a relief to be engaged in a kind of music which doesn't 'play itself', which requires the player's dedication, and which yields up more and more to anyone prepared to make the effort. The meaning is often generated as the music moves along; its process is one of engaging with the musical material in a state of transformation. There may be well-known shapes or structures underlying such music, but it can't be written to a formula.

As a teenager I became uncomfortably aware that 'classical music' was feared or resented by quite a few people. I saw it all the time in people's reactions to news of my musical activities. The idea of coming to a concert seemed to make them anxious. It was clear that classical music was not regarded as open to all. Anyone with serious classical ambitions was stepping aside from the circle where 'everyone' crowded together to listen to the new 1960s pop radio stations, Radio Caroline and then BBC Radio 1. These were aimed at young audiences, thrilled and intoxicated by the idea that there was a kind of music which 'belonged' to them and, even better, was disapproved of by adults. It appeared that classical music, on the other hand, didn't even belong to ordinary people, let alone young ones. I was puzzled by this. Where did the idea come from that classical music was not for everyone? The music itself seemed innocent of any such judgement. I couldn't find any trace of it in Schumann's *Kinderszenen*, Grieg's *Lyric Pieces* or Chopin's Nocturnes. I couldn't detect any 'exclusiveness' in Mozart's piano concertos, Bach's Inventions or Beethoven's sonatas. There was no disdain lurking in the pages of my Strauss waltzes or the albums of Delibes and Tchaikovsky ballet music. Why did people say it was 'snobby'?

Most of my university friends had had similar experiences. We had discovered classical music in different ways, and liked it for itself rather than for anything it might have represented to adults. We'd all stumbled upon the fact that a love for classical music could be a bit of a social handicap. In my teenage school years, all the talk about music was based on whatever BBC Radio 1 was featuring that week. I was never 'allowed' to say what I'd heard at the Friday night symphony concerts, or if I did, my remarks were greeted with indifference or scornful smiles. By the time I left school I had got used to passing over my musical studies in silence. One of the pleasant surprises about university was that I suddenly found myself among people who, like me, had learned to keep quiet about their liking for classical music. Now suddenly we discovered one another as kindred spirits. It was liberating to find myself in a new place where everyone living on my corridor had their record player and their favourite classical records with them, and was looking forward to singing or playing in all sorts of musical ventures, or at least to attending concerts. For the first time, my piano-playing was an asset, not something to hide.

In history classes I learned that a lot of the music I particularly loved had been written for the court or the church, performed for a rather specialised audience of educated or aristocratic people. Composers (rarely posh or affluent themselves) had mostly had to rely on wealthy patrons and their wealthy friends, who were the audience and sometimes the performers for the newly written pieces. Playing the piano was considered an important accomplishment for the young, particularly the daughters of socially ambitious families. The story of the piano, an instrument which cost money to buy and more money to have lessons on, was bound up with the history of people who could afford such luxuries and had leisure to practise. The poor did not spend their evenings accompanying one another in tasteful performances of songs or chamber music. As I came from a working family I began to worry about what would have happened to me had I been born in a hovel or in an era when there would not have been the slightest chance of my ever having a piano to play, or having been allowed to play it. All this threw some light on why classical music was regarded as belonging to 'them'.

I was grateful not to have known any of this at the start, because my conscience is clear: I liked classical music for its own sake. This recollection has been very useful to me in what sometimes feels like a rising tide of antagonism towards so-called 'elitist' music. The tide has risen against a background of neglect of music in school education, though there are some striking exceptions. Children don't come across classical music as a matter of course, and in many schools, music lessons have been driven into the sphere of private enterprise, where the extra expense has led to music lessons acquiring a 'luxury' image. This has been very unfortunate. Musical education of all kinds should be as central to the school curriculum as the famous 'Three Rs' of 'reading, 'riting and 'rithmetic' – because study after study has proved the benefits of music, particularly of making music yourself. Every child should be offered opportunities to play and sing, get involved in youth orchestras and bands and groups and choirs. They should be offered good music of all kinds, with no judgements made about whom it belongs to. What would Bach or Mozart say if you accused them of trying to shut people out from their music? They would be horrified. Like all great musicians, they wanted to appeal to human souls of every kind.

Now this is not to say that when you go to classical concerts you do not see a rather homogeneous audience of educated, culture-loving people, but this is for reasons quite separate from the music itself. I personally would like my audiences to be more varied than they have been for the past couple of decades. Like most of my colleagues I worry when I look out from the stage over a sea of silver-haired heads, and I worry about how to bring in younger, more multi-cultural audiences. The typical classical audience does have a certain look to it. There are exceptions, such as The Proms, London's summer festival of concerts in the Royal Albert Hall, which attracts an enormous audience of all ages, but outside of such rarities, classical audiences are often very 'niche'. People often say that classical music is something that you 'come to' when you're more mature, but people won't tuck it away in the back of their minds if they've never come across it in the first place. You can only mature a taste for something you've tasted. I feel it's very dangerous to leave classical music off the agenda and say that people can educate themselves in it later if they wish, once they are old and wise enough to appreciate it. Maybe a few people manage it, but the majority simply never encounter any kind of music other than popular. I have lots of classical-musician friends who, guided partly by their children, have embraced all sorts of other musical forms, at least as listeners. I don't see much traffic in the reverse direction, of adults deciding that they want to explore classical music for the first time.

I've never understood why, alone amongst the arts, it is acceptable to know nothing about classical music. Any British person with pretensions to culture will have been educated to some degree at school about the theatre, literature and the visual arts, and will continue to take an interest in those things, but it seems fine to be ignorant of classical music. Commentators will write in the press about how excited or proud they are to have tickets for this or that famous actor's Shakespeare performance, to be going to the premiere of an art-house movie, or to have been in the queue to buy so-and-so's latest novel, but you don't hear them saying how excited they are to have tickets for Haitink's Beethoven Nine or Harnoncourt's *Fidelio*. Books, films, art exhibitions and plays are standard dinner party topics, but the subject of classical music rarely comes up. 'Music' means today's popular music. This is so despite the fact that 'old' paintings, 'old' theatre plays

and 'old' books are comfortably revered. Nobody thinks the Globe
Theatre is geeky for choosing *Hamlet* as the play to perform on its
two-year-long tour of the world.

Exhibitions of 'old' art attract huge crowds and are so popular that
timed tickets have to be allocated, even for somewhat obscure or challenging things like (to take some London examples) the Tutankhamun
exhibition, the Chinese Terracotta Warriors, the 'Bronze' exhibition,
the British Museum's 'Ice Age' exhibition or its 'Life and Death in
Pompeii and Herculaneum' exhibition. Few of these are exactly 'easy
listening'. They all require effort on the part of the viewer, a willing-
ness to be taught some history and context. The art is often centuries,
even millennia, old. Strangely, that hasn't made it unpopular. But 'old'
music has been moved to the margins, its oldness is cited as a reason
why it should accept defeat gracefully. Why classical music should be
singled out for this kind of discrimination I don't understand.

Somewhere along the way I lost the feeling that classical music and
popular music were coexisting amicably in my life. I used to picture
myself standing between two equally broad flowing rivers, one of classical and one of light music. I could dip into one or the other. But
that balance was lost when popular music became truly predominant.
As it filled the airwaves and the pages of newspapers and magazines, I
started to feel that classical music and musicians were being eclipsed by
something we'd never seen before, a tsunami of 'pop'. We had never
seen such publicity machines. Never before had we seen 'celebrities'
manufactured with such ease and speed, and with so little apparent
link to musical skill or content. Image was paramount and it seemed
that more effort was expended on the publicity than on the music
itself. Songs became famous for their videos, which people imitated
joyfully at parties and in pubs. TV channels sprang up playing music
videos all day long. The disco and the club scene arose, arousing an
insatiable appetite for 'dance music' of a new kind. It was puzzling to
people like me who preferred a bit of swing in their dance music; the
new 'dance' genre seemed quite primitive and thumping in comparison, exhausting rather than enlivening. Music for teenagers lost the
edge of rebellion against the Establishment and gradually became the

Establishment itself. I realised this was so when British prime ministers started identifying with pop groups and inviting them to tea in Downing Street. Now we often hear commentators using the phrase 'pop royalty', a potent combination of words surely indicating that the most celebrated pop artists have been granted Establishment status.

Parallel to these developments came the hunger for loud music – really, really loud amplified music. Clubs and gigs seemed to compete to have the most powerful sound systems and the biggest speakers. The loudness of music at gigs became a draw in itself, a draw which persists despite evidence that large numbers of people suffer some degree of hearing damage as a result. The fact that young people consider hearing loss an acceptable price to pay for having been at certain celebrated gigs tells you all you need to know about the domination of pop. Had this degree of hearing damage happened outside of pop music, it might have been regarded as assault. Extreme volume has, indeed, been used by the military as a weapon and a form of torture, yet there is a generation of young people willing to consider loud music a sensory thrill and seek it out as an experience. How could it be acceptable to go to a rock concert and come out with tinnitus? But people did and still do.

All this was bewildering to witness from the sidelines. I resented the way that amplified music, played on electronic instruments, became the norm. In comparison, classical music with its acoustic instruments began to seem tiny and fragile, powered only by the human arm or hand. Classical musicians started to feel as though towering edifices of pop had been built around them, blocking out the light. (I imagine jazz musicians must have felt something similar.) I lost the sense I previously had of the benign partnership between classical ('heavy') and 'light' music. 'Light' didn't seem to be the right word for something as loud, driving and aggressive as commercial pop/rock. It was almost as if 'light' and 'heavy' had swapped places. If anything was 'heavy', it was surely the pounding amplified beat of pop and rock music. If anything was 'light', it was now classical music, whose mode of expression seemed delicate and self-effacing in comparison. I felt as if something had been lost.

Of course rock music can be extremely sophisticated, and some classical musicians are also rock fans – a university music lecturer told me recently that many of his students were keener on rock than on classical – but many others feel pushed aside by pop culture. Our long training in the subtleties of 'Western art music' has unfitted us to be passive customers of the pop machine. If you spend your childhood years learning week after week and bit by bit about music theory, harmony and counterpoint, being taught about word-setting and its musicality, analysing pieces of music to see how they do what they do – not to mention the slow process of mastering an instrument – well, it develops your taste for complexity. It feels a bit like emerging from an apprenticeship in Leonardo da Vinci's studio to find that people are flinging a few daubs of primary colour at a canvas and becoming rich and famous overnight for it. Are we jealous of their success? Yes, of course. But it also makes us feel sad and a bit eccentric for having invested so much in a type of music which is being slowly pushed into the margins. The music hasn't changed, but society seems to be looking the other way. Sometimes it feels as if classical music has subtly morphed into a kind of 'outsider art'.

When I consider all the forms of folk and ethnic music, and how rich and varied they are, I find it disappointing that by far the most globally successful types of music are the various genres of pop/rock emanating mostly from the USA and the UK and now spread around the world. Much of today's pop music is a manufactured genre relying on formulas, which makes its extravagant commercial success even harder to digest. It is not a genuine outgrowth of previous musical forms but merely an appropriation of them. I think I could live much more easily with globally dominant flamenco or Irish folk music or Burundi drumming, Malian praise songs or Indian raga – ancient forms which bring with them a sense of place and a compelling national spirit. You might object to this and say that surely pop music has grown out of blues and ragtime, but even though it may have started off that way, it has long since moved away from the 'spirit' and emotional integrity of blues. There are exceptions, of course: artists like Amy Winehouse who have drawn inspiration from jazz and blues. Today, however, it often seems to me that the basic chords and the 12-bar form are all that blues and pop have in common.

We live in a world in which everything seems to be speeding up, or at any rate is delivered in easily digestible nuggets, each supplanted by the next at greater speed. We flick restlessly from one thing to another, grazing on bite-size summaries as they scroll across the bottom of our screens. Vast online libraries of recorded music enable us to flick from one piece to another without even bothering to wait for the end of a three-minute song, let alone a symphony. It has never been easier for people to explore the musical archives of the past, and perhaps for that very reason, they don't do it. My students are often surprisingly hazy about music and musicians of the past, although the information and the recordings are just a click away. As one of my teaching colleagues said recently, 'Considering that they live in "the information age", they're surprisingly ill-informed!'

It's almost as though the sheer availability of information has somehow come to supplant knowledge itself; people seem to feel that because they *could* find out anything in a fraction of a second, that's pretty much the same as knowing it. They don't see the point of having things in their memory when electronic memories can store so much more and supply it to them at any moment and in any location. Things seem to be shrinking, getting cheaper, less nutritious and more disposable. The phrase 'everything comes to those who wait' often seems like outmoded advice in a world which disregards loyalty and prioritises new customers. Perhaps the three-minute song will shrink to the one-minute song and finally to a single snort of sound which people inhale like addicts.

In Scotland (where I grew up) there's an ancient, highly developed tradition of pibroch (piobaireachd) – music played on the pibroch, a form of bagpipes. Today the bagpipes are associated with medleys of Scottish tunes played on ceremonial occasions, at military tattoos and for tourists looking for photo-opportunities. However, piobaireachd is an old art-form similar to the passacaglia or 'variation form' of classical music or jazz: a melody (often sad) is used as the basis for gradual elaboration, resulting in a lengthy meditation on the tune. Players and listeners alike hold the shape of the tune in their minds through all the twists and turns of the exploration. 'Entertainment' in the modern sense has nothing to do with it; this is an attempt to build something complex and illuminating.

In the Gaelic tradition there is a distinction between this kind of music and tunes simply used for dancing or singing; the long-form is called 'big music', while the other is 'small music'. I use this example to explain what I felt I was witnessing in the changing musical landscape: the triumph of 'small music'. It's anything but small, of course, in terms of commercial power and audience numbers. Its artists have fan-bases whose obsessive support is a wonder. It's not 'small' in cultural importance, as I discovered when I wrote something sniffy about it in a newspaper article and was told, 'You can't say that. Too many of our readers love this stuff.' My remarks were cut: censored, I felt, for political correctness. Nevertheless I started to feel it was important to remember that a lot of this music is what in the old Gaelic tradition would be classed as 'small music'. That doesn't mean that small music is not the dominant trend at the moment. Clearly it is. But it is not 'big music' in terms of what it tries to do artistically, nor in terms of the mind-space it occupies.

As for the long-acquired training of the classical musician, such craft seems to have sunk in popular estimation, and this is part of a more general trend. Talent shows on television have encouraged people to feel they can have a go at something and become celebrities almost overnight with no training. In fact, evidence of 'training' (such as a controlled vibrato in the voice) is often greeted with mocking whoops from the audience. It often seems as if an ounce of talent has become more laudable and lovable than a ton of it. There's some kind of weirdly inverse relationship between preparation and reward which I daresay would baffle many of the musicians of ages past. In such an atmosphere, how are young people to be persuaded that it is worth tackling the long and complex training to play classical music?

On the plus side, counter-movements seem to be arising in protest against speediness and disposability. People are starting to be interested in home cooking, in organic vegetables, in community projects. They want to make their own sourdough bread, write their own creative fiction and sing together in choirs. They seem to feel the need to resist the speeding-up and trivialising of so many things. When I started writing this chapter I asked a random selection of people whether they had been introduced to classical music, or indeed any other types of long-form music, when they were at school. The answers were not reassuring. Even older people said 'not much' and younger people sometimes said 'not at all'. Some of the younger ones told me that with computer programs it was possible to get a school qualification in music without reading music, playing an instrument or knowing anything about the history of music. Introductions to classical music had come about mainly through the efforts of parents, but of course if parents themselves have not been exposed to this kind of music, they won't think of introducing it to their children.

I find all this baffling at a time when research keeps proving that involvement in classical music, especially if you play it yourself, has beneficial effects on the brain. Singing in choirs has received a lot of good press lately, partly thanks to the efforts of TV choirmaster Gareth Malone who has enabled lots of people to discover how good it feels to make music together with others and to realise that they are 'musical' when they had once thought they weren't. Even listening to music has beneficial effects, and more mysteriously, just *imagining* music can do us almost as much good. Scientists keep telling us that classical music can promote concentration, improve socialisation, help people to prepare for operations, assist them in recovering from illness, alleviate depression, and there's a wealth of anecdotal evidence from people who've stumbled upon those proofs for themselves. Classical music seems to bring a whole raft of benefits you'd think any education minister would be desperate to make part of the National Curriculum. Surely music should be as central to education as literature, maths or sport? I don't really care what kind of music is central to the curriculum as long as it is complex music, music with heart and soul, music which is more than a simple three-minute song written to a computer program. It should be music which is rewarding to learn and satisfying to be involved in. For me, no kind of music has yet proved as satisfying as 'classical', but I'd be happy for any good music to be in children's lives.

Or perhaps our approach should be more counter-intuitive. I heard recently about the ancient tradition of Javanese puppet theatre, where the craft of puppetry is often handed down from one generation to another in the same family. Young people are not entrusted with the puppets; they have to wait years to be initiated into the mystery of how to handle them. The puppets are not playthings, and are treated with great respect. Audiences often stay up all night to watch performances, and the puppeteers have high status. I heard of one family of specialist puppeteers where the young son had been strictly forbidden to touch the puppets or handle them on his own when there was nobody else about. Naturally he sneaked into the puppet cupboard to have a go when nobody was looking and, over time, working in secret, was able to copy what he had seen older members of the family do when they put on performances. Eventually came the long-awaited moment when he was allowed to begin his formal training. At that point he confessed that he already knew how to handle the puppets and make them speak, only to have his proud father announce that he had been expecting that to happen, and that it was always so. This was an intriguing example of 'less is more'. It made me think that perhaps the trick of boosting the image of classical music would be to ban the young from listening to any whatsoever.

Music hath charms

A few years ago I became intrigued by the number of people coming up to me after concerts and telling me that listening to the music had helped them to feel better. Sometimes they were quite specific. They mentioned having felt unwell at work, feeling unsure if they ought to go to the concert or just go straight home instead and rest. They said that they took their seats in a pessimistic frame of mind, were drawn in by the music, caught up by the interaction between the musicians, somehow soothed by the effect of the music and gradually realised that the horrible headache had gone, the fatigue had lifted, that they were no longer feeling so down about whatever it was that had been on their minds.

I had often been aware of the power of music to 'soothe a savage breast', but it seemed that there was a crescendo of such remarks from members of the audience. It could have been that people had gradually come to trust me enough to share such thoughts with me. Yet by no means all of these remarks were made by people I knew; mostly they were made by strangers. Sometimes I received letters from people I didn't know, attesting to the power of music. I couldn't attribute the effect entirely to live music either, because sometimes they wrote about recordings. The experience had clearly been striking enough that people had been moved to pick up a pen and paper to write to me, a complete stranger, because I had played on the recording.

Around the same time I noticed a proliferation of features in the media about music's power to help in contexts such as education and medicine. Various kinds of researchers were becoming interested in it. It seemed that you didn't have to have any musical experience, or even consider yourself 'musical', to feel the benefits of one or other aspect of music (some seem particularly sensitive to melody, others to rhythm). Music, I learned, came before speech in human development, and we can't help but respond to music at a deep instinctive level. Speech itself has a musical element, of course. I had long known about the power of 'worksongs' throughout history to encourage and enliven soldiers on the march, slaves rowing big boats, peasants working in the fields, labourers working together at manual tasks. Singing as they worked or marched along seemed not only to bolster their physical stamina but to produce 'entrainment', the instinctive ability to move in synchrony with others.

I now started to be more aware of reports that listening to music, and more particularly playing or singing music, can enhance the development of a child's brain. Learning to distinguish the sound patterns in music can help a child with learning to read. Learning to hear your own sound pattern as distinct from the patterns played by others (the kind of skill you learn in any music group, such as an orchestra) is helpful in training children to pick out speech sounds against a background of noise. Teachers report that after children have been involved in music-making they are better able to concentrate in the classroom. Listening to music can improve fine motor coordination in activities like origami. Music can calm socially disruptive behaviour. In healthcare settings, it's reported that listening to carefully chosen music before an operation can reduce anxiety. I had an enjoyable correspondence with an eye surgeon, a skilled pianist, who had brought his own piano into the hospital in order to play music to some of his own patients before eye operations. He found that their blood pressure, heart rate and breathing rate all decreased after listening to soothing piano music. Patients reported that the whole experience of the operation was much less stressful than they had anticipated.

Listening to music after an operation can, it seems, reduce the time spent in recovery and convalescence. Patients suffering from depression can alleviate their moods with the right kind of music, both by listening and by joining in music-making with others. Those with Alzheimer's and other kinds of dementia, whose memories for words, times and places are very impaired, are often remarkably receptive to music, 'coming alive' when it is played to them and being able to remember long stretches of music when they are unable to recall long stretches of anything else. I saw for myself that my father, though unable to recall events from the past, still had a lively recollection of tunes he learned in his youth and was able to sing many verses with all the words intact. Parkinson's sufferers appear to gain moments of relief from their symptoms while listening to or making music. Music's ability to make people want to dance, tap their feet or move their bodies in time is being harnessed in all sorts of contexts from pre-natal 'stimulation' to helping the elderly to keep mobile. Taking up a musical instrument, no matter how late in life, was reported by a University of St Andrews study in 2013 to stave off and even to reverse age-related cognitive decline. In September 2013 the *British Medical Journal* reported a study which suggested that older professional musicians had cognitive advantages. Researchers in Toronto had compared professional musicians with non-musicians of similar age (mean age sixty), education, vocabulary and general health. 'In almost all tests of cognitive function, the musicians did better' was their cheering conclusion.

In November 2013, the *Journal of Neurological Science* reported that older adults aged fifty-five to seventy-six who took music lessons during childhood seem to have a faster brain response to speech than those who never played an instrument, and this was true even if they had not picked up an instrument for forty years. The study was carried out at Northwestern University and led by Nina Kraus, who said that 'It suggests the importance of music education for children today, and for healthy aging decades from now.'

Even animals appear to be susceptible to music. Cows are said to give more milk when music is played in their milking sheds. Veterinary hospitals report that music can calm agitated dogs and cats, lower their heart rate and their respiration rate. Zoos report that many animals respond positively to music, though it has to be music tailored to their hearing ranges and the pitch of their vocalisations. For music to be therapeutic, whether for animals or humans, it has to have the right kind of pacing and trajectory, and the right kind of affirmative qualities. The music found to be most effective was almost always classical, though there were positive reports about 'new age' sound collages using electronic sounds to evoke the forest and the ocean, the waves and the wind, and so on. I had come across these 'rhythms of life' compilations when sitting in the waiting rooms or lying on the treatment couches of various physiotherapists. Perhaps I was not the ideal subject, but for me they had the opposite effect of the one intended, setting my nerves a-jangle with their clumsy collages of whooshing ocean sounds and choruses of soothing 'female voices' hovering at the edge of audibility. I disliked hearing beautiful music shorn of its context. I was far from lulled as I listened to Mendelssohn's 'Fingal's Cave' overture overlaid with Californian deep breathing. However, other patients sat peacefully beside me with their eyes closed, so I concluded that I was just being too fussy.

All around me were unsolicited declarations that classical music had beneficent powers. Could it be that classical music, though struggling to generate new audiences, was beginning to be recognised by a different group of people as a repository of healing potential? I started to think it would be interesting to gather together all these bits of evidence to mount a defence of classical music as something we must preserve for the sake of qualities only now becoming widely appreciated by the community. Of course, there are several very persuasive books written on the subject already, for example by Oliver Sacks, whom I've admired ever since *The Man Who Mistook His Wife for a Hat* came out in 1985. His 2007 book *Musicophilia* is a collection of fascinating anecdotes and expert speculation about the effect of music on the brain and nervous system. Many of his observations echo my own experience of what listeners have said to me about the effect of music.

I realised that I knew a number of medical experts who could tell me things, or give me introductions to people who specialised in various fields of research. I was particularly keen to talk to neurologists and scientists studying how music is dealt with by the brain. Using various contacts, I was able to set up a round of interviews, and I set off with notebook in hand. As it turned out, the scientists were sceptical about my project. They were convinced that it was beyond the powers of a layperson to account for the effect of music on the brain, still a mystery even to those most deeply knowledgeable about how the brain works. They explained to me that although techniques such as magnetic resonance imaging have enabled researchers to see how areas of the brain 'light up' in response to music, this is not as revelatory as the general public might believe, because nobody really knows what that lighting-up activity really *means*. They explained that music seems to have a uniquely powerful effect in that it appears to stimulate every part of the brain. This indicates that left and right hemispheres are coordinating, that music appeals to 'activity centres' of different kinds and seems to excite responses from spatial and movement as well as verbal and memory centres. Many human activities excite a cerebral response focused in a particular part of the brain but, if I understood correctly, music seems to *unite* different parts of the brain, primitive as well as sophisticated. So far, so good. Beyond that simple summary, however, the scientists I spoke to were unanimous in saying that the actual science was a subject of fundamental disagreement between them and still in its infancy as a body of knowledge.

It's probably a fool's task to try to pin down exactly how music works, partly because the science is still unclear and partly because any individual's response to music is such a complex matter, with cultural components which make the response very difficult to measure. The more I thought about it, the more I realised it would be hard to say anything precise or universally applicable about music and health. Perhaps words were the wrong medium. On the other hand, I didn't want (nor did I have the skill) to produce a dossier of electro-chemical data and charts of neural connections. I felt the scientists were probably right to discourage me. I began to tell my friends that I was abandoning the idea of writing about music and health. At which point a number of people – all women, as it happened – begged me not to drop the project. They said they were sure that music had spiritual and aesthetic powers which could affect the body and the mind. They had experienced it for themselves, or had known people who had experienced it. It might be hard to analyse, but that didn't mean it wasn't real and important. As for the idea that such a book 'could only be anecdote and speculation', they asked what was wrong with that. Anecdote and speculation could be so thought-provoking and evocative.

At the time I had been thinking more than usual about music and health because of Jacob Barnes, a young pianist I had got to know on various chamber music courses. I didn't know him well, but he struck me as a type of musician similar to me, someone who had 'got the point' of chamber music straight away and was in his element when collaborating with others. He was an excellent musician, a gifted pianist and an avid sight-reader, very popular on music courses because of his enormous appetite for music. He was always keen to play anything and everything, new or old repertoire, with anyone who wanted to play chamber music. He could have opted for a career as a solo pianist, but his heart was in chamber music. This was sufficiently unusual for me to follow his progress with sympathetic interest, and he occasionally came to my house for a lesson.

Unfortunately, when he was just a first-year student at the Royal Academy of Music in London he developed flu-like symptoms which refused to go away, and eventually he was diagnosed with leukaemia. He rapidly became very unwell and underwent a series of very unpleasant treatments which at times interfered with his ability to play music, or even to hear it. Whenever he was well enough, he returned to playing the piano and, if possible, to playing chamber music. He maintained that the prospect of playing music was one of the most important things keeping him going, and his family felt he was right. His friends would arrange to go and play music with him when he was feeling up to it. As his illness developed and he became weaker, his doctors commented that he was withstanding the effects of the treatment with surprising strength. They speculated that 'it's music which is keeping you with us'. Everyone in his circle was deeply impressed by the idea that music could be healing. Around this time, I had one of my interviews with a medical expert, in this case an eminent brain surgeon. I told him about Jacob, and said we all hoped that music was proving to be a powerful form of treatment in its own right, especially for one so sensitive to it. The brain surgeon gently put me right, explaining that while music was undoubtedly good for the spirit, there was no way that music could vanquish such a pitiless disease. The illness would take its course. Music was not to be ranked with chemotherapy or steroids as a form of intervention. He sharply warned me against fuzzy New Age-ism which would make my claims look ridiculous.

Very sadly, he was right about Jacob, who died of his leukaemia not long afterwards. A few weeks before he died, when he was feeling well enough to take some lessons and even join in with some performances at the Royal Academy of Music, we met for lunch at the British Library. I asked Jacob if he would be willing to talk about the role of music in his fight against illness. He told me that when he was feeling most unwell, he did not want to hear any music. It was only in his phases of feeling better that music started to call to him again. He said that music was actually no help in his worst times; the prospect was not even alluring. He had come to associate music with *wellness*. This was its great power: that the prospect of playing music pulled him towards 'the world of the well'. Music was *not* a form of treatment; it was a light at the end of the tunnel. I was surprised, but I came to understand how powerful this experience must have been. Perhaps it was important in Jacob's case that he was a musician himself, not just a listener. He told me it had become clear to him that 'playing on your own means nothing' compared with making music with others. When he had the strength to play, his beloved chamber pieces were the ones he instinctively turned to, though his playing of solo pieces was remarkable enough in itself. It was, however, the prospect of sharing music with his friends that made him want to play again and gave him the greatest pleasure. 'Music is for sharing,' he said. His friends understood this and rose magnificently to the occasion whenever there was one. Jacob's passion was inspiring, and I felt that his grasp of the value and significance of chamber music showed an unusual maturity in one so young, especially when his pianistic gifts could easily have lured him onto a starrier path.

Although Jacob may have felt that illness and music-making dwelt in two separate realms, his condition nevertheless had an extraordinary effect on his playing. I was in the audience for a remarkable chamber concert he gave with friends in the last weeks of his life. His practice time had of course been restricted, and he was too fragile to have full control over the details of the piano part, but strangely this didn't detract in the least from the effect; instead, he seemed to have transcended 'mere notes' and to be alert and active at a deep structural level hidden from most of us. His playing that evening struck all the musicians in the audience as wise and insightful – a lesson in what to focus on. Illness had not created a barrier between him and music; in fact, it seemed to many of us as if it had somehow intensified his musical gifts.

I have known other people for whom music *was* very helpful when they were ill. I don't know if it is a coincidence that those people were not practising musicians themselves. They were music-lovers, concert-goers and record collectors. For some months I had a correspondence with a man (whom I never met in person) who was receiving cancer treatment. At his lowest ebb he found great consolation in listening to Beethoven's late string quartets, often in the small hours of the night. He wrote that he found them a more accurate description of deep spiritual anguish than any other; Beethoven was able to express things which would be very difficult to put into words but made perfect sense as music, and indeed the music made him feel that Beethoven was speaking directly to him about things which they both understood. For this man, music was indeed a companion in a time of trouble, and I have heard from other people about the solace that listening to music gave them, or their relatives, during challenging episodes of their lives. Therefore I don't think that music is 'situated in the world of the well' for everyone. It probably depends partly on whether you are a musician yourself, on whether your illness has cut off your ability to play and struck at one of the roots of your relationship with music.

I do vividly remember an experience when I was on a concert tour in India, years ago. I fell ill with paratyphoid and was hospitalised in Delhi. When I was starting to feel better, my colleagues found a cassette player and brought me a tape of David Oistrakh playing the Sibelius Violin Concerto. The choice of music didn't have any particular significance – I think it just happened to be the only cassette of classical music they could get their hands on. I played it over and over again, and still remember the feeling that it was not just beautiful music – it was also some kind of ... how to put it? It was some kind of nourishment. It was not just music; it was a message, it was information. Information about what? It seemed to be reminding me that there were things to look forward to. My days in the hospital were dull and quiet, my thoughts muted. I was far from home and pretty depressed. The Sibelius Violin Concerto burst on me like a lively and detailed message from the world of the well.

When I began to mention to some of my professional colleagues that I was thinking of writing something about music's healing powers, they snorted bitterly and said that in their own cases, playing music had landed them in all sorts of trouble. 'Nearly killed me' was a phrase I heard several times in various guises, said 'jokingly' of course. They were racked with aches and pains as a result of playing their instruments. They were plagued by episodes of RSI (repetitive strain injury) during which they could not even stir a cooking pot with a wooden spoon, let alone play the violin. They suffered from all manner of nervous and psychological problems as a result of their performing careers. Some of them were taking beta blockers to enable them to get on stage, even if they were members of symphony orchestras with plenty of others to 'cover' for them. Many of my colleagues had regular appointments with chiropractors, masseurs and physiotherapists specialising in the hand, arm and back problems of performing musicians. Most instruments have to be held in the air, supported, or played by fingers, hands and arms twisted into unusual asymmetrical positions and held in those positions for hours at a stretch. Nature didn't intend people to play the violin, for example, though it is astonishing how good some can be at playing it, considering the angles their hands and arms have to adopt. Among my colleagues, cellists often had really sore knees. Double bass players had sore backs. Wind players had trouble with their teeth and jaws. Pianists had back problems from hunching over the piano and pounding the hard ivory keys for hours on end. As in other strenuous activities such as ballet or sport, it seems that, to the participants, the pressures of modern professionalism can come to obliterate the benefits of what they're engaged in.

It seemed that almost every instrument carried its own set of occupational hazards, and no doubt singers have their own problems too. Many of my instrumental colleagues commented that, far from healing them or maintaining them at optimum functioning, music had reduced them to nervous wrecks. I heard the 'nearly killed me' phrase again in a *Guardian* interview with Sarah Wills, a horn player in the Berlin Philharmonic when the orchestra came to Britain in 2011. She commented that belonging to such a great orchestra made her wake up every day feeling happy and proud, but that it was also very stressful, so stressful that she sometimes thought 'it will kill me'. This vividly illustrated the potent combination of good and bad stress in the life of a performing musician. Why would anyone persist in a line of work they sometimes thought would kill them? It could only be because the fear and anxiety were offset or surpassed by the deep thrill of achievement. I had had my own moments of wondering if I might be about to collapse in public after exerting myself to play a very fast, difficult or exciting piece; sometimes in the silence which followed such a piece my heart would beat so violently that I felt slightly ill. (It's happened to me recently after performing the finale of Schubert's E-flat Trio, the fastest movements of the Shostakovich Piano Quintet and Piano Trio, and the 'Pantoum' movement of Ravel's Piano Trio.) I realised that for many professional musicians, life in music was often a fine or precarious balance of ingredients, even a struggle between opposing forces. Becoming and remaining a professional musician was definitely not a simple matter of wishing to dream away your time while being marinated in lovely music.

I became aware that these days it is increasingly rare to see an elderly member of an orchestra. This is partly to do with retirement policies, but it is also due to today's orchestras' very high requirement for stamina and accuracy at all times. In the past, an older musician might have been retained in an orchestra, even if they were prone to the occasional slip, simply because everyone valued their good musicianship and their long service. (A few decades ago the Hallé Orchestra, for example, used to print asterisks beside the names of those of its players who had been awarded long-service medals.) Now there is less tolerance for 'the occasional slip', and older players feel less secure. Even younger players feel less secure once they discover how many recent music college graduates are snapping at their heels; these days there are often several hundred well-qualified applicants for a good orchestral job. The drop-out rate amongst orchestral players is partly linked to the punishing schedule that many of today's leading orchestras are forced to adopt, particularly in the UK. For an individual orchestral player, the lack of motivation to persevere in such a strenuous job may be linked to a sense of not being crucial to the event, and if they are not crucial, perhaps there is insufficient reason to put up with the demands for accuracy and dependability. I fully understand that many orchestral players are very proud of their orchestras, but they must also be aware that they are cogs in wheels, not driving the train.

I had my own struggle with stress, which is partly why I was so interested in the subject of music and health. My problem was irritable bowel syndrome, which I had suffered from ever since my teenage years. Some doctors called it 'spastic colon'. I was often felled by a nervous tummy and painful abdominal cramp in the run-up to a performance. Once the cramp took hold, it would usually 'lock in' until bedtime, or at least until I was able to lie flat for a long period. The cramp felt like a sheet of pain across my middle, often making it difficult to breathe properly. I had lots of tests done. Nothing dreadful was found, though my colonic spasms were clearly visible on medical scanners. Doctors reassured me that it was 'not an organic illness', though it often felt indistinguishable from one. They advised me to follow a high-fibre diet (which I did) and to reduce the stress in my life, easier said than done for a concert pianist. The pain was sometimes severe and impacted on my mood; 'irritable' was the right word for me as well as for the condition. There was very little I could do to alleviate a painful cramp once it had taken hold. If it happened on a concert day I had to make the best of it, knowing it would be 'locked in' for the rest of the day. The following morning the pain would be gone, though it left behind a ghostly after-effect, a feeling of being bruised and tender across my middle, 'as if I had been kicked by a horse', as I often put it to my family.

I had realised that one of the triggers for the pain was leaving too long a gap between meals. My feeling of hunger became more and more acute until it suddenly tipped over into abdominal pain. Unfortunately, long gaps between meals were built into my professional life. Travel plans often meant that we were en route across mealtimes. Also, most of my colleagues preferred not to eat until after the concert, so we tended to rehearse right up until close to the concert time, leaving just a short pause in which to get changed. Usually there wasn't enough time for me to have a meal during that pause, and in any case there was often no way of obtaining food in a concert hall. I took to bringing snacks in my suitcase to reduce the chance of a painful cramp being triggered by hunger before the concert began. Sometimes it helped to lie face-down on the floor, doing deep breathing exercises or stretching abdominal muscles, but not always. In any case, lying on the backstage floor in one's neatly ironed concert clothes was not conducive to a pleasing appearance on the platform. I often went onstage in some degree of pain or discomfort.

It wasn't only concerts that brought on the pain but any kind of stressful event, such as a meeting I was worried about, or a combative situation. I didn't associate the pain with music as such, but with the effort of 'public performance', be it when I had to force myself to speak up in an argument, give a talk, or play a demanding piano part. I knew better than to blame music, though when I realised that I was in some degree of pain for about eight out of every ten concerts, I had to wonder whether my body was telling me I was in the wrong job. Much as I looked forward to my concerts, my body kept informing me that I was literally knotted up about performance. Why did I press on? Music is very lovable and engrossing, of course. I enjoyed the feeling of communicating with musical partners and with audiences who liked us, and I got a tremendous buzz out of performances which went well, but it was also the case that having invested so much time and energy in it, I felt I couldn't turn back. As Macbeth says, 'I am in blood stepped in so far that, should I wade no more, returning were as tedious as go o'er.' That quote popped into my head from time to time. The situation was hard to discuss with friends because in the music profession, where so many are freelance, there's a strong taboo against admitting to health problems.

I knew a doctor who was a consultant to one of the big London orchestras, advising them on performance-related problems. He told me that all his orchestral patients implored him not to mention their health problems to any of their colleagues, or to anyone who might employ them. Some of them were going deaf because of 'workplace noise levels' (meaning the decibel levels produced by a symphony orchestra, especially by brass and percussion), but they didn't want anyone to know this and were training themselves to compensate for their advancing deafness by becoming more and more alert to visual clues, 'which', as my doctor friend said, 'they can do with amazing skill'. As concert halls have become bigger, so has the emphasis on pro-jecting sound to the back of the room; musicians need to know how to play more loudly than they once did, and they often find themselves having to develop this skill in small practice rooms. Many musicians suffer some degree of hearing damage, simply through the process of practising loud instruments in tiny studios for years on end. Pianists' ears take quite a battering from the volume of sound produced by a grand piano in a small room, and violinists often suffer from the high frequencies they produce on strings right under their own ears. These days, orchestras are more aware of the risk of damage to players' hearing, and some orchestras offer special ear plugs, which I have seen lying in a box on a table just at the players' entrance to the stage, where even those who might need them tend to walk past them with a show of insouciance. No-one wants to be seen as fragile or unreliable, because people might stop offering them work. I came to realise that under the surface of professional life, many musicians are concealing performance-related health problems.

At the time of writing, I have escaped from my own performance/ pain cycle after finding a gifted osteopath/healer who has somehow been able to release the physical tension which had been plaguing me for such a long time. So, as doctors had said, it wasn't an organic illness, but on the other hand it *was* something real. I was happy to learn it wasn't psychosomatic. My osteopath hasn't promised the effect will last for ever, especially if I keep reproducing the circumstances which trigger the problem, but at the moment I am doing very well, and the relief has made me feel comfortable enough to speak about it.

I began to realise that the 'performance' element was largely responsible for my fellow musicians' stress-related problems. There are parts of the world where music is primarily a community activity, not a performing art in the sense that we understand it in the West. In some societies where people come together to sing and dance, to mark special festivals, rites of passage and commemorations of the dead, music requires no special training and is not regarded as a high-status option available only to the talented few. Obviously people have to learn the songs and dances, but their participation in community music is automatic, not restricted by competitive audition. Nobody tells them that they are not good enough to be allowed to join in. Moreover, their music-making is not subject to criticism and review.

When one considers how the profession of music has developed in Western countries, one realises that musicians are subject to an enormous amount of 'knowledgeable' evaluation and comparison. You can't get up on stage and play your favourite piece at the Wigmore Hall, or any other prestigious concert venue, just because you're in the mood. There are many gateways that stand between a musician and a desirable concert opportunity. Every concert opportunity has many applicants but only one winner. Many would-be performers are rejected, either at the audition stage, or by a mysterious process of evaluation by the 'gatekeepers', who are not obliged to disclose their reasons. Professional musicians depend on getting paid for their skills, so for most of them it's not an option simply to go and play their programme for fun and for no money. They can choose to do so out of goodwill or for charity (and many do), but if music is their livelihood, it doesn't relieve them from the ongoing effort to find paid concerts, which is almost always a matter of prevailing over others in a competitive process. The situation is of course much more critical for non-orchestral musicians (such as soloists and chamber groups) who have to create their own work and identify their own performance opportunities. Unfortunately, nobody 'needs' a musician in the same way as they need a plumber or a garage mechanic.

When a performance opportunity is finally achieved, performers have to submit themselves to public criticism. In order to reach the point of being invited to review a concert, most reviewers have had to jump through far fewer hoops than the performers have had to encounter in their quest to play that same concert. Some reviewers seem to get the job on the basis of 'being knowledgeable about music'; however, what one needs from a critic is not just knowledge but judgement. I can think of a few critics with excellent judgement, but I can also think of some, particularly in specialist magazines, who seem to submit every kind of performer to rigid agendas, no matter what the performer may be trying to achieve. I've often felt that the most discerning comments come from members of the audience who have very little formal knowledge of music, but have open minds or hearts. Being criticised in the national press is an experience for which nothing can prepare you, and as yet in the music profession there are no teams of 'sports psychologists' to advise you on how to protect yourself.

It was bad enough in the days when the readership was limited to citizens of the country in which the newspaper was published, but the internet has increased exponentially the size of the audience with access to the critic's sharp digs and amusing cameos. It takes a long time to build up the defences necessary to shrug off such moments, and some performers never build them up. Sadly, good reviews tend to be all too easily forgotten, whereas bad ones lodge in the memory and return to torment us in low moments. Many of my colleagues can still quote, word for word, critical sentences which particularly stung them, or which they felt were unjustified. Some years ago, taking part in Gidon Kremer's Lockenhaus Festival, I admired his counter-tactic of asking that year's performers to send in their worst reviews, which were published in the festival programme amid much hilarity. Some of the meanest things had been written about Kremer and submitted by the man himself. Clustered together, the bad reviews looked like a pitiable outpouring of spite and rancour, and their dubious motivation was revealed. This was therapeutic for us all.

As for physical problems, my guess is that professional musicians have never played for such long hours as they do today. The rise in the number of hours spent practising instruments has various causes, from the development of music conservatoire and degree programmes to the awareness of global standards. In the past, musicians had no idea how musicians played in other places, or what their conditions of work were. No musician had any reason to think of music as anything other than a transient thing. You played it and it was gone. People might remember it or not. In any case there was no way of recapturing it, and this has always been part of its beauty. But since the development of recording techniques the situation has been very different. When it became possible to capture a performance and make multiple copies of it for people to buy and collect, musicians started to become aware of other styles and standards of performance. For the first time, they could compare their own musical skills with those of others far away in place and time. It wasn't sufficient any more to have a locally pre-vailing standard which was 'good enough'. Moreover, when musicians started to listen back to their own recordings, their attention would be drawn to the mistakes which were mercilessly recorded along with the good bits. They realised that every time the recording was played, the mistakes would be heard again.

Much as one might welcome the rise in playing standards, it is a pity that we've all become so used to glossy perfection. Recording and editing techniques themselves made it possible to 'polish' perfor-mances, erasing the evidence of human frailties. The resulting discs sailed out across the world to impress and intimidate musicians who had no way of knowing whether the astonishing perfection was real or manufactured, and would set about trying to live up to those standards. Audiences got used to hearing recordings and started to expect that musicians could reproduce those standards when they played live. I know from my own experience that my level of accuracy definitely went up as I got used to being recorded, though I doubt whether my level of poetic inspiration went up commensurately; in fact it was often a struggle to keep thinking lofty poetic thoughts while also worrying about errors and extraneous noises. Today I am often amazed by the technical level of students who, growing up with awareness of global standards, have built up the stamina to be able to reproduce polished playing time after time. Admirable as this is, musical inspiration remains as elusive as it ever was. As György Sebők said, 'The standard of mediocrity is rising all the time.'

Today at any leading music college you can find people coming in at 7.30 in the morning to practise, and others stay until 10pm. I know students who make practice timetables for themselves and don't allow themselves to leave the practice studio until the plan is fulfilled. In many cases, the long hours may be excessive. Students often seem to be in the dark about how to practise most effectively, and if you wander the corridors of a music college you can hear people practising 'the difficult bits' over and over again. They seem to think that if they 'put in the hours' they will reach their goal, and indeed Malcolm Gladwell's 2008 book *Outliers* has made many people aware of the sheer amount of practice which expertise demands. However, by practising for such long hours, many students are laying the foundations for physical problems. As a result, many music colleges now employ Alexander Technique teachers and other types of physiotherapists to deal with the effects of over-practising. I've known several young musicians forced into periods of 'lay-off' in their teens and early twenties because they were already suffering from tendonitis after too much playing.

Long hours of practice are part of the zeitgeist. Everyone feels they have to do it because everyone else is doing it. Liszt's wise advice to 'think nine times and play once' seems far away from today's beehives of practice studios, buzzing from early in the morning. Rarely do you see people sitting quietly with the score, or just looking out of the window, letting their imaginations do some of the work. To overlook this opportunity is a mistake, because I'm convinced that most musical maturity comes through work away from the instrument, not work with the fingers. This was borne out recently by a comment of guitarist Julian Bream, winner of *Gramophone*'s Lifetime Achievement Award 2013, that although he no longer plays the guitar, he is a better musician in his eighties than he was in his seventies. (This he attributed to 'having changed from a player into a listener', an interesting observation.) It's a pity that practising the instrument has become the overwhelming goal of music students. In the old days, music students didn't only play but also composed and improvised and played chamber music. If you read accounts of studying at the German conservatoires in the nineteenth century, students mention going for walks, reading books and attending concerts, theatres and opera performances as if they were natural ingredients of a musical education. Today we are more specialised – for good or ill.

By being so perfectionist in their practice, young musicians build up more and more intensity about the forthcoming performance itself, which is supposed to be the culmination of all that practice. Very often it isn't. Most of the possibilities they've considered and tried out during hours of practice have, of course, to be jettisoned at the moment of performance, when they can choose only one of the possibilities. The relationship of practice to performance has become top-heavy for most of us, and the weight of expectation placed on the concert itself doesn't make for a playful spirit or a relaxed atmosphere.

Much of this perfectionism is linked to our feeling about 'the classics'. The best of classical music has become 'a canon', a body of work which is greatly valued and minutely known. Universities and scholars all over the world pore over its scores, analyse its 'reception' and measure elements of performances, often using computer software to do so. It's undeniable that as we move further away in time from the period when most of these works were composed, we have more respect for them, more sense of their cultural significance and more fear of damaging them or disrespecting them by getting things wrong when we play them. Beethoven's works may have been written in the white heat of inspiration, but for the twenty-first-century performer there is no freedom about which notes to play; the world knows these notes and expects you to get them right.

No matter how much a player may love a piece of classical music, there is still an overwhelming sense of *having to get things right* before one can even start to consider interpretation and other matters. The jazz musician Miles Davis may sometimes have played only half a dozen well-chosen notes on his trumpet if he was in an especially laconic mood, but it's not within a classical player's gift to decide to play fewer of Beethoven's notes one night for the same reason. The high value attached to accuracy is a mark of how greatly these pieces of music have come to be esteemed, and classical musicians willingly accept the importance of being faithful to the original score. But perfectionism is a straitjacket for the player, and must surely add to the stress that many performers experience. I know myself that no matter how pleased I may be with my interpretation or the mood I managed to create in a concert, I am also relieved at having been able to deliver, one after another, thousands of correct notes. And let nobody think that just because you are 'musical', you can effortlessly play any piece you want. Not so: every note of a piece of classical music has to be learned, the sequence of notes practised, the finger and hand movements plotted. These are someone else's notes, and knowledge of them does not come automatically, nor does the physical dexterity required to play them.

For a few years I had to have occasional treatment on my wrist after slipping and falling down the icy stone steps of a concert hall one winter. I was having tiny bones in my wrist 'unlocked' one day when my chiropractor commented glumly that many of his clients were 'dropping like flies' all around him, and he sometimes thought that only the musicians were doing pretty well. 'We're probably like the old tractor which is only held together by mud,' I said glibly. 'Maybe it's only the music which is holding us together.' He looked serious and said, 'You know what, I bet you're right. I think music *is* holding you together.' After a further thoughtful pause he said, 'It's very important that you guys have the outlet of performance – to get rid of so much tension. Lots of people don't have that sort of outlet. You probably build up an awful lot of nervous tension in the run-up to performances, but then releasing all that tension becomes cathartic. You have the chance to *express* something, and all the tension gets resolved. From my perspective, you're lucky creatures. I spend half my time trying to treat people who never arrive at any sort of cathartic moment. Their problems grumble on and on for years, believe me.'

I realised that, despite all the stress of performing, he was right. Thinking of friends who are not musicians, I realised that while their working lives are much more stable and dependable than mine, not characterised by the wild up-and-downs of a musician's performing life, they also lack cathartic outlets. I could imagine how those low-key unresolved tensions could start to eat away at a person. It was interesting to consider the energy of performance and the highs of a successful concert as *health-giving opportunities*. I don't think I or any of my musician friends had ever considered them in that light, but I could see how my physiotherapist might see our performances as constructive uses of worry and tension. I had been focusing on the worry and tension without considering the element of release which a concert provides.

To feel that sense of release you probably have to have a sense of achievement, and I imagine this varies quite a bit between musicians. If you are a soloist, you know for sure that everything depends on you. Technical standard, interpretation, atmosphere: it's all down to you. If it goes well, the achievement is entirely yours and all the credit goes to you personally. When you play chamber music you also know that your input is essential. Nobody else plays the same notes as you, and nobody directs you. Moreover, you know your contribution can and will affect the others in the group, both for good and ill, which increases (or should increase) your sense of responsibility. If you are a member of, say, the string section of an orchestra in which there are eleven other people all playing exactly the same part as yours, the sense of achievement must, I suppose, be tempered by the knowledge that your individual contribution is not evident in itself. If you stopped playing, others would continue; no notes would be lost. If the performance goes well, you can feel pride at having been part of it, but the credit will go largely to the conductor. I've sometimes wondered if it is any coincidence that soloists and conductors are the two principal types of musician sometimes still active in concert life well into old age. The conductor and the pianist in their eighties, even their nineties, are cherished phenomena of the music world. Conductors, who receive a lot of adulation, often seem to be buoyed up into old age by a sense of being powerful and meaningful, and let's not forget the motivating effect of their vastly greater earning power as well.

There is, of course, a lot less stress in amateur music-making. Choirs, orchestras, bands, rock groups, amateur string quartets – these ensembles bring enormous benefit to their participants. Sometimes performance is involved, sometimes not, but in any case it is understood by participants and listeners alike that this is music-making for fun, not to be subjected to exacting criticism. And then there are all the people who enjoy dance in its many forms. They may not actually make music themselves, but in terms of benefit to body and mind, their physical response to music must run very close to actual music-making. There are also all the people who don't make music themselves but derive great interest and satisfaction from listening to it. They may listen in private on their iPods or go to concerts to enjoy being part of larger audiences. Many listeners develop passionate attachments to the music and musicians they follow. The enormous chunk of society constituted by all these amateur music-lovers and music-makers far outweighs the number of professional musicians. And all these 'hobby' music-lovers would no doubt be surprised to learn that many performers find life stressful. They might protest that music is, if anything, health-*giving*. Research backs them up, proving time and time again that music, particularly making music yourself, does nothing but good. In the light of that, it is poignant to reflect that the professional musicians who are *bringing* music to all these different audiences are themselves often struggling with performance-linked health problems. Is this any different to medical professionals being stressed as they deliver healthcare to the general public? Perhaps after all it is not too fanciful to suggest that there are things in common between the two professions.

It's easy to see that the cultural value of classical music, the growth of global standards and the easy availability of innumerable recordings have led to a high level of perfectionism and therefore stress amongst classical performers. I sometimes fear that as we move further away in time from the eras when our favourite works were composed, and as we develop more respect for them, we are also losing our sense of ease with them. A lot of effort goes into preserving these precious works, but it's sometimes a strange kind of effort, clouded by veneration. I was very struck by psychologist Daniel Kahneman's remark, in his book *Thinking, Fast and Slow*, that 'one recipe for a dissatisfied adulthood is setting goals that are especially difficult to attain. Measured by life satisfaction twenty years later, the least promising goal that a young person could have was "becoming accomplished in a performing art".' This was sobering to read. My own sense is that 'goals that are especially difficult to attain' are also doubly satisfying if you manage to attain them. But of course there are also many ways in which you can fail. For every musician who can actually get up on that stage and play Brahms' Violin Concerto or Rachmaninov's *Rhapsody on a Theme of Paganini*, there must be hundreds who visualised themselves doing so but never realised the dream.

Of course, there is much to enjoy in making music before the matter of 'goals' arises. Many people really enjoy the *process* of learning to make music. They love their weekly music lessons. The craft of music-making, the engagement with the instrument or voice – these are engrossing hobbies, to be enjoyed quite independently of any goal. Sadly, it seems clear that the trouble is often caused by goals. Anyone who wishes to become a professional musician needs to consider goals, because merely engaging with the craft and the process of music-making is not enough to cause money to start rolling in. This is a great pity, because being obliged to focus on goals often eclipses, or even ruins, your enjoyment of the process. It's easy to understand why many professional musicians eventually come to envy amateurs for the sheer pleasure they get out of their hobby.

Kahneman writes about those whose goal to succeed in a performing art was thwarted before they ever reached the stage of turning professional. Did they fail? Well, is it beneficial to grapple with a dream? Does it enhance your life to immerse yourself in an art form you really admire? I'd guess that even those who reported that they 'didn't attain their goal' were enriched by the attempt. Grappling with powerful works of the imagination can change the texture of your thoughts and open your eyes to other ways of looking at the world.

For many people, music is the art above all others. It is both mentally and physically stimulating. It has a positive, perhaps profound, effect on brainwaves and biorhythms. But if we are trying to sum up its effect on health, it seems to make a big difference whether you are a performer, a player-for-fun or a listener. For the listener, it seems to be wholly beneficial. If you sing or play for pure pleasure, the effect is surely life-enhancing. It's the role of the professional performer that straddles an uncomfortable divide. Love of music draws you into being a performer in the first place, but the professional performer's life creates situations which may compromise your health even as they bolster your resilience. Perhaps the trick is not to have 'excess of it, that, surfeiting, the appetite may sicken, and so die'.

It's important to bear in mind that the stress of performing is not caused by the music itself. And even though classical musicians might resent the degree of perfectionism expected of them, it is that same perfectionism which gives rise to some of the most thrilling and uplifting performances one will ever hear. Those same high standards allow the performer to experience the fulfilment and release of a really fine concert performance, a catharsis which many outside the arts never experience.

Coda

I read recently that the ancient Greeks used sometimes to sleep in temples in the hope that the powerful atmosphere would help them to 'incubate dreams'. Such dreams would provide imagery and symbols to help them interpret whatever it was that was puzzling them. I sometimes feel that my life as a classical musician has been a similar kind of 'sleeping in temples', the temples in my case being the works of great music which have occupied me and my fellow musicians. When I say 'sleeping', it is not meant to sound like a retreat from the world, rather a desire to recharge my batteries by connecting with powers bigger than myself.

When I look around my musician friends, however, I realise that none of us is religious, or not in the formal sense. Perhaps the analogy of 'temples' is therefore a strange one to use. But I think that for many musicians, the great works of Bach, Mozart, Beethoven, Schubert and so on are as close as we come to sacred texts, and their individual notes can feel like words of truth. The attempt to come to terms with them, to transmit them, has something of the feeling of a sacred task. This may sound a little solemn in an age of loud disposable music. A friend of mine, giving the welcome speech at a gathering of classical chamber musicians, compared our endeavours to sailing beautiful intricate four-masted ships, the nineteenth-century clippers which graced the seas and set people's imaginations alight. He meant it positively, but it gave some of us a 'turn', for of course we were all aware that those ships no longer sail the seas and are mostly to be seen in museums, if at all. 'Museum music' is not how we think of it. On the contrary, we love this music for the way it comes alive in the present. Using our craft to bring it alive feels very much like a task of *now*, not a task whose purpose has been lost in the mists of time. Many of us feel that classical music is a high point of music altogether, and has provided us with a treasury the equal of anything in literature, theatre or visual art. I don't know anything better than this music for 'incubating dreams'.

In this book I've tried to speak about what this kind of music does, what it feels like to work on it, why I love it, and about some of the challenges of being a classical musician. I imagine it has always been challenging. Even in the case of Mozart, whom one might think to be above earthly trammels, his employers called the shots, decreeing whether he was allowed to go to Vienna or not, and telling him what kind of music he was to provide. Now we face a new kind of difficulty. There have probably never been so many young classical musicians, from all around the world, playing to such a high standard – I know this from the teaching I do at conservatoires in different countries and from serving on competition juries – but just at the point where there is an unparalleled depth of accomplishment, the massive growth and grip of the commercial pop industry, whose beginnings I enjoyed as a teenager, make many classical musicians feel overwhelmed and afraid of what the future holds.

Pop started as a rebellion against the status quo. When Elvis, The Beatles and The Stones got going, the elegant light music of the recent past began to look a little stuffy, and older forms of music even more so. But things have changed. Pop has become the Establishment, and other kinds of music have to fight to make their mark. It almost feels as if it's time for another rebellion, this time to assert the value of long-term thinking and music which lasts for centuries. Unlike in Mozart's day, this music is already available to everybody, not just the fortunate few.

People who have mastered instruments are changed by the process; that is part of this book's DNA, if I could put it like that. Mastering an instrument is, of course, impossible without also learning – or at least attempting – to master oneself. This makes the task doubly engrossing since one hardly knows whether inner is fuelling outer development or the other way round. Speaking for myself, I can say that much of the way I think and analyse things can be attributed to my long training in classical music and to my work with it over the years. I feel fortunate to have come across this kind of music, which has been a joy for the imagination and a mental companion like no other. It has introduced me to a way of thinking about emotional landscapes and journeys which, though cast in music, seem somehow fundamental to an understanding of life.

. . . .

'Nach Arbeit ich frug
Nun hab ich genug
Für die Hände, fürs Herze,
Vollauf genug.'

I asked for work,
And now I have it.
For the hands, for the heart,
Enough and more.

Wilhelm Müller, 'Danksagung an den Bach',
from *Die schöne Müllerin*, 1820

. . . .

Index

Wizard of Oz, The 115
Wonder, Stevie 199, 203
Wurman, Felix 122
Young, La Monte
   Piano Piece for David Tudor #1
    87

Young Concert Artists 65
Young Jazz Musician of the
   Year (Greater London Arts
   Association) 200
Zehetmair Quartet 61